Living God's Way

Going on God's Way

Into Battle

This omnibus edition first published 1998.

ISBN 0 85476 783 5

Designed and produced by Bookprint Creative Services
P.O. Box 827, BN21 3YJ, England for
KINGSWAY PUBLICATIONS
Lottbridge Drove, Eastbourne, E. Sussex BN23 6NT
Printed in Great Britain.

Reproduced from the original typesetting
of the single-volume editions.

Living God's Way

A Course for Discipling New Christians

ARTHUR WALLIS

KINGSWAY PUBLICATIONS

EASTBOURNE

Contents

SECTION 3   GROWING IN GOD

Introduction

1 A Word about the Course

This course has been designed for use in a local church setting where the new Christian is being *personally* discipled, not necessarily by a leader or recognized teacher in the church, but simply by another believer older in the faith. This method will result in the greatest benefit both for the disciple and the teacher.

It could involve couples discipling couples as well as an individual brother or sister, married or single, discipling another of the same sex. I have tried to keep the language and concepts simple, so that it should be quite possible for an older teenager to disciple another teenager, or for Christian parents to use the course with their teenage children.

Perhaps you question the rightness of someone who is not a leader teaching someone else. The letter to the Hebrews was not written to church leaders but to believers in general. The author rebuked them for their slowness to learn, telling them, 'Though by this time *you ought to be teachers*, you need someone to teach you the elementary truths of God's word all over again' (5:11–12). It is clear from the New Testament that believers in general are expected to 'teach and admonish one another' (Col 3:16).

Sadly, our churches are full of believers, like the Hebrew Christians just mentioned, who are more in need of being taught the basics of the faith than being able to teach others. I am hopeful that the 'disciplers' will get as much from this course as those they disciple.

We have come to an exciting day of evangelistic endeavour. The fields are surely 'ripe for harvest'. There is a growing expectation for the outpouring of the Holy Spirit, with the massive ingathering that that would bring. But are our churches ready? Not if they are only prepared for conversions by the handful instead of by the hundreds and thousands.

It will be nothing short of a tragedy if, with a record catch on our hands, the nets break and the catch is lost. The remedy is within our grasp. Alongside the current emphasis on every-member evangelism we must be prepared for every-member discipling. The call to rank and file believers to teach others is not beyond their spiritual capabilities. I believe hundreds of Christians, frustrated by a feeling that they are of little worth, or weighed down with personal problems, could find a new release and great fulfilment as 'a teacher of infants' in the faith (Rom 2:20).

Personal discipling is not without its dangers, but these can be overcome if it is done in a church setting, and carefully monitored by the elders. More of this aspect later. While not discounting the value of a small group going through the course together, the advantages of the one-to-one method are:

1. As soon as converted the new disciple can begin the course without waiting for a new 'converts class' to commence.

2. The course can proceed at the speed suitable for the convert, and can adjust for delays owing to holidays, sickness, etc.

3. There is an intimacy and a friendship that can develop

between teacher and disciple. The convert will be more ready to open up on personal needs and problems.

4. That first audible prayer comes much more easily in such a setting than in a house group or converts' class.

The emphasis of the course is practical. The pressing need in the first days of the Christian life is teaching that relates to the business of 'living God's way' in an alien society. Although the course is full of Scripture, the emphasis is practical rather than simply doctrinal.

There is some homework with each of the studies. However, this is not of the usual variety: a question, a scripture reference and a blank to fill in, where it is possible to score 'ten out of ten' without making any spiritual progress! The questions will require the disciple to apply the lessons to his or her own life, and will usually necessitate having direct dealings with God over the issues raised. And when the teacher and disciple meet for the next study they can go over this ground together. This should help the person teaching to know how much truth is really sinking in and what real spiritual progress is being made.

2 A Word to the Disciple

Welcome to this course of study. If you are a new Christian, may I say how delighted I am to know that you are now a part of God's family, and to greet you as a brother or sister in Christ. I believe that God will make the course a great blessing to you. Twenty sessions may seem a formidable task to face, but you will be free to take it at your own speed, and you should discuss this frankly with your teacher.

There was a parable told by Jesus about two builders. The wise one built his house on the rock, and when the storm came it stood firm. The foolish one built his house on the sand, and when the storm came it collapsed. Let's apply this to you, in the way Jesus did to his hearers. Whether you, as his disciple, are the wise or foolish builder, depends on *whether or not you hear and obey* what Jesus says. This course will help you to learn what Christ wants from his disciples, and then it will help and encourage you to obey. Look upon it as a foundation-laying course for your Christian life.

Many commit their lives to Christ, but never become firm and secure in their faith. Others sadly give up altogether when temptations assail. They make the mistake of never paying attention to their spiritual foundations. Laying them is a demanding and time-consuming task. But because you're building a house that you're going to occupy, your own safety and security depends on the foundations. How glad was the wise man in the middle of the night when he heard the wind howling and the flood waters rising, that he had taken all that trouble over the foundations.

If this good news about Jesus is something completely new to you, you will find your teacher a great help in grasping some of the truths, in finding your way around the Bible, and in facing some of the practical difficulties of 'living God's way' in our modern world. We have all had to face these same battles. That's where we are able to help one another. Before very long *you* should be able to help another new Christian in the same way that you have been helped. That's exciting, isn't it? All that you will require for the course is your own copy of this study manual, your own copy of the Bible (preferably the New International Version [NIV] on which the course is based; quite inexpensive editions are available), a notebook for the home tasks and something to write with.

The course is divided into three sections, each having an introduction explaining the ground to be covered.

Similarly, each study has its own introduction. Read this before you meet with your teacher. If you can also read in advance the study itself, in order to get the gist of it, that will be a great help.

One of the main purposes of the course is to teach you to talk to God yourself about the things that he is saying to you, and to learn to listen to his voice. The home task is geared for this, and is therefore very practical. Do these diligently, recording any answers in your notebook. Be ready to share your findings with your teacher when you next meet.

With each study there is also a verse to memorize. I have found the memorizing of Scripture a great blessing in my service for God, and I would encourage you in this. But if it's more than you can cope with, forget it. For those who do want to do it, may I suggest that you write out the verses on small cards. If you prefer to memorize in a version more familiar to you than the NIV, then do that. And as you proceed, keep refreshing your memory on the ones already learned. Continual rehearsing is the secret of memorizing. And don't forget to include the scripture reference.

At the end of this introduction to the course is a list of abbreviations of the books of the Bible and versions of the Bible used in the notes. You may need to refer to these when looking up scripture references.

It now remains for me to commit you to God and to his word which can build you up in your Christian faith, and make you strong in Christ. God bless you.

3 A Word to the Teacher

May I welcome you also to this course as a teacher. To be called to share with someone else what you have learned about how to live God's way is an exciting and demanding task. Be assured that God is with you, and will give you all the wisdom and strength you need as you look to him in faith. Let me share with you some key things to help you to make the sessions as fruitful as possible.

If you are leading someone through this course in a church setting, there should be an elder or other mature leader appointed to oversee your discipling. If this has been overlooked, speak to your leaders and ask for a particular leader to take this responsibility. You and your disciple will both feel more secure in the knowledge that you are covered in this way, especially if you run into problems that you feel unable to handle.

Before you undertake any discipling take time to *go right through the course*, looking up the scripture references, and ensuring that you are clear about the truths being taught. Paul has a word for the person who aspires to be 'a teacher of infants'—and that's what everyone is who disciples a new Christian. He says, 'You, then, who teach others, do you not teach yourself?' (Rom 2:21). In other words, you must be 'practising what you preach'. There are parts of the course that you will find a challenge to your own Christian life, so remember you will communicate to your disciple not only what you say, but what you are.

There's another important reason for going right through the course before you commence. You can note anything that you yourself do not fully understand and talk it through with your elder. That's much better than being caught out in the middle of a study! Better still, perhaps your church could run a training seminar and go right through the material with all those who are to be involved in discipling.

A key to the progress of the one you are discipling will be the relationship that is established between you. Make it one of true friendship. It is not difficult to receive and respond to instruction when you know that the one giving it really loves you and is wholly for you. Take time to find out about his or her background, family, interests, conversion to Christ, present struggles, etc. Not only will this express your loving concern, but enable you to pray for your disciple intelligently and apply the teaching in the most helpful way. Why not have a meal together before you start the course proper, or at least set apart some time to get acquainted? It is equally important that you share about yourself, and how you came to Christ.

As you go through the studies together, encourage your new Christian to pray with you out loud—even if at first it's only a one-sentence prayer. Teach your disciple to talk to God in an easy conversational way, and in the language that they would use with any other friend. Before moving on to the new study check the home task from the previous study. Encourage the disciple to share his (or her) findings, and talk through any difficulties encountered. Your concern is to know whether he (or she) has entered into the good of what you have taught.

Now you are ready to read through the introduction to the new study together and work through the teaching, helping your disciple to look up the scripture references, and to understand what God is saying. A list of the Bible books with their abbreviations found at the commencement of the course will help here. Watch that you don't get sidetracked on to some other interesting related topic. This may prolong the time unduly. Keep it for discussion at the end, if time permits.

It is very important to share your own experience, as it relates to the theme of the study, even experiences of failure, and how God brought you through into victory. The new Christian will identify with this and be encouraged.

Pray much over these times together. Ask God continually to enable you to impart the truth in a spirit of faith, so that your new Christian will also receive it in a spirit of faith, and start to walk in it. Otherwise the burden on the disciple of all that he (or she) is required to do will appear to get bigger and bigger, without a realization of the grace that is available to make it work.

It is important that you report regularly to the elder concerned as to how you are progressing. In the Community Church here in Southampton, where we have a number already going through the course, we have drafted a simple monthly progress report, with an account of each study completed, and an end-of-the-month report on general progress made.

Finally, remember the fellow Christians, leaders and others, who have had a part in shaping your Christian life, and bringing you thus far along the road. God is now going to use you to shape another life for eternity. What a privilege! Give yourself to the task humbly, prayerfully and conscientiously—and God be with you.

4 Abbreviations

Scripture references

Genesis	Gen
Exodus	Ex
Leviticus	Lev
Numbers	Num
Deuteronomy	Deut
Joshua	Josh
Judges	Judg
Ruth	Ruth
1 and 2 Samuel	1 and 2 Sam
1 and 2 Kings	1 and 2 Kings
1 and 2 Chronicles	1 and 2 Chron
Ezra	Ezra
Nehemiah	Neh
Esther	Esther
Job	Job

Psalms	Ps
Proverbs	Prov
Ecclesiastes	Eccles
Song of Solomon	Song
Isaiah	Is
Jeremiah	Jer
Lamentations	Lam
Ezekiel	Ezek
Daniel	Dan
Hosea	Hos
Joel	Joel
Amos	Amos
Obadiah	Obad
Jonah	Jon
Micah	Mic
Nahum	Nahum
Habakkuk	Hab
Zephaniah	Zeph
Haggai	Hag
Zechariah	Zech
Malachi	Mal
Matthew	Mt
Mark	Mk
Luke	Lk
John	Jn
Acts	Acts
Romans	Rom
1 and 2 Corinthians	1 and 2 Cor
Galatians	Gal
Ephesians	Eph
Philippians	Phil
Colossians	Col
1 and 2 Thessalonians	1 and 2 Thess
1 and 2 Timothy	1 and 2 Tim
Titus	Tit
Philemon	Philem
Hebrews	Heb
James	Jas
1 and 2 Peter	1 and 2 Pet

1, 2 and 3 John	1, 2, and 3 Jn
Jude	Jude
Revelation	Rev

Note: 'a' or 'b' at the end of a reference indicates that only the first or second half of the verse is meant, for example, Eph 2:3a or Col 2:6b; 'f' or 'ff' at the end of a reference indicates that the verse (f) (or verses ff) following should also be read.

Bible versions

AV	The Authorized (or King James) Version
RSV	Revised Standard Version
NASB	New American Standard Bible
Phillips	*The New Testament in Modern English* by J. B. Phillips
NIV	New International Version

SECTION 1

Coming into Christ

(Studies 1—6)

In ancient times if you wanted to qualify for membership of certain secret societies there were rites and ceremonies that you had to go through. Some of these were things that were done to you, while others were things that you had to be willing to do yourself. Only then did you fully belong. You had been 'initiated' into that society. Christianity is not a free for all. There is what we might call 'Christian initiation'. The heart of this is, of course, the new birth, on coming into Christ. Though you may have experienced this, it is essential that you understand clearly what has happened to you. But there are other things too that are not optional extras, such as water baptism and the fullness of the Holy Spirit. These are essential if you want to enjoy the full privileges of the kingdom of God. This part of the course will deal with the foundations of your Christian life. It is so important that you get these right.

Introducing Study 1

THE BIG CHANGE

The Bible calls it conversion, being saved or being born again. To understand what God has done in you and for you we must first take a glance back and recall *how you were* before the big change took place. It's not a question of how you then saw yourself, or how your relatives or friends saw you, but how *God* saw you. That, and only that, is how you really were. Then we must look at what God says *you are now*. That means looking at your new spiritual identity. You are not yet what you will be. But nor are you what you once were. A miracle has taken place inside you. It's not that you decided to become 'religious', go straight or turn over a new leaf—and keeping your fingers crossed that you will be able to keep it up! God has made you a brand-new person. It's not that you necessarily *feel* tremendously different. It's not a matter of feelings but of facts. It's because you *are* different you have begun to live differently—to live God's way.

This study has more than the usual number of scriptural references to look up. Don't be daunted by this. The study itself is not difficult, and getting accustomed to finding your way around the Bible is an important aspect of the course.

STUDY 1

The Big Change

Read 2 Corinthians 5:14–21

Sin and its cause. It's a disease that all men have contracted (Rom 3:23). 'Fall short' is like an arrow not reaching the target. 'A miss is as good as a mile'. All of us have failed to measure up to God's standard of righteousness, called here 'the glory of God'. Our good deeds cannot make up for our failures. Even our good deeds are not acceptable to God (Is 64:6). Men are not sinners because they sin, but they sin because they are sinners, i.e. were born with a sinful nature (Ps 51:5). As sheep have an inborn tendency to go astray, we have an inborn tendency to do our own thing and go our own way (Is 53:6).

'*The old has gone, the new has come!*' (2 Cor 5:17) is the key to what has happened to you:

The old has gone

Before you came to Christ you chose darkness. You were therefore responsible for the state you were in, and quite helpless to put it right. The Bible says you were:

1. *Dead* (Eph 2:1), that is, unable to respond to God, to obey God or to please God.

2. *Defiled* because sin is spiritual uncleanness. The

body may be clean while the mind and the conscience are corrupted or defiled (Tit 1:15).

3. Enslaved by sin, and unable to get free (Jn 8:34), 'enslaved by all kinds of passions and pleasures' (Tit 3:3).

4. Blinded by Satan (2 Cor 4:4), and so unable to 'see' the truth.

5. Under God's judgement with the threat of divine punishment hanging over your head, because God was angry about your sin (Eph 2:3b).

6. Cut off from God 'Separate from Christ...without God...far away' (Eph 2:12–13), like the lost (prodigal) son in the far country (Lk 15:13). If you had not repented and received Christ this separation would have resulted in eternal death (Rom 6:23), that is, hell.

The new has come

Though you may have the same physical appearance, temperament and personality, you have become a brand-new person, 'a new creation', with new attitudes, new relationships, new outlook, new purpose in life, new interests and new friends. 'The big change' is described as being:

1. Forgiven (1 Jn 1:9a). When God forgives he also forgets (Is 43:25). Don't let your memory condemn you (Rom 8:1, 33–34). The burden has lifted.

2. Justified, or declared righteous before God (Rom 3:24). At the cross Jesus took your sin that you might take his righteousness (2 Cor 5:21). What a wonderful exchange!

3. Cleansed. Mind, memory, imagination and conscience are purified through Christ's blood (1 Jn 1:7). Isn't it good to feel clean?

4. Reconciled. Before you were God's enemy, now you are his friend (Rom 5:10). You'll never find a friend to compare with him.

5. Born again (Jn 3:3). Physical birth gave you the life

of your parents, but this new birth gives you the life of God, eternal life (Jn 10:27–28).

6. *In God's family.* God is now your Father, you are his son or daughter (2 Cor 6:18), and that means all other believers are your brothers and sisters. As Father he is committed to love, protect, provide for, and train you.

7. *Bound for heaven.* Jesus has gone to prepare a place for you (Jn 14:2–3). Meanwhile he is preparing you for that place. The best is yet to come (1 Cor 2:9).

All these are not simply what preachers say, but what God says of you as a true believer.

Memorize: *Therefore, if anyone is in Christ, he is a new creation; the old has gone, the new has come!* (2 Cor 5:17). (Try to memorize the reference as well as the scripture.)

Home task

1. Under the heading 'The Old Has Gone' there are six descriptions of your old life. Look up one scripture under each description and write it out in full in your notebook. Remember, that's how it is with your relatives and friends who are still without Christ. Make a list of them and start asking God to save them as he saved you.

2. Under the heading 'The New Has Come' there are seven descriptions of you as a brand-new person. Find a quiet place on your own. Look up one scripture under each description and *confess out loud* what it says you are, followed by the scripture. For example, the first would be:

'I am *forgiven*, because 1 John 1:9 says, "If we confess our sins" etc.' Then write it out in your notebook before moving on to the next one until you have completed all seven. Finish up with a big thank you session with your Father for all the blessings of this big change in your life.

Introducing Study 2

HAND-PICKED

'How did you find Christ?' someone asked an African Christian. 'I didn't find him,' came the answer, 'he found me!' In salvation God always makes the first move. He was seeking you before you began seeking him. In fact, it all goes back long before the seeking/finding process began. You may have thought that you chose Christ, but that was only because he had first chosen you.

That is the theme of this study. Believers call it 'the doctrine of election'. You may wonder how God could choose you before you were born or had any existence. Or how he could 'elect' you and then give you free will to choose yourself to love and serve him, and no one lives and serves God without choosing to do so. Don't worry. These things have perplexed the minds of the greatest Christians down the centuries. I don't have to understand the laws of electricity to enjoy its benefits. Praise God we don't have to unravel the mystery of election to enjoy the blessing of knowing that God has chosen us simply because he loves us.

Hand-Picked

Read Deuteronomy 7:6–9

God took the first step

Salvation is not man groping after God, but God reaching down to man. The Bible teaches that God chose some men (election), but he gave to all a will to decide and holds them responsible for how they exercise it. The truth lies in both these facts, however difficult it may seem to reconcile them. We are required to believe, not necessarily to understand.

When were you chosen?

It wasn't after you had lived a while and looked a promising candidate for salvation! It was before you were born, and had done anything good or bad (Rom 9:10–12). It was even before the world was created (Eph 1:4).

What was the basis of God's choice?

Since he chose you before you were born it could not be because of your good deeds. It was on the basis of God's mercy and grace (Tit 3:5; 2 Tim 1:9). You will hear a lot

23

about grace on this course. It means God's abounding love towards those who are unworthy of it. 'Something for nothing for those who don't deserve anything.' He chose you because he loved you when there was nothing to love. Did you notice in the reading that that was why he chose Israel (Deut 7:7)?

You were a love gift

You were a love gift from the Father to the Son (Jn 6:37). You came to Jesus, not primarily because you decided to, but because the Father drew you (verse 44). No one comes without that drawing. It is a work of the Holy Spirit.

God didn't get a shock!

In his foreknowledge God knew all about you when he chose you (1 Pet 1:2). Couples marry, only to discover what they've let themselves in for! Despite your weakness, frailty and sinfulness, God wanted you. Out of millions he has chosen you! You are 'special', hand-picked.

Learn to accept yourself

God chose you, created you as he wanted you to be, and now he has redeemed you. Don't crave for someone else's looks, personality, temperament, natural gifts, etc. Having chosen you, God formed you as a person according to his own will and design. Don't question this (Rom 9:20). Instead praise him for it (Ps 139:14).

The pressure is off

You no longer need feel, 'It all depends on me. Have I got what it takes?' Instead, 'It's over to God who chose me, knowing me better than I knew myself. His grace is more than enough for all my needs' (Jn 1:16; 2 Cor 12:9).

God has a perfect plan for you

Choice has to do with purpose. The carpenter chooses a tool with a job in mind. God didn't save you, and then wonder what to do with you. He chose you for a purpose, and when you were saved that set the plan in motion (Eph 2:10) You may not know what that plan is, but God will unfold it step by step. As you carry out that plan you will not only be secure, but fruitful and fulfilled (Jn 15:16).

Memorize: *For it is by grace you have been saved, through faith—and this is not from yourselves, it is the gift of God—not by works, so that no-one can boast* (Eph 2:8–9).

Home task

Use your notebook to answer these questions:

1. What are the wonderful things that should result from the fact that God has chosen you? See Ephesians 1:4 and Romans 8:29.

2. What are the four wonderful things that 1 Peter 2:9 says God's people are because he has chosen us?

3. Jot down all *the things that you like* about the way God has made you. Then list *the things (if any) you don't like*, or wish were different. Then thank him for *all* of them, and tell him, 'Father, you have done all things well.'

Introducing Study 3

WHAT GOD DID

In the last study we said that salvation did not begin with you but with God. He chose you because he loved you. Now we must consider what he did to express his love and to make his choice effective and meaningful.

We will not be thinking so much of what God has done *in* you by making you a new creature in Christ, which we called 'the big change' (Study 1), but what he has done *for* you in sending Jesus into the world to be your Saviour. We shall be thinking about the basis of salvation, the great historic event of the cross and its meaning. Why was it necessary for Jesus to come? Why did he have to die? How can we be sure that his death and resurrection have accomplished anything? It is so important that you understand this. God's act of choosing you could not in itself restore you to himself. The cause of separation between him and you had to be removed. He had to find a way of justifying you while remaining himself a just and holy God.

What God Did

Read Romans 5:1–9

The problem of sin

God made man to enjoy fellowship with him, but sin brought estrangement (Gen 3:8). How could there ever again be fellowship? Only by the cause of the estrangement being removed. Man was 'powerless' to do anything about it (Rom 5:6). It would have been like trying to lift himself up by tugging on his bootlaces. Only God could deal with the problem.

The solution

Though God loved you and chose you, he could not disregard your sin (Hab 1:13a). Sin always has to be paid for. You were bankrupt, so God paid the sum himself so you could be forgiven your debt. How did God do it?

Blood must be shed

When God planned to redeem Israel from Egyptian slavery a lamb had to be sacrificed by every household (Ex 12:3ff). This pointed forward to 'the Lamb of God' who was to come (Jn 1:29). Later God taught Israel that there could not be forgiveness without the shedding of blood (Heb 9:22b). Since the law of God insists that the penalty of your sin is death (Ezek 18:4), Jesus, the only sinless man, had to suffer to save you from your sin and bring you back to God (1 Pet 3:18a). It is only through the blood of Jesus that you are cleansed from your sin (1 Jn 1:7b).

Justified by his blood

Did you notice that the word 'justified' came twice in your reading? Justification is the act by which God declares sinful men righteous. Verse 1 says that you are 'justified by faith'. That's your side of it, and we shall be looking at that more particularly in the next study. But verse 9 says that you are 'justified by his blood'. That's God's side of it. In the matter of righteousness you were declared bankrupt. But Jesus came and discharged your debts on the cross. All his righteousness was paid into your account.

How can you be sure?

The proof that God accepted the sacrifice of Jesus to justify you is seen in the fact that he raised him from the dead (Rom 4:25). Sometimes, after a man's death, the terms of his will are not carried out. Jesus, when he died, left you a legacy of salvation. Then he rose again to make sure you got it! (1 Pet 1:3–4.) Now he's in heaven ensuring that all the terms of the will are carried out.

His love—your response

The cross of Jesus is the supreme act of God's love (Rom 5:8). The man in the dock, so the story goes, was found guilty. The judge, though an old friend, didn't treat the offence lightly. He fined him as heavily as he could, and then handed him a cheque for the full sum. Because God was holy he had to punish sin with the sentence of death. At the cross God the Judge stepped down from the bench and paid your debt in the blood of Jesus. That's what grace is all about. What should your response be? In his great hymn, Isaac Watts wrote, 'Love so amazing, so divine, demands my soul, my life my all'. See Paul's response in Phil 3:7–9.

Memorize: *For God so loved the world that he gave his one and only Son, that whoever believes in him shall not perish but have eternal life* (Jn 3:16).

Home task

Use your notebook to register your answers to the following questions:

  1. The fact that Christ died and rose again entitles him to what position in your life? (Rom 14:9.)

  2. What do you think that means in practical terms? Include in your answer the areas of your life that ought to be affected by this.

Introducing Study 4

WHAT YOU DID

In the last lesson we saw how God, having set his love on you, took action to free you from your sin and bring you to himself. But salvation, as you well know, is not a work that God carries out independently of us; it requires our willing response and co-operation.

A Christian was talking to a soap manufacturer about his faith. 'Don't think much of your Christianity,' he said to the Christian. 'It's been around all these centuries, and look at the mess the human race is in.' At this point they passed two or three children playing in the mud at the side of the road. 'What about your soap?' replied the Christian. 'It's been around longer than Christianity, but look at the mess those kids are in.' 'Ah,' retorted the manufacturer, 'my soap is only effective as and when it is applied.' 'That's exactly how it is with Christianity' came the answer.

In this study we shall be looking at the question of how the work that Christ has done for us is personally applied. It is important that we check out the whole area of our responsibility.

STUDY 4

What You Did

Read Acts 20:17–21

Introduction

If Christ died for all, why are not all saved? Though salvation is *sufficient* for all, it is only *effective* for those who respond in the right way to the good news. Remember the story of the judge who fined his friend? What would have happened if the convicted man had torn up the cheque? As well as the work that God performs in salvation, Scripture emphasizes the part that we are required to play in salvation. We must always *work out* what God *works in* (Phil 2:12–13).

Acts of the will

Mind, emotions and will are all involved. When a man hears the good news his *mind* may be convinced, his *emotions* may be stirred, but if his *will* is not moved he is not converted. The lost son said, '*I will* set out and go back to my father' (Lk 15:18), and that was the turning point in his life. 'Whosoever *will*, let him take' (Rev 22:17, AV). In conversion this decision of the will must be expressed in *repentance* towards God, *faith* in our Lord Jesus and *confession* towards men. Let's look carefully at these actions.

Repentance

'Turn to God in repentance' (Acts 20:21). The word means 'a change of mind'. Instead of rejecting or ignoring God, we turn to him in acknowledgement of who he is. That will also mean a change of mind about ourselves, that we *are* sinners and *need* salvation. It's more than just thinking 'I'm wrong', or saying 'I'm sorry'. It's *a change of mind that leads to a change of course*. A father and son were living in a log cabin. The son took no notice of the father's repeated request to fetch logs and stoke the fire. Father: 'You either fetch those logs or quit this place!' The son stormed out. Weeks later he returned weak and hungry. Son: 'Dad, I'm sorry'. Father: 'All right, son, then fetch those logs' (Cf. Mt 21:28–29). There must be 'fruit in keeping with repentance' (Mt 3:8). Repentance must be followed by *confession* of our sin to God and *forsaking* it (Prov 28:13). If others have been wronged we must confess to them too. Damage must be made good, e.g. money or goods stolen must be restored with interest (Lk 19:8).

Faith

'Have faith in our Lord Jesus' (Acts 20:21). Most people are trusting to their 'good deeds'. 'Are you a Christian?' 'I hope so, I'm doing my best.' This fosters pride. Salvation is a gift, not a wage or a reward (Rom 6:23). It is received by faith, not worked for (Eph 2:8–9). Faith is not simply a mental acceptance. Believing *about* Christ is not the same as believing *in* him. 'I believe *about* Satan, but *not in* him' (Cf. Jas 2:19). Believing in Christ is a thing of the heart more than the head (Rom 10:10) and it leads to committing

32

myself to him. If I am unwilling to commit myself and *submit* myself to him to rule over me, I haven't really *believed in him*. True believing always results in 'calling on the Lord' (Rom 10:13).

Confession

This completes the process. To confess Christ is to let other people know that you side with Christ as your Saviour and Lord (Rom 10:9–10). This often has a profound effect on unbelievers and may lead to their salvation. It always gladdens the heart of Christ, and he then confesses your name before his Father (Mt 10:32).

Memorize: *He who conceals his sins does not prosper, but whoever confesses and renounces them finds mercy* (Prov 28:13).

Home task

The Bible says 'Make your calling and election sure' (2 Pet 1:10), and 'Examine yourselves to see whether you are in the faith' (2 Cor 13:5). This will either confirm us in the faith or save us from thinking that we are all right when we are not.

1. Review your past life before you came to Christ, and ask yourself, 'Have I renounced and forsaken all that I know to be sin?' Call on God for grace to deal with any areas in which you are not yet clear.

2. Ask yourself, 'Have I really committed myself to Jesus Christ?' Is he really Lord of every part of my life? Again, take to him in prayer those areas over which he is not yet ruling.

3. If then, you are still having a struggle over certain matters, share them with the one who is discipling you for his (or her) counsel and prayer. Be assured, God has chosen you to be free.

Introducing Study 5

BAPTISM IN WATER

We have now completed our study of that work of God in us called 'the new birth'. But there are still other matters that are part and parcel of our coming into Christ and which, therefore, belong to this opening section. They are of great importance in our new life in Christ. The first is the rite of water baptism.

Although it might appear a simple outward act or just a religious ceremony, baptism is an act of the utmost importance and significance for us. It not only speaks of what has happened to us now that we have come into Christ, but it is also designed to 'trigger off' faith in us for the future, to live from now on in the full blessing of our salvation. In non-Christian lands people don't always take a lot of notice when a person of another religion professes to believe in Christ, but when he (or she) follows this by being baptized the opposition breaks out. Everybody understands that baptism is the outward sign that you mean business.

As you read the New Testament epistles you will find that nowhere are believers exhorted to get baptized. It is taken for granted that this happened when they were born again. We don't come across any unbaptized Christians in the New Testament churches. If you are *not* yet baptized, this study will help you to see the importance of obeying this command of Christ. If you *are* baptized, this will help you to understand more perfectly what has happened, and what should result from it.

Baptism in Water

Read Romans 6:1–11

Introduction

Because of confusion and controversy among Christians about baptism, we need to be clear as to what the Bible teaches. The question is *not* 'What does *church tradition* say?' but 'What does *the Scripture* say?' (Gal 4:30). There is no confusion or uncertainty about it if we rely on Scripture alone. It tells us how baptism is to be practised and what it really means.

Babes or believers?

The only infants baptized in the New Testament were 'babes' in Christ (i.e. newly 'born again' believers). Baptism in Scripture always *follows* repentance and faith (Mk 16:16; Acts 2:38). It was *after* a person became a disciple that he was to be baptized (Mt 28:19). We never find the order reversed.

It is by immersion

Baptizo (Greek) translated 'baptize' means literally to

dip, immerse, submerge. New Testament believers were, therefore, *immersed*. So John needed plenty of water to do the job (Jn 3:23). This is confirmed by the description of Jesus' baptism. He came 'up out of the water' (Mk 1:10). So with Philip and the eunuch (Acts 8:38–39).

Who should do it?

A responsible person, but not necessarily holding a position of leadership. Jesus did not personally baptize, but left it to his followers (Jn 4:2). If a believer is able to disciple another he should be qualified to baptize him (Mt 28:19). The great apostle Paul was baptized by one simply described as 'a disciple' (Acts 9:10, 18).

What does it mean?

1. *I've been initiated.* Baptism is a ceremony of initiation (admission to membership). We are not baptized 'into a denomination', but 'into Christ' (Rom 6:3), and thus into his body, the church.

2. *I've been sealed.* It's like circumcision was to Abraham, 'a seal of the righteousness that he had by faith' (Rom 4:11). It should confirm and strengthen your faith. Let's say, here's a letter representing *you*, and an envelope representing *Christ*. The letter is placed in the envelope, just as in conversion you are placed in Christ. Then the envelope is sealed. That's like water baptism. It makes you feel secure.

3. *I've been cleansed.* Bathing the body is an essential part of hygiene. Conversion, 'the washing of rebirth' (Tit 3:5b), deals with the grime of sin, and baptism reminds you that you are now to live as a cleansed person. Read Ananias's words to Paul at his baptism (Acts 22:16). They show how new birth and baptism belong together. We must not separate them. Once you're born again you

qualify for it.

4. I confess Christ. New birth may be in the seclusion of your own room, but you can't have a 'private baptism'. In the New Testament it was in rivers and city pools. It's no 'hush-hush' affair. It's like an enlisted soldier putting on the uniform (Gal 3:27). You can't wear the uniform and be a secret soldier.

5. I am united with Christ in his death and resurrection, as in our reading (Rom 6:1–11). Think of the pool as the grave and your body as the corpse. What do you do with the corpse? Bury it. What do you do with your old life, with its sinful ways, now that you are a Christian? Bury it in the act of baptism. Christ rose again. Going under is followed by coming up. That's reassuring! United with Christ you rise to 'live a new life' (Rom 6:4). *Believe* for the symbolic act to be a reality in your life.

Conclusion

Baptism is not an 'optional extra' to salvation. It is a command of our Lord and Master. Complete the following verse: 'If you love me, you will . . . .
. . . .' (Jn 14:15).

Memorize: *Don't you know that all of us who were baptized into Christ Jesus were baptized into his death? We were therefore buried with him through baptism into death in order that, just as Christ was raised from the dead through the glory of the Father, we too may live a new life (Rom 6:3–4).*

Home task

1. Make a list of all those 'relics' of your old life that still cling, though you know that they can never be part of your new life in Christ.

2. Go over the list, and if you have already been baptized tell God concerning each one, 'That old thing went down into death when I got baptized.' *Believe* that God has now made you free.

3. If you have not been baptized, read Acts 22:16, and make up your mind to obey God. Meanwhile, renounce all those 'relics' of the old life on your list, believing that you are going to leave them all in the baptismal pool.

Introducing Study 6

BAPTISM IN THE SPIRIT

The Bible tells us that there is 'one baptism' into Christ. Being immersed in water is only one part of it. The other is baptism in the Spirit.

Although there have been great changes in your lifestyle since you were born again, you may be aware of a lack of power to live for Christ and witness for him in the world. Jesus' disciples, though they believed in him and loved him, were just like that before he left them. He gave them the promise of the Holy Spirit to come upon them and empower them. It happened a few days after he had gone back to heaven, on the day of Pentecost. What transformed men they became! Like the cross of Calvary, Pentecost is not just an historical event or a date in the church calendar, but a present reality. We are to *experience* Pentecost and its power just as surely as we have experienced the cross and its pardon.

Like water baptism, this is not an optional extra, but something God wants us to experience and enjoy at the beginning of the Christian life, as the early Christians did. This study is all about this wonderful promise Jesus gave us, and how we can experience it.

Baptism in the Spirit

Read Acts 1:1–9

Introducing the Holy Spirit

Of course, you have met him already! Your salvation and all the blessings that have followed have been his work. If we do not have the Holy Spirit we are not Christians (Rom 8:9). What Christ did *for* us, the Holy Spirit now does *in* us. He is not just God's power or influence. We are told not to grieve him (Eph 4:30), and you can't grieve an influence. He shares the Godhead with the Father and the Son (2 Cor 13:14). That's why we speak of the Holy Spirit as 'him', not 'it'. Now for Spirit baptism.

How baptism in the Spirit is described

Sometimes we read of the Spirit *coming upon* people (Acts 1:8), their being *clothed with power* (Lk 24:49), their *receiving* (Gal 3:2) or being *sealed with* the Spirit (Eph 1:13). Why *receive* the Spirit if we now *have* the Spirit? Receiving means *receiving in fullness and power*.

Is it once for all?

We don't need to be baptized in water every week, nor do we need a weekly baptism in the Spirit. But the first experience does need renewing or recharging, usually called being *filled* or *anointed*. Many fillings or anointings, but only *one* baptism. Peter was filled twice soon after his first filling at Pentecost (Acts 4:8, 31).

Our Lord's description

Jesus not only had the experience himself (Lk 3:21—22) but describes for us the Spirit-filled man: 'Streams of living water will flow from within him' (Jn 7:38). Such a man brings the water of life to others and quenches their thirst. God intends *you* to be like that.

What it does

Through this baptism the Holy Spirit will:

○ make Jesus increasingly real to you (Jn 15:26);
○ give you power and boldness to witness (Acts 1:8);
○ open up the Bible and make it living (Jn 16:13);
○ give you a new prayer/praise language (Acts 10:46);
○ make your praying effective (Rom 8:26);
○ lead you to right decisions (Rom 8:14);
○ set you free, especially in praise and worship (2 Cor 3:17);
○ fill you with God's love (Rom 5:5) and joy (Acts 13:52);
○ equip you with spiritual gifts (power tools) to do your job in the church (1 Cor 12:8–11).

You may not come into all this at once, but it's all there for you.

To serve the body

The purpose of this 'baptism' is not to make people think 'You're a great guy', but to equip you to serve Christ's body (1 Cor 12:7). The human body has many parts, each gifted to do its special job. So you are one of many parts in Christ's body, with a special job earmarked for you. (Remember 'election' in Study 3.) The Holy Spirit will equip you with the gifts you need. That's exciting! (See 1 Cor 12:12–13.) My foot is just as important as my hand, but not so prominent. Don't think that only the prominent members or the spectacular gifts are important (1 Cor 12:21–22).

How to receive

'If a man is *thirsty*, let him *come* to me and *drink* . . . By this he [Jesus] meant the Spirit, whom those who believed in him were later to receive' (Jn 7:37–39). He gave you three things to do:

1. *Thirst*—a deep longing for God to meet you in this way. God creates thirst and satisfies it. If you're not thirsty, ask God why. If you have been filled, thirst for more.

2. *Come*—to Jesus, who baptizes in the Spirit, and *ask*. God gives to those who ask (Lk 11:13). But more than asking is needed.

3. *Drink*—that means to lay hold of the blessing by faith. Jesus says, 'Whatever you ask for in prayer, *believe* that you have received it [that's when you start drinking], and it will be yours' (Mk 11:24). Drinking is an act of faith (Gal 3:2). Praying is no good without faith.

Finally, *laying on of hands* is a ministry to help you to receive. The person laying on hands becomes a channel of faith for the imparting of the Spirit. Your teacher will be ready to pray for you in this way. Expect to be filled with

God's power. Expect to receive a heavenly language. Expect the rivers of living water to start flowing out.

Memorize: *You will receive power when the Holy Spirit comes on you; and you will be my witnesses* (Acts 1:8).

Home task

Under 'What It Does' there are nine things that you should expect. Write out those that are *not yet* true for you, underlining the statements, and copying out the scriptures. Then pray that God will bring you into this part of your inheritance. Remember, believing is receiving!

SECTION 2

Getting along together

(Studies 7–13)

You have seen that 'coming into Christ' is very much a personal matter. The Holy Spirit showed you your need, revealed the Lord Jesus to you and finally brought you to repentance and faith. That *could* all have happened without anyone else being directly involved. But once born again you are part of God's family, the church, and that means getting along with other believers. When someone joins the Forces, he has to 'sign on', which is a personal decision, but that leads to 'joining up', which means living with others. It's like that when you become a Christian and join the Lord's army.

Your personal relationship with God is of course very important. You will be learning a lot about that in Section 3 of the course. But in this section we want you to think about the exciting and very important matter of 'getting along together' in God's family. Most of your growth and development as a Christian will now come through your relationship with other believers. This will happen, not only because of what the leaders and people share with you, but because of what *you* share with them, for that will also help you to grow.

Introducing Study 7

THE COMMITTED BODY

When someone mentions 'church' what do you think of? The drudgery of attending some place of worship while others are enjoying themselves? Singing dreary hymns? Listening to boring sermons? Be prepared for a whole new 'think'. Real church is not like that at all. In the first place it is a commitment—not just 'going to church' once a week but discovering a new and joyful way of living in harmony with other Christians. It will be the most demanding and fulfilling thing you've ever experienced. Those who get most out are those who put most in!' As you explore the real thing you'll never want to opt out again.

The Committed body

Read Matthew 16:13–20

What is the church?

It is not a religious club (pay your dues and obey the rules), but a body of committed people who have *all* found a new togetherness with God and with one another. You can't get in without being 'born again'. The New Testament speaks of Christ as the head and the church as his body (Col 1:18)—i.e. people who share his life and come under his control. As the parts of a human body are varied, so are we. We can think of the church in two ways. Jesus said:

1. *'I will build my church'* (Mt 16:18) meaning *the universal church* for whom Christ died (Eph 5:25), i.e. all believers, regardless of 'label' or race, past or present. It has a unity that is invisible but real. Meet a Christian, even from another race or culture, and immediately there is a oneness.

2. *'Tell it to the church'* (Mt 18:17) must refer to a *congregation who gather together*, whether it's a city church (1 Cor 1:2), or a church in a house (Rom 16:5). It's a visible body of committed people. 'Church' in the New Testament is a company of 'born again', not simply religious, people. It never refers to a building. Jesus

49

promised that when the church met together he would be there with them (Mt 18:20).

What about denominations?

These have come through divisions in the history of the church, and were not in God's original plan. Jesus only founded one church, 'one body' (Eph 4:4), to which *all* true Christians belong. Your loyalty is first to Christ and his universal church, and then to the local church where he has put you. Open your heart to all believers and pray for them (Eph 6:18). Don't be put off by 'labels'. One day all will be united (Jn 17:20–21).

Any place for 'loners'?

Christians who don't have a church? Imagine my hand decides to 'go independent', and not receive signals from my head through my arm. And if all the other parts did the same, the body would be paralysed and die. 'Church' is not meetings or activities, it is *people in relationship*.

The New Testament doesn't say, 'Go to church and so be a good Christian'. It says in so many words, 'you Christians belong to each other' (see Rom 12:5), 'so get it together' (see Eph 4:2–3).

Giving and receiving

This is what the church is all about. If you want to receive in a big way you must learn to give in a big way, and we are not simply talking about money. That's what Jesus said (Lk 6:38). Start asking, 'What can I put into this?' not 'What can I get out of this?' and then you will get far more out than you put in. You may ask, 'What will I be expected to give?' We'll be answering that in greater detail in the following studies in this section. But first and most important, you must *give yourself* (2 Cor 8:5).

Wholehearted commitment

'The team won because of their total commitment' (sports commentator). This is what Jesus expects of his disciples (Lk 14:33). Didn't he give himself totally for us (Gal 2:20b)? Imagine a wife saying to her husband, 'I am fond of living with you but I don't like living with your body!' Your real attitude to Christ is seen by your attitude to his body, the church. You cannot be wholehearted to the one and half-hearted to the other (Mt 25:40; 1 Jn 4:20).

Commitment means faithfulness

That means: (a) *Being faithful in meeting* with your brothers and sisters to encourage them (Heb 10:25). (b) *Being faithful in sharing* your life, your time, your gifts, your money (Heb 13:16). Fellowship ('two fellows in one ship!') is sharing. (c) *Being faithful in submitting* to the elders and leaders who are shepherds of the flock (Heb 13:17). In a later session you will learn more about this.

Memorize: *For where two or three come together in my name, there am I with them* (Mt 18:20).

Home task

1. The New Testament tells us that Christ is the head of the church, which is his body (Col 1:18). Write down in your notebook what you think this means in practical terms (see also 1 Cor 12:14–27).

2. You have seen that being part of the church means

51

being wholly committed to your fellow believers. Write down in your notebook what you think such a commitment would mean for you. Pray over each point that God will help you be committed.

Introducing Study 8

LEARNING TO RELATE

We have been saying that *church* is all to do with getting along together, that is, relationships. Later you will see how essential relationships are if the church is to do its job. But in this study we will show that *love* is the cement that holds the building together.

It sounds so nice and easy—till you start doing it! Perhaps you think to yourself, 'If only everyone was as easy to get on with as I am!' If you think that, you don't yet know yourself—not fully. But you soon will—with the help of your fellow Christians! They will bring to the surface things deep down inside you that you did not know were there. You will learn to love them just as they are. And in the same way they will learn to love you. It is this kind of relationship that makes the church strong.

Learning to relate

Read 1 Corinthians 13

Introduction

Have you ever flared up when someone said something unkind about you? It wasn't really the unkind words that did it; they only caused 'something inside' to surface. It's learning how to deal with that 'something inside' and to get along with others that God will use to change you and make you like Jesus.

Holding together

Keeping 'the unity of the Spirit' keeps the church strong. 'United we stand. Divided we fall.' The devil, our arch-enemy, is always at work among Christians to cause division. Therefore, 'Make every effort to keep the unity of the Spirit' (Eph 4:3). How do we do that?

Love is the cement

The church includes all sorts. Some of your fellow Christians you would never have chosen as your friends, but God has chosen them for you, to shape you. But this calls for love. The cement that holds the church together is not natural or human love, but God's love. Love is his very character (1 Jn 4:7–8). When the Holy Spirit came to you he brought that love (Rom 5:5).

Love must be expressed

It's not just a warm feeling deep inside. It is not words without deeds (1 Jn 3:18). A young man in love with a girl who does not respond will look for ways to stir up a response. You must learn to do that to your brothers and sisters (Heb 10:24) by acts of thoughtfulness and unselfishness.

Love will be tested

It's not only your *actions* you need to watch, but your *reactions* to what others do to you or say about you. This is where love is put to the test. It's not just being kind to those you like, but learning to love those you don't like, who 'rub you up the wrong way'. It helps to remember (a) How patient God is with your faults. (b) Others have to put up with them too. (c) You tend to think of your faults as trivial and the other person's as big, but see what Jesus said (Mt 7:3–5).

Love always forgives

Think how Jesus expressed his love in this way on the cross (Lk 23:34). Where would we be without a forgiving God (Heb 10:17)? A forgiving spirit is what you must have in your heart, even before the other person says sorry. Jesus always taught that if you do not forgive your brother you won't be forgiven by your Father in heaven (Mt 6:4–15).

Handling the breakdown

Jesus knew that there would sometimes be a breakdown in fellowship between believers, and so taught us how to handle it. He spoke of two situations:

1. When you know it's your fault. (Read Mt 5:23–24.) 'Offering your gift' means praying, worshipping or serving God. God's acceptance of your 'gift' must wait until you get things right, so go first and make up the quarrel ('be reconciled'). Don't say, 'It's half your fault!' Simply confess your part and leave the rest with God.

2. When you believe it's his fault. (Read Mt 18:15–17.) Sometimes, in spite of how strongly you feel, it's fifty-fifty who's right and who's wrong, and so you don't get things right the first time. Taking 'one or two others along' the second time may help here. Even if it is all his fault your attitude must be right. You're not out to 'tear him apart' or 'show him up', but to *win* him—back to you, and back to the Lord. You must have a forgiving spirit and want to be one with him.

Who is responsible to act?

According to this teaching of Jesus, *you* are the one to act when fellowship breaks down—always! If *you're in the wrong or it's fifty-fifty,* you must go to the other person. If he's in the wrong you still go to him. You may say, 'But what about the other fellow?' Sure, he is equally responsible, but you don't have to answer to God for his obedience to this teaching, only for your own.

Memorize: *Be kind and compassionate to one another, forgiving each other, just as in Christ God forgave you* (Eph 4:32).

Home task

Find a quiet place, taking your notebook and ball-point:

1. List the names of those you have not forgiven. Ask God to bring them to mind. Decide there and then that you will forgive each one. It is often hardest, yet most important, to forgive those who are, or have been, closest to us, such as husbands and wives, fathers and mothers, brothers and sisters, fiancés or boy/girl friends. Call on God to give you a forgiving spirit, to drive all anger and bitterness out of your heart, and to fill it with his love.

2. Ask God to show you if there is anyone with whom you are not on speaking terms where it's *your* fault. Pray for God's help to put all such matters right. If you can go and see the wronged person do so, telling them you are sorry and asking their forgiveness. Otherwise write or phone. If more than an apology is needed, such as money to be repaid, do that also. Tell them that you are now a follower of Christ and are doing this to obey his word.

Introducing Study 9

THE COVENANT MEAL

Water baptism and the Lord's Supper (also called Holy Communion or breaking of bread) are the two great 'ordinances', or recognized religious ceremonies, of the church. We dealt with water baptism in the first section of the course, as it is very much part of Christian initiation or 'coming into Christ'. Now we are going to deal with this second ordinance, which I have called 'the covenant meal', for it belongs very much to this second section, expressing something very important about our commitment to each other, and our relationship together in the body of Christ.

The two ordinances of baptism and the Lord's Supper have certain common features. They both point directly to Christ, and are intended to remind us of what he did on the cross. Both illustrate different aspects of our present union with Christ by faith, which spring from the cross. Both are witnesses and proclamations of Christ by the believer. However, one essential difference is that water baptism, since it has to do with our initiation into Christ, does not need to be repeated, while the Lord's Supper points to our ongoing communion with Christ, and so we do it again and again. The truth that 'you are in Christ', which we find continually in Paul's epistles, is illustrated in water baptism. The corresponding truth that 'Christ is in you' giving you spiritual life and energy, is one of the great truths we shall see pictured in the covenant meal.

The Covenant Meal

Read Luke 22:7–20

The meal foreshadowed

The night God brought Israel out of Egypt a lamb was killed in every Israelite household, its blood sprinkled on the doorpost to save that family from the angel of death, and then the lamb was roasted and eaten. Every year afterwards they celebrated the Passover feast to remind them of their deliverance from slavery. This event in Israel's history was but a picture of the deliverance of God's people from the slavery of sin by Christ at the cross. It was while celebrating the Passover, as we saw in our reading (verse 7), that Christ replaced the Passover Feast with this covenant meal.

The first occasion

How Christ, the head of the church, observed this meal provides us with some keys as to how he wants us to observe it. Note these features:

1. *The day.* It was neither Sabbath nor Sunday. Any day is suitable.

2. *The place.* A private home, so no special place of worship is necessary.

3. The circumstances. An event of simplicity and informality in an evening of conversational teaching.

The meaning of the meal

The two elements are the bread, representing Christ's body, and the cup (of wine) representing his blood. His body was given up to death and his blood was shed to save us. The bread, 'the staff of life', teaches us that we have life by his death. The cup teaches us that we have cleansing and forgiveness by his blood. Observing the supper is therefore:

1. An act of remembrance. Jesus said, 'Do this in remembrance of me' (Lk 22:19). He wanted the event of the cross to be always fresh in our minds. It is one way in which we say a big thank you. The cup is called 'the cup of thanksgiving' (1 Cor 10:16).

2. An act of confession. Since only those committed to Christ have a right to share in the meal, doing so becomes a confession of Christ as Saviour and Lord. By this means 'you proclaim the Lord's death' (1 Cor 11:26).

3. An act of participation or fellowship, with Christ. You don't just gaze at the elements, you eat and drink, and so participate in the body and blood of Christ (1 Cor 10:16). Jesus had spoken earlier of eating his flesh and drinking his blood, and so having his life (Jn 6:53–54). That happened at your conversion. But the covenant meal teaches us that we need to feed on Christ continually by faith, and find our nourishment in him.

4. An act of covenant. In your reading Jesus said, 'This cup is the new covenant in my blood' (Lk 22:20). You don't take the Lord's Supper on your own, but with those who are in the same new covenant. The loaf not only speaks of the physical body of Jesus that was crucified for us, but also of his spiritual body, the church, of which we are all members (1 Cor 10:17). In the meal we are celebrating that we are not only in covenant relationship with Christ, but also with one another.

Learning from Corinth

Turn to 1 Corinthians 11. Paul had to rebuke the Corinthian Christians because of the way they were observing the Lord's Supper. Some went hungry while others got drunk. By doing this they were despising the church and humiliating other believers (verses 21–22). They may have been having a communal meal, but instead of expressing covenant they were denying it. They were bringing God's judgement on themselves because they were not recognizing in their brothers and sisters the presence of the body of Christ (verse 29). As a result many had been taken ill, and some had even died (verse 30).

To avoid eating and drinking in an unworthy manner we must examine ourselves (verse 28), and put right anything wrong, especially in our relationships with other Christians.

Blessing and healing

It is often said that the Supper is 'a means of grace'. That is, it is designed by God to bring us blessing. But there is nothing magical or mechanical about it. There is no virtue in the bread and wine in themselves, even after they have been prayed over, and you don't receive blessing automatically by eating and drinking. It is only by faith that the life of Christ is imparted. By eating and drinking unworthily the Corinthians brought sickness and death on themselves. On the other hand it is possible to come to the Lord's table in faith and receive healing as well as other spiritual blessings. If you need healing look to God for it as you share in the Supper, for it comes as a result of his death (Is 53:4).

A few practical matters

As to how often we should observe the Lord's Supper, Jesus simply said 'whenever' (1 Cor 11:26), without saying how often. In times of revival believers may want it every day. This was the case after Pentecost (Acts 2:46). And they did it at home, which means it hasn't necessarily or always to be at church as in 1 Corinthians 11. Nowhere does Scripture require a minister or leader to be present. It could be a family affair, or after a time of fellowship with friends.

Memorize: *For whenever you eat this bread and drink this cup, you proclaim the Lord's death until he comes* (1 Cor 11:26).

Home task

Use your notebook to answer the following questions:

1. 'A man ought to examine himself' (1 Cor 11:28). What do you think that means practically? (Ps 139:23–24 will help you.)

2. What kind of things do you think would disqualify you from breaking bread?

3. If you come to take the Lord's Supper wanting to receive healing for your body or some other blessing in your Christian life: (a) What is the spiritual quality you most need (re-read your notes)? (b) How do you get it?

Introducing Study 10

YOUR LEADERS

God might have arranged things so that we Christians get all our instructions from God direct, and are responsible to him alone. But God has planned something very different. Though he does speak to us directly and personally, he also raises up leaders to act on his behalf. They have a very important part to play in teaching us God's will. The Bible often speaks of God's people as a flock and the leaders as the shepherds. How we respond to those whom God sets over us will have a great effect on our spiritual development.

Every believer has to learn to come 'under authority'. Only when we have learned this can we be entrusted 'with authority' over others. In this study you will learn about the leaders in the church, what they do, and how God wants you to relate to them.

Your Leaders

Read 1 Timothy 3:1–12

Order in the universe

It is a law of God's universe that in every area of life some people have to lead, and that means *authority*. All authority comes from God, and even governments are appointed by God (Rom 13:1). Where authority is lacking there is disorder and evil (Judg 17:6). In the church God raises up leaders and equips them to care for his people. We shall speak briefly of *travelling leaders,* and then concentrate on *local leaders*, as these are the ones with whom you will directly relate.

Travelling leaders

(Read Eph 4:11–13.) Note that these men have received gifts from Christ (verses 7–10) for special tasks. Apostles, prophets and evangelists all travel beyond their local churches. *Apostles* are spiritual builders like Paul, sent to found new churches and help them to grow strong. *Prophets* bring an immediate word from God to direct or correct what God's people are doing. Both are concerned with the building up and uniting of Christ's body. *Evangelists* reach out to bring new people to Christ, and train the churches to do the same. In New Testament times it was the travelling leaders, not some big church head-quarters, who linked the churches and made them feel one.

Now we must look at the local leaders, that is, the elders and the deacons (Phil 1:1).

The elders

These are also called 'overseers', translated 'bishops' in our older versions, though quite different from what people understand by bishops today. Elders have to be mature and stable men, able to teach others. Though the apostles single them out and appoint them, it is God who makes them (Acts 20:28). Their task is to shepherd the flock of God (1 Pet 5:2). This means:

1. *Feeding*. Not only giving them food (i.e. teaching) but leading them into 'green pastures' (Ps 23:2) where they can learn to feed themselves from God's word. As one newly born into God's family, you will especially need feeding with the right food. Babies need milk, not a mixed grill! (1 Pet 2:2.)

2. *Tending*, as a doctor tends the sick. In every flock there are 'sheep' who are spiritually weak and sickly (1 Thess 5:14). Elders are committed to getting the sheep whole and strong. We have to learn to accept their remedies.

3. *Protecting*. Sheep are easily attacked by robbers or wild animals. Paul told the elders at Ephesus, 'Guard yourselves and all the flock' (read Acts 20:28-31). Elders must watch over the flock as those who have to answer to 'the chief shepherd'. Christ (1 Pet 5:3-4).

4. *Leading*. Shepherds in Bible lands always led the flock (Jn 10:4). It was the butchers who drove! Leaders have to take the lead. This means two things. They set an example for us to follow (1 Pet 5:3). They cry 'Come on',

not 'Go on!' Second, they give direction for the flock as a whole, and steer them on the right course.

5. *Ruling.* Sheep, if they want to be shepherded, must come under the shepherd's staff (Ezek 20:37), that is, under his authority. If the sheep do not submit, the shepherd cannot lead. So give your shepherd entry into your life, to correct and discipline you. This is not a harsh authority, but a loving rule to make you strong and secure.

The deacons

The word means servant. Deacons are a clearly recognized body appointed to assist the elders by serving the church in special ways, according to their gift. Elders are always men (1 Tim 3:2), but deacons may include women (Rom 16:1; 1 Tim 3:11 NIV margin, or NASB). Some would be gifted in administration, others to help the elders in shepherding and teaching. Deacons do not rule, or make decisions for the flock, but if they serve well they 'gain an excellent standing', leading to something higher (1 Tim 3:13).

Responding to your leaders

How we respond to them is how we respond to God who appointed them. We are commanded in Scripture to:

1. *'Respect' them and 'hold' them in the highest regard in love because of their work* (1 Thess 5:12–13). They have to work hard (verse 12).

2. *'Obey' them and 'submit' to their authority (Heb 13:17).* Obedience is an act, submission an attitude. You may obey with a bad attitude. See how Jesus obeyed his Father (Ps 40:8). You might also disobey with a right attitude, but that would be in the unlikely event of a leader requiring you to disobey God, as happened with the apostles (Acts 5:29).

3. Be loyal and faithful. If you do the first two, this will follow. You won't criticize or murmur, or listen to others who do this (Jas 4:11; 5:9). If you have difficulty with anything elders say or do they will always want you to go straight to them and talk it out.

Memorize: *Obey your leaders and submit to their authority. They keep watch over you as men who must give an account* (Heb 13:17).

Home task

1. Read about the false shepherds in Ezekiel 34:1–6 and write down the six things that they did *not* do (verses 3–4), and the two things that they did that were wrong (verses 2, 4b).

2. Go through in the notes the five things that elders do, and write down against each why you need that sort of shepherding care.

Introducing Study 11

PLAY YOUR PART

Church was never intended to be 'a show' with a stage performer and an audience, plus a little bit of audience participation, such as singing hymns and saying 'amen' at the end of prayers. Church does not consist of 'priest and people'. It consists of people, all of whom are priests.

Already you have learned that the New Testament speaks of Christ as the head, and the church as his body. The purpose of your physical body is to express what your head is thinking, but this requires every part of your body to be working properly and obeying the signals coming from the head. It is just like that in the body of Christ. You are now a part of Christ's body, with a definite role to play, even though you may not be too clear as yet what that role is.

In this lesson you will learn that there is a spiritual contribution that you can begin to make, as well as human skills and abilities you can use, to glorify God as well as to serve and bless your brothers and sisters. A life of serving is the most fulfilling life there is.

Play your part

Read Romans 12:3–13

A special task

There are no spare parts in the body of Christ. You have
been hand-picked and placed in that body for a special
purpose. (Remember Study 3.) It is not simply that you
might go to heaven, but also that you might serve God on
earth (1 Thess 1:9).

Finding your place

Children playing a 'pretend' game often squabble over
who's to be leader, and what part each is to play. In the
church God chooses what each is to do (1 Cor 12:28).
Your role will be suited to your gifts and personality. As
you grow spiritually that will become clear, if not to you,
at least to your shepherd. Meanwhile, whatever lies to
your hand, or whatever you are asked to do, do it with all
your heart (Eccles 9:10).

Learning to serve

More important than what we actually do is *how* we do it.
Motive is what drives us, like the mainspring that makes

the clock go. Our motive must not be primarily our own happiness and self-satisfaction, but a desire to *serve* our fellow Christians, and thus serve Christ. Of course God wants us to be happy and fulfilled, but when we make these things our goal we miss them. Someone said, 'I looked at the Lamb of God, and the dove of peace flew into my heart. I looked at the dove of peace and it flew away!' In Study 7 we saw that spiritual gifts were not given to us for our benefit, but to enable us to serve Christ's body. Jesus taught that serving others was the path to promotion in his kingdom, and that he himself had not come to *have* a servant, but to *be* a servant (Mt 20:25–28). Serving is love in action, a love that does not seek its own interests (1 Cor 13:5), but the interests of others (Phil 2:4). The Holy Spirit is able to fill you with that love (Rom 5:5).

You are a priest

In the Old Testament the priests were a special class of God's people qualified to offer sacrifices for the people who could not do that for themselves. As believers in Christ we no longer need a priest between us and God as the Israelites did, but are all made priests (Rev 1:6) and so have direct access to God (Eph 2:18). Being priests does not necessarily make us leaders, but does qualify us to offer spiritual sacrifices (e.g. praise, worship, service) to God (1 Pet 2:5).

Offering up spiritual sacrifices

Don't think to yourself, 'I could never do that'. You have begun to do it already without realizing it! Each time you prayed or thanked God on your own you were acting as a priest and offering a sacrifice. Start doing it with your teacher in these times together, and you will find it won't be a big step to do it in a cell or home group. There are few things that will thrill your fellow Christians more than to hear you participate for the first time. This in turn will give you confidence to open your mouth to share, testify, pray, give thanks or even exercise a spiritual gift in the congregation (1 Cor 14:26). As you grow the Holy Spirit will teach you when and how to participate under the authority of your leader.

Practical service

'If it is serving, let him serve' (Rom 12:7). This includes practical ways, as well as participating in meetings. If God's love is in your heart there will be many opportunities to meet the needs of others, e.g. moving house, baby-sitting, ironing, cooking, cleaning, gardening, shopping, providing hospitality or transport. Some have particular skills, e.g. plumbing, wiring, carpentry, decorating, typing, dressmaking. You will have great joy and fulfilment whenever you do any of these things out of love for others, for you will be serving Christ.

Memorize: *I tell you the truth, whatever you did for one of the least of these brothers of mine, you did for me* (Mt 25:40).

Home task

1. Go through the reading again in Romans 12. In verses 6–8 and verse 13 there are some eight or nine ways in which we may serve the body of Christ. List them under two columns in your notebook, first those that mainly refer to Christian *meetings*, and then those that could be

outside of meetings. Ask the Lord to help you to serve his body in both areas.

2. Make a list of the practical ways in which you think you would be able to serve others. There's no need to confine your list to the ways listed in the notes. Then ask God to fill your heart with his love, so that when the need arises you will be eager to serve, knowing that you are truly serving Christ.

Introducing Study 12

MONEY MATTERS

Of course money matters! It matters to you and it matters to God. That's why the Bible has so much to say about it. There's nothing wrong with money. We all find it pretty useful. But it's the craving some people have for more and more of it, the things they do to get it and how they then use it that can be evil.

In the world the man with money is usually respected as a man of influence, while the poor person is often despised. Though it's not like that in the kingdom of God, your attitude to money and how you handle it is seen as a test of your character. When Christ bought you for himself, he bought you right out, your possessions and all. You cannot therefore give yourself wholly to him without giving your money and your possessions. This means that you no longer own anything, you just manage it for God. One day he is going to summon all his 'managers', you and me included, and ask us to give an account to him of how we handled what he entrusted to us. This lesson is to help you to become a good manager, so that you won't blush when you have to give your answer.

Money Matters

Read 1 Timothy 6:3–10

Money can be dangerous!

The Bible speaks of money as being both an instrument for the kingdom of God (Lk 16:9) and 'a root of all kinds of evil' (1 Tim 6:10). That proves it isn't the money itself, but our attitude to it and how we use it that makes the difference. Here are some important safeguards:

1. Don't love it or get infected by the 'get rich quick' fever of the world. See what the reading 1 Timothy 6:6–10 says are the tragic spiritual results of wanting to be rich. Note too the remedy for this wrong attitude—learning to be content with what God provides.

2. Don't make a god of it. 'You cannot serve both God and money' (Mt 6:24). Whatever you put in the place of God is an idol. Don't be an idolator. Many Christians have drifted far from God because they put money and prosperity in that first place that rightly belonged to God.

3. Don't hoard it up. Men 'lay up treasure on earth' for security, but your treasures can be corrupted and your money taken from you (Mt 6:19). Instead of hoarding up what is 'so uncertain' (1 Tim 6:17) we should invest what we do not need in the kingdom of God. That's laying up treasure in heaven. That will not prevent us from making adequate provision for our families (1 Tim 5:8).

4. *Don't run into debt.* Christians who are always running into debt are poor managers and bad advertisements for the kingdom of God. The only ongoing debt we are allowed is 'to love one another' (Rom 13:8). House mortgages are not debts, but watch those credit cards. Don't let them tempt you to buy what you can't afford.

Your money is God's

As a Christian you and all that you have belong to God. Your money is like the 'talents' (Mt 25:14 ff) Your Master entrusts you with it and gives you freedom to use it, but it is really his. He is testing you to see whether you will be 'faithful' (1 Cor 4:2) as his manager, or 'wasteful' (Lk 16:1). One day we shall have to give an account.

Learning to give

God is the greatest giver (Jn 3:16), and you are called to be like him. You don't do God a favour by your giving. You are simply recognizing that it's all his anyway. Some have a special gift of giving (Rom 12:8), not necessarily because they are wealthy, but because they have faith for this. Offering hospitality is an additional and valuable means of giving (1 Pet 4:9). How to give?

1. *Freely and cheerfully* (2 Cor 9:7). It's not meant to be like having a tooth out!

2. *According to what you receive* (1 Cor 16:2). Heaven estimates our giving by comparing what we give with what we keep (Mk 12:41–44).

3. *Systematically and prayerfully.* Not rummaging round in pocket or handbag at the last moment (1 Cor 16:2).

4. *Secretly.* Not making a big show of how generous you are (Mt 6:1–4).

75

Sowing and reaping

This is how Scripture likens giving (2 Cor 9:6–11). For every grain you sow, you may expect to reap many more. Generous reaping depends on generous sowing (verse 6), and you reap spiritual blessing, not just financial (verse 10). See what a generous return God promises you (Lk 6:38).

Tithes and offerings

Tithing is giving a tenth of what you receive back to God. Offerings were additional gifts—how much and how often is a matter of free will, hence 'free will offerings'. In the Old Testament tithes were for the support of priest and Levites. Similarly in the church, tithes are for the support of people (full-time shepherds or those who are in need) and offerings are generally for church expenses, special projects, or for the work of God outside your own congregation that you may want to support. When the people failed to bring their tithes and offerings into God's house to support his servants, God said they were robbing him (Mal 3:8–10).

Memorize: *Give, and it will be given to you. A good measure, pressed down, shaken together and running over, will be poured into your lap. For with the measure you use, it will be measured to you (Lk 6:38).*

Home task

1. How does Proverbs 3:9a describe our giving to God?

Write it down, and tell God that this is what you intend to do.

2. Read 2 Corinthians 8:1–7. It tells of the giving of the Macedonian churches in north Greece to help their brothers and sisters in need. Write down:

(a) how Paul describes their response (verse 9);

(b) what their own financial position was at the time (verse 2);

(c) how Paul describes their giving (verse 2);

Work out what would be a tenth of your income, and determine to put it aside for God. You don't have to be earning. You can start while at school, as I did, with pocket-money and money gifts.

Introducing Study 13

THE KINGDOM IS COMING

In this closing section on 'getting along together', let's take a look at the worldwide task that calls for such togetherness. It is summed up in one phrase, 'the kingdom of God'.

Only twice did Jesus speak directly of 'the church', but again and again he spoke of 'the kingdom'. What is the kingdom? Does it differ from the church? And what did Jesus mean when he told us to pray, 'Thy kingdom come'? Finding answers to these questions will enlarge your horizon, way beyond your own personal life or your own congregation, to see that you are part of a worldwide movement that is fast gathering momentum, and will end in total victory, just as God's word has promised. You can afford to ignore those lies of Satan that suggest you are part of a weak and failing cause. The fact is that you are part of a kingdom whose glory will one day fill the earth, as the waters cover the sea. This will inspire you to play your part in the coming of Christ's kingdom both by the way you live and the way you witness.

The Kingdom Is Coming

Read Matthew 28:16–20

Understanding the kingdom

In Scripture 'kingdom' is not so much the territory over which a king rules, as *the rule itself*. The kingdom of God is the rule of God, firstly over the lives of those who, like you, submit to his rule (Mt 7:21), and then over the whole world and its course of events. Here he overrules what men do to bring to pass his purposes in the earth (Dan 4:34–35). The church and the kingdom are closely related, but the kingdom emphasizes *the thing God is doing*, while the church emphasizes *the people he is using* to do it.

How the kingdom comes

You have seen that your conversion involved repentance for the past, and then coming under God's rule (Study 5). In this way you entered God's kingdom (Col 1:13). The coming of the kingdom means making the rule of God effective *in* the lives of men, and then making it effective *through* their lives, so that the will of God is done on earth (Mt 6:10).

The Bible does not teach that the world will be converted

or Christianized (Rev 22:11), but it does promise such a turning to God that nations become Christ's inheritance, and the ends of the earth his possession (Ps 2:8). Despite opposition and persecution the church in the New Testament became the most powerful movement of its day. So it will be throughout the earth in these end days. The crowning victory will be the personal return of Christ (Study 20). How, then, does God use his church to bring in his kingdom?

Kingdom lifestyle

Your new-found faith has brought you a new way to live. Your lifestyle has already changed, and will continue to do so. Certain practices, habits, ambitions and attitudes have dropped off, and new ones are forming, as you allow Jesus to rule. The influence of God's kingdom is not negative but positive. We are to be known because of what we do, not because of what we don't do. 'For the kingdom of God is... righteousness, peace and joy in the Holy Spirit'—qualities the world does not have but desperately needs. It goes on to say that such qualities are 'pleasing to God and approved by men' (Rom 14:17–18). This is a powerful way of influencing men, and happened with the first Christians (Acts 5:13). But there is something else:

Speaking boldly

Witnessing, i.e. telling others what Christ has done for us, is our joy and privilege, as well as our responsibility. The Holy Spirit was given to empower us to do this (Acts 1:8). The first Christians, though they had received the Holy Spirit, still prayed for more boldness, and were filled again with the Spirit for this purpose (Acts 4:29, 31). You will need to do the same. You don't need to know a lot or be able to answer difficult questions. Just to share what Jesus has done for you. The blind man that Jesus healed admitted that he couldn't answer the questions fired at him, but he added, 'One thing I do know. I was blind but now I see!' (Jn 9:25). There's no answer to that.

Memorize: *For the kingdom of God is not a matter of eating and drinking, but of righteousness, peace and joy in the Holy Spirit (Rom 14:17).*

Home task

1. How much has your lifestyle changed as a result of becoming a Christian? Write down in your notebook:
(a) Where you know God has changed you, e.g. habits, language, attitudes, ambitions, relationships, handling money, business methods etc. Thank God for each change.
(b) Where you still need to change. Ask God to make each one happen.
2. How is your witnessing going?
(a) If you have already witnessed to relatives, friends, workmates etc., ask God to show you the next step. He may want you to speak again, invite them to a meeting or give them a booklet to read. There may be others that you still need to witness to for the first time. Write down what you believe God is telling you to do.
(b) If you have not witnessed to relatives and friends, decide to make a start. Ask God to show you with whom to begin, to give you an opening and courage to take it. The first time is like breaking the ice. It's not so hard after that.
(c) Whether you come under (a) or (b), ask God to fill you afresh with his Spirit and make you bold.

SECTION 3

Growing in God

(Studies 14–20)

A gardener noticed that one of the young plants in his greenhouse was wilting, while all the others of the same variety were thriving. When he tapped it out of the pot and looked at the roots he found that they were being attacked by a small insect. He destroyed the insect and the plant thrived.

As a plant draws its nourishment from the soil, so you draw your life from God. If there's something wrong with your spiritual roots, you won't thrive. This section is all about your life in God, how to make sure that nothing hinders its flow, learning how to nourish it day by day by having fellowship with God and feeding on his word.

It's the leaves, flowers and fruit of the plant that we see and enjoy. Because the roots are hidden we don't always realize how important they are. There may be many aspects of your Christian life that are more obviously interesting and attractive, but none that are more important than your spiritual roots. In this final section of the course you will learn how to keep them healthy and strong, so that you thrive as a Christian, and don't wilt.

Introducing Study 14

A CLEAR CONSCIENCE

The burglar alarm rang in the middle of the night at a certain business premises, and the police were soon on the spot investigating. But it wasn't an intruder this time, just a fault in the circuit.

Conscience is like an alarm bell that God uses to wake us up to the fact that something is wrong. Everybody has a conscience, but when it comes to registering what is right and what is wrong, different consciences may come up with different readings. Sometimes the bell doesn't ring when it should. Sometimes, like the business premises just mentioned, there is a false alarm.

What is conscience? How does it work? Why do different consciences sometimes tell their owners different things? Why is it that your conscience is troubled now by things that never bothered you before you became a Christian? This study will provide you with answers. Most important of all, it will explain why it is so important to keep a clear conscience, and how that is done.

A Clear Conscience

Read Romans 2:12–16

What is conscience?

It's an inner prompting to do what we think to be right and to avoid what we think to be wrong. It's an inner voice that is 'bearing witness' to you, 'accusing' you, if it thinks you are wrong, or 'defending' you if it thinks you are right (Rom 2:15). If you heed these promptings you have 'a good [or clear] conscience' (1 Tim 1:5). If you disregard them you have 'a guilty conscience' (Heb 10:22). Every human being, however primitive, has a conscience.

Is it reliable?

A head hunter may have no conscience about scalping a man from another tribe, but may feel guilty about killing a monkey, because he has been taught that monkeys are sacred. What is fed into the mind concerning what is right or wrong will determine how the conscience works. It's like a computer. Only if you feed it with the right information will it come up with the right answers. Since you have come to know God and to read his word, you will have a much clearer idea of what pleases and what displeases him than you had before.

What happened at conversion?

In the run up to your conversion the Holy Spirit used your conscience to make you feel guilty. It's his work to 'convict [or fully convince] the world of guilt' (Jn 16:8). It was his convicting that drove you to Christ. It was the truth of the gospel fed into your mind that enlightened your conscience, and brought about a new awareness of sin that you hadn't had before.

As you grasp more and more truth about the will of God your conscience will become more and more enlightened. This doesn't necessarily mean that you feel guilty about more and more things. It also works the other way round. Paul speaks of believers with 'a weak conscience' that was not fully enlightened. They felt guilty when there was no reason to (1 Cor 8:7–8). An enlightened conscience would free them from this. Remember the burglar alarm that went off when there was no burglar! How important it is to be 'filled with the knowledge of God's will' (Col 1:9).

Is a clear conscience important?

Very important. Our salvation is to set us free from condemnation (Rom 8:1), but if your conscience is not clear you will always be under condemnation. This will affect:

1. *Your fellowship with God.* You won't enjoy God's presence. It's like when you were a small child, you never felt comfortable with your parents when you had a guilty conscience.

2. *Your faith.* A guilty conscience and a strong faith just don't go together. Put the matter right, and at once faith is restored.

3. *Your prayer life.* A man came to Christ, and the Holy Spirit reminded him that as a boy he had stolen a bag of nails from Woolworths. Every time he tried to pray he

saw a bag of nails! Only when he went back to the store and put the matter right could he get through in prayer.

4. Your desire for God's word. A troubled conscience can rob a person of his appetite for natural food; how much more for spiritual food.

5. Your witness. You may want to open your mouth to speak for the Lord, but Satan whispers, 'You have no right to witness. You're a hypocrite.'

If you set your alarm clock at night, but persistently ignore it in the morning, the time will come when you will sleep right through it. If a person wilfully goes on ignoring 'the inner voice', it will stop speaking. That means 'a seared conscience' (see 1 Tim 4:2).

How to keep a clear conscience

There are four important steps:

1. Immediate confession of sin. Do it the moment you become aware of sin (1 Jn 1:9). By praying, as Jesus taught, 'Forgive us our debts', we can keep short accounts with God. Then, when you have confessed:

2. Trust in the promise of cleansing. God is faithful and just to forgive and cleanse us (1 Jn 1:9). Our very consciences are cleansed by the blood when we confess (Heb 9:14). Then:

3. Obey your conscience. Do what you failed to do, or stop doing what you ought not to do. It's not enough to confess our failure. We must stop failing (Jas 1:22).

4. Continue to walk in the light (1 Jn 1:7). That means keeping open to God, sensitive to the Holy Spirit (that 'still small voice' inside) and ready to obey immediately.

Memorize: *I strive always to keep my conscience clear
                 before God and man* (Acts 24:16—the
                 words of Paul the apostle).

Home task

1. Make sure you have a clear conscience. If there is
nothing troubling you, don't become 'inward looking' by
searching for what isn't there! Just praise God for the
blessing of being in the light with God. But if you don't
have a clear witness that all is right, pray the prayer of
David in Psalm 139:23–24 and, as God answers, take the
four steps mentioned above.

2. You are trying to help a friend who says he has
confessed his sin to God but has no assurance of forgiveness. Write down in your notebook what you would say
to help him. You will find 1 John 1:9 useful.

Introducing Study 15

AMAZING GRACE

Ever stopped to think what is meant by the Old Testament (or covenant) and the New? God made the old covenant (or agreement) with the Israelites when he gave them the law. If they obeyed they would be blessed. If they disobeyed they would be cursed.

The new covenant that came with Jesus was a covenant of grace, not a covenant of law. That is, it was more about promises than commands. It spoke more about what God had done for men than what men could do for God. It promised to put inside men the desire and ability to please him.

Let's take a look at the home where Mother Law rules the roost. She's very strict, has little notices everywhere telling everybody what to do, and what not to do. She is always scolding, but never seems to encourage or help the children.

It's very different in the home where Mother Grace is in charge. Here the children are happy. They tend to be good and obey because their mother has that effect upon them. She encourages them with promises and helps them with their difficulties.

We all know which mother we would prefer to be under. But here's a strange thing. Even today there are believers who have come into God's family under Mother

Grace and then have taken themselves off and gone back under Mother Law. Whatever for? Little wonder Paul says to some Christians who did this, 'O foolish Galatians!' It's like taking a plant out of rich fertile soil and planting it in the desert. And we wonder why the church doesn't thrive!

What is grace? How can we make sure of always living under it? This lesson, one of the most important in the course, will help you to find answers.

Amazing Grace

Read Romans 7:1–6

Only two religions in the world

The religion of law and the religion of grace. Every religion, including the old covenant religion of the Jews (Jn 1:17) and modern cults like Jehovah's Witnesses, belong to the religion of law. It is one of do's and don'ts, by which men try hard, but without success, to please God. The gospel alone is a religion of grace, not emphasizing what we have to do for God, but what he has already done for us. Because the law depended on human effort it was 'weak and useless', and man had to be provided with 'a better hope' in Christ (Heb 7:18–19). He needed some power outside of himself (Rom 8:3). Although grace sets a higher standard than the law (Mt 5:27–28), it also works in us to enable us to live up to that standard (Phil 2:13).

> 'Run, John, and live', the law commands,
> But gives me neither legs nor hands.
> Better news the gospel brings,
> It bids me fly, and gives me wings!

What is grace?

It is the love of God in action towards those who are totally undeserving. It is 'something for nothing for those who don't deserve anything'. Because no man has ever deserved God's mercy, salvation had to be a gift (Rom 6:23). Even the repentance and faith required to receive that gift had to come from God (Acts 11:18; Eph 2:8). We owe everything in our salvation and in our Christian life to grace. It is God's unlimited supply of mercy, love, strength, wisdom, in fact, all we need, flowing freely to us (Jn 1:16). This makes us a joyful, praising people all our lives.

Back under law

The fact that some believers in New Testament times, having come into the kingdom through grace, then went back to a life of rules and regulations, was one of the greatest hindrances to the early progress of Christianity. The letters to Galatians and Hebrews, as well as part of Romans, were written to keep us from that. Even today it is still one of the biggest causes of deadness and defeat among Christians. Believers who are constantly defeated by temptation need to know that Paul never said, 'Try a little harder.' But he *did* say, 'Sin shall not be your master, *because you are not under law, but under grace*' (Rom 6:14). Grace *teaches* and *enables* us to say no to sin and to live a life that pleases God (Tit 2:11–12). To the Galatian Christians who were stupid enough to go back under law, he puts this question, 'Are you so foolish? After beginning with the Spirit, are you now trying to attain your goal by human effort?' (Gal 3:3). When we live by rules and regulations, and that always means human effort taking the place of the power of the Holy Spirit, we are back under law. We call this 'legalism'. We lose our freshness, joy and freedom.

Why does it happen?

For the same reason that many refuse the grace of God in salvation, and prefer to trust their own righteousness. It gives them something to brag about. They show off their righteousness like a street artist does his pictures, with a notice, 'All my own work'. See what God says about that (Tit 3:5). Grace takes away all cause for boasting and throws us wholly on God. Believers also go back under law because they never really understood what Jesus did at the cross. It came in our reading, so let's look at it.

There's a new marriage

In our relationship with the law we are likened to a woman who cannot marry the one (Christ) she really loves, until her present husband (the law) dies (Rom 7:1–3). A death has taken place (at the cross), Paul tells us, by which our union with the law is broken, freeing us to marry the One who rose from the dead, our Lord Jesus, and so become happy and fruitful Christians (verse 4). In other words, Christ's death not only loosed us from our sins, but also loosed us from the law, that old demanding husband. Now we are under a new husband who doesn't ask us to keep house on a pittance, but hands us his cheque book. What do we have to do? Believe completely what Scripture says about our married state—we are 'not under law, but under grace'—and learn how to make out cheques!

Enough—and to spare

'What was your fare?' asked the church treasurer. 'Sixty pence,' replied the visiting preacher. He went home with his bus fare paid. At the next church, knowing that the preacher had a financial struggle, they announced, 'Let us bless our brother with a love offering.' His fare had cost him the same, but he went home with his pocket bulging with bank notes, and a praising heart. Grace goes 'over the top' in generosity. It is God's 'abundant provision' (Rom 5:17). It is 'the riches of God's grace that he *lavished* on us' (Eph 1:7–8). Isn't that absolutely marvellous? God is such a great giver, but we have to learn to be great receivers. No matter what the temptation or testing—no matter what the opportunity or challenge—God's supply of grace is 'enough and to spare'.

Memorize: *He said to me, 'My grace is sufficient for you, for my power is made perfect in weakness' (2 Cor 12:9).*

Home task

This is to be an exercise in making out spiritual cheques.

1. Take a careful look at every area of your Christian life, and note down those where you feel you *greatly need* the grace of God. For example, it could be relationships—in the family, in the church or at work. It could be in your spiritual activities—worshipping, witnessing, praying, reading the Bible. It could be in your own daily life—speech, behaviour, inner thoughts. Don't be discouraged if the list gets very long!

2. Pick out two, or at most three, that you feel are the areas of *most urgent* need. Alongside each write down what is the provision that you want God to supply. Your list could read something like this:

(a) My mother—keeping my cool when she nags!

(b) Jim at work—grace to handle it when he mocks or talks smut.

(c) Discouragement in my Christian life—a tendency to be up and down.

3. Take these areas to God one by one in prayer, and tell him in your own words:

(a) That you are weak. That you haven't got what it takes.

(b) That you know that he has an abundant supply of grace for you. Name exactly what you want—self-control, courage, steadfastness, or whatever.

(c) That you now receive that supply of his grace by faith, that you thank him for the answer, and that you are expecting to see this need supplied.

Note: It would be wise not to add to your initial list of two or three. Just replace them as they get answered. You're in for an exciting time!

Introducing Study 16

TALKING WITH GOD

In Rome there is a sculpture of Moses carved in marble by Michelangelo. When he had finished it he was so overcome by its life-like features, so the story goes, that he exclaimed, 'Speak! Why don't you speak to me?'

Perhaps it broke his heart that he couldn't talk with that object of beauty he had created. The great longing of God's heart is to have fellowship with man. This is the purpose for which we were created. At the beginning we see God enjoying man and man enjoying God. Then sin came, and man ran away and hid from God. That fellowship has now been restored through our Lord Jesus and his salvation. But if you never meet, never write or never phone a friend your friendship fades away very quickly.

Because we have been reconciled to God we cannot take our friendship with him for granted. We must spend time with him. We must learn to listen to what he has to say. We must develop the habit of talking freely with him. Don't think about it as a duty you perform but as an experience you enjoy. Two people in love don't talk to one another because it's a duty but because it's a delight. An old church teaching says, 'The chief end of man is to glorify God and enjoy him for ever.' God wants you to enjoy him and he wants to enjoy you. This study will help to show you how.

Talking with God

Read Psalm 63:1–8

It's a two-way traffic

From the moment you responded to God in repentance and faith, a line of communication between you and God was opened up (Eph 2:17–18). To be in communication with God is a two-way traffic. It is not just you talking with God but it is also God talking with you. So let's think about:

Listening to God

A little intercom in my study links me with my wife in the kitchen, but we have to take it in turns to speak. I have to stop talking in order to listen. It's like that with God. Despite what Jesus said about it, many believers don't take time to listen (Jn 10:27). A wife, suing for divorce, accused her husband of not speaking to her in five years of marriage. 'What have you got to say?' asked the horrified magistrate. Meekly the husband replied, 'Well, er, I didn't like to interrupt...'! In your times of prayer does God ever get a word in?

    1. How God speaks. He uses many ways. He may speak through Scripture, through spiritual gifts such as prophecy, through conscience, through the counsel of a leader or through that quiet inner voice. Because you read the Bible or listen to a sermon does not necessarily mean that you hear God speak. It's when the Holy Spirit makes the words burn in your heart (Lk 24:32), and you feel you want to do something about it.

2. It's friendship with God. Moses met regularly with God, and God spoke to him as a man would speak to his friend (Ex 33:11). In this way Moses came to know God intimately (Ex 33:13). Isn't it wonderful to know that we can have the friendship of the Lord in the same way (Jn 15:15)?

3. It's receiving direction. God has not given us ability to direct our own steps (Jer 10:23). We are not to trust our own wisdom but to trust God for guidance (Prov 3:5–6). David always 'inquired of the Lord', that is, asked God for guidance, before making any major decision (1 Sam 23:2). That's the way to make right decisions. When it says, 'God said to David' it was not usually an audible voice, but an inner voice in his heart. In this way God is able 'to fill you with the knowledge of his will' (Col 1:9).

4. It's receiving correction. If, when praying about something you've planned to do, you become uneasy, it could be God waving a red flag. 'Let the peace of Christ rule [act as umpire] in your hearts' (Col 3:15). When your peace is disturbed it's like the umpire stopping the game. See how Paul's plans were corrected (Acts 16:6–7).

5. It's learning to listen. If you are not hearing from God it's probably because you're not 'tuning in'. God is always 'on the air'. How do you tune in? In your times with God learn to be quiet before him. Pray like Samuel, 'Speak, Lord, for your servant is listening' (1 Sam 3:9). But then, be still and give God a chance to speak. This is what Scripture means when it says 'wait for the Lord' (Ps 27:14). Older versions have 'wait *on* the Lord'.

Praying to God

1. A practice for all seasons. It requires no special technique, no special time, no special place and no special language. Old Bible English is not needed. 'Hear my prayer' is so much better than, 'Wouldest thou have regard unto the petition of thy servant'. Pray at all times (1 Thess 5:17), travelling to work or school, waiting for an interview, wrestling with an exam, in time of danger or temptation. You don't have to close your eyes or kneel. Notice the situation in which Nehemiah prayed (Neh 2:4–5). Prayer should be as natural as breathing. God wants you to share your life with him, and that means joys and sorrows, successes and failures.

2. Time set apart. Besides calling on him in a crisis or talking to him while on the job, it is important that you have regular time set apart when you give him your undivided attention. Jesus had such times (Lk 5:16), and he taught us to pray behind the shut door (Mt 6:6). Some only pray when they feel like it. But there's something in the Scripture called 'self-discipline' or 'self-control' (Gal 5:23). Often in the Christian life you have to learn to say no to yourself (Mk 8:34) by overruling your human desires and inclinations for something which you know to be more important. One evening I was preparing one of these studies when my wife asked if I would go for a walk in the park. I knew she had seen little of me all day, but I did so want to complete what I was doing. I said to myself, 'My wife is more important than my preparation.' Once I made the decision the rest was easy, and we enjoyed our walk together. It's often like that with God. Keeping a time set apart for God doesn't need to be legalistic.

3. How to draw near to God. It is good to start with praise and thanksgiving (Ps 100:4). In fact, always mix your requests with thanksgiving (Phil 4:6). God answers the prayers of grateful people. Don't be self-centred in your asking. Pray for others, not just for yourself. This is called 'intercession'. As you pray for others you will surely be blessed.

4. The greatest of all. 'If only I had some great intercessor to help me.' You have. The greatest intercessor on earth dwells within you to help you to pray according to God's will (Rom 8:26–27), and that ensures answered prayer (1 Jn 5:14). Trust him to guide you, inspire you and give you faith.

Memorize: *Do not be anxious about anything, but in everything, by prayer and petition, with thanksgiving, present your requests to God (Phil 4:6).*

Home task

Even if you have never done it before, take time this week to wait on God. Find a quiet place where you are not likely to be disturbed. Don't try to make your mind a blank, but just be still before God, asking him to speak to you, as Samuel did, and expect that he will.

1. Ask God if he has anything to say to you personally at this time, and then wait before him. Jot down what you believe he is saying, and do anything you believe he is asking of you. At the next session with your teacher share through what you believe God gave you. If he didn't give you anything the first time, don't be discouraged. Persevere in waiting on God and he will begin to speak.

2. Ask God to show you those he wants you to intercede for regularly. Again, jot down the names as they come to mind. Be prepared for him to give you some names you have never thought to pray for.

3. Bring those names to God one by one, and ask him to show you any needs they have individually. You may not hear from God about everyone, but list the things he does give against the names of the people concerned. Use that list as you pray.

Introducing Study 17

HANDLING THE BIBLE

It's sixty-six books, and yet it's one Book. It has many authors, and yet it has one Author. It is the oldest book in the world, and yet it's more up to date than tomorrow's newspaper. Already you will have discovered what a practical book it is, and how it speaks into your present life, and shows you things about yourself that you didn't know, as well as things about God.

The Bible is without doubt the most wonderful book in the world. Do you realize how privileged you are to possess a copy? Many Christians in other parts of the world would give almost anything to have a copy of their own. The best way to show your gratitude to God for the Bible, is not to preserve it in its nice cardboard box, or give it an honoured place on your bookshelf, or carry it around like a lucky charm. The Bible does nothing for you until you receive its truth into your heart and let it change you, as I'm sure you have been doing throughout this course. If in the past you have found the Bible boring or too difficult to understand, it will be very different now as the Holy Spirit begins to unlock its treasures for you.

This study will be a very practical one on *how to handle the Bible* so as to get the most out of it. It won't tell you how to master the Bible, but how to let the Bible master you!

Handling the Bible

Read 1 Peter 1:22–2:3

The power of the book

From the moment you became a child of God you experienced the Bible's power. Verse 23 in the reading reminded you that your new birth was through the action of God's word. How do we explain its power? Although its words came from the lips and pens of men, those words were 'inspired' or 'God-breathed' (2 Tim 3:16), that means that as these men spoke or wrote they were controlled by the Holy Spirit (2 Pet 1:21). God was speaking through them. That alone explains how so many different authors from so many different countries, and living in so many different periods of history, could produce a book in which all the parts harmonize so perfectly.

Getting acquainted with the Author

This is the greatest thing that the Bible does for you. 'I've not met you before,' said someone to me at the close of a meeting, 'but I feel I know you. I've read so much of what you've written.' Acquainting you with the Author is the greatest thing that the Bible does for you as a believer. It's so much more important than filling your mind with infor-

mation about God. The Holy Spirit makes God's word
spirit and life to you (Jn 6:63). Every time you open the
Bible expect to meet the Lord in the Scriptures and hear
him speak.

The importance of right attitudes

If they're not right, no method you use will make your
time with the Bible profitable. If your Bible reading is
dull, the fault is not with the Book or the Author, but with
the reader. The heart attitude with which you approach
the Scriptures is the key to the time being profitable and
enjoyable.

   1. Clear the decks. Look at the above reading again and
notice the things to be rid of before you come for the milk
of God's word (1 Pet 2:1). All these things have to do with
our relationships with others. Bad attitudes will affect
your appetite for God's word. Rid yourself of them by
repentance and confession.

   2. Be hungry. 'Like newborn babies,' continues Peter,
'*crave* (or have a hearty appetite for) pure spiritual milk'
(1 Pet 2:2). If you are regularly opening the Bible with no
spiritual appetite, and your reading doesn't stir it up,
there's something wrong. Watch what else you are reading
and viewing. Feed your mind on garbage and you lose
your love for God's word. To be hungry is to be healthy.
Notice how healthy the Psalmist was (Ps 119:131). If
you're not hungry, ask God to show you why.

   3. Be expectant. Don't just come hungry to the
Scriptures, but come believing that your hunger will be
satisfied. Jesus promised this (Mt 5:6). With God *believing
is always receiving* (Mt 21:22). If you didn't receive, you
didn't really believe, however much you thought you did.

   4. Be submissive. Approach the Bible with a readiness
to obey. Tell God that's how you're coming. Because they
don't have a heart set to obey is the reason why many do

not understand, or even misunderstand God's word. Because the Psalmist had an attitude to obey he could pray confidently for understanding of God's word (Ps 119:34). Obey the light and you will receive more light. That means, obey what you understand of God's will and you will understand more. Disobey, and your light (understanding) can turn to darkness (Mt 6:23b).

The practical needs

Of course, these apply to all the times you set apart for God, whether for Bible reading or prayer or both.

1. A regular time. Don't wait till you feel 'inspired' to read the Bible, but make a daily habit of it. I'm not legalistic because I take regular meals. My stomach looks for it and my health benefits from it! The Bible encourages us to meditate regularly (Ps 1:1–3) as well as to pray and praise regularly as Daniel did (Dan 6:10). It requires a little self-discipline at first, but in time it becomes second nature, like meal times. Note that if Job didn't have time for Bible and breakfast he chose Bible! (Job 23:12.) Many like to read and pray before breakfast. They find their minds are fresh and uncluttered, and that there's less chance of being disturbed by phone or door bell. Some get on better last thing at night. Sometimes Jesus prayed after the day's work was over (Mt 14:23), and sometimes he got up early to do it (Mk 1:35). You must choose the time most suitable to you.

2. A suitable place. This must be a place where you won't be disturbed. In the last scripture Jesus found 'a solitary place'. He told his disciples, 'Go into your room, close the door and pray' (Mt 6:6). We are not to make an exhibition of our devotions. Walking can be a very good way of meditating and praying, but it will require mental discipline to concentrate. It is an answer for those who can't get alone at home.

105

3. A reading plan. It is good to have a plan, but not to be rigid about it. Without a plan you may waste time wondering what to do, or become haphazard, jumping from one passage to another. An approved workman is one 'who correctly handles the word of truth' (2 Tim 2:15). Books of the Bible were written as books, and it is important to read them as books. But where to begin? As a new Christian your urgent need is to learn what it means to be a disciple (learner) of Jesus. So choose a gospel (Matthew, Mark, Luke or John) and go through it. Then take a short epistle, say 1 or 2 Thessalonians. Then go to an Old Testament book, perhaps the Psalms (Israel's prayer and praise book) or Proverbs, which is full of practical teaching on life. You need to be mostly in the New Testament without neglecting the Old Testament. But in your consecutive reading don't be rigid. If some other verse or passage comes alive to you stay with that for a while, then return to your consecutive reading. Let the Spirit lead (Rom 8:14).

4. A helpful method is to read and meditate. Have a notebook with your Bible. As you read slowly, ask God to speak to you (Ps 119:18). Keep on reading until something strikes you, then stop and meditate. That means to turn the words over and over in your mind as though chewing a mouthful of food to get all the goodness out of it. Twice the Bible tells us that we must learn to 'meditate day and night' if we want to be successful for God (Josh 1:8; Ps 1:2–3). The more you do it the easier it will become. Write down in your notebook the thoughts that God gives you. If you get through a whole chapter and nothing has struck you, go through it again. Persevere with it until the Book starts to speak to you.

Memorize: *Do not let this Book of the Law depart from your mouth; meditate on it day and night, so that you may be careful to do everything written in it. Then you will be prosperous and successful (Josh 1:8).*

Home task

1. 2 Timothy 3:16 uses the word 'God-breathed' or 'inspired by God' to tell us why Scripture is different from all other books. Explain what you think this means.

2. The same verse also tells us that Scripture is useful for four things. Explain in the simplest of terms what these four things mean and why they are important in the Christian life. Try to give practical examples.

3. Make a start on the 'read and meditate' method. Start at the beginning of Mark's gospel. Read till something strikes you, and then meditate on it. Write down the thoughts that come to you. Cover two or three different points that strike you.

Introducing Study 18

BEATING TEMPTATION

Temptation, as you will know, is not 'a little surprise' that Satan reserves for committed Christians. Everybody faces it. Perhaps it has troubled you to find that temptations have not eased off since you became a Christian. If anything they have probably increased. Perhaps you have thought, 'If I'm still tempted like this, can I be a real Christian? Has anything really happened?'

In the first place, temptation is not sin. It only becomes sin when you yield to it. In the second place, an increase in temptation is an encouraging sign that something has indeed happened. Your commitment to Christ has made you a threat to the kingdom of evil. Satan, the ruler of that kingdom, has therefore to redouble his efforts to drag you down.

But if God is all-powerful, why doesn't he see Satan off for good? Or why doesn't he rob temptation of all its power? One day he *will* destroy Satan for good, but he has not done so yet because he has a very important purpose in allowing us to be tempted. In this study we shall learn where temptation comes from, and that the grace of God that we studied in the last lesson is there to enable us to beat temptation. Learning to face it and conquer it puts something into us.

Beating Temptation

Read James 1:1–15

God and temptation

Verse 13 teaches that God cannot be tempted, and he does not tempt anyone. He may lead us into temptation (Mt 4:1), but he is always there, controlling and limiting it, and helping us to master it (1 Cor 10:13).

The rebel ruler

Since becoming a Christian you have become aware that you were in a spiritual battle. Before your conversion you were part of a rebel kingdom, serving Satan. Once he was one of God's angelic rulers, but he rebelled and was cast out of heaven (Lk 10:17–18). Satan's great aim, with his army of spirit beings (Eph 6:12), is to entice people away from God, and get them to serve him. He is called 'the tempter' (Mt 4:3). He does this by appealing to 'the cravings of our sinful nature' (Eph 2:1–3).

Satan's landing strip

The 'sinful nature' (called 'the flesh' in older versions) is that within you that does not and cannot respond to the

Holy Spirit (Gal 5:17). It is like an enemy landing strip within you that gives Satan an avenue to tempt you. Read again James 1:14. How do you deprive him of that landing strip? That old nature of yours cannot be reformed or changed, it can only be crucified through the cross of Jesus (Gal 5:24). When Jesus died on the cross that sinful part of you died with him. 'If it's dead,' you may say, 'it won't lie down!' Believe what God says and you will find that it is indeed dead. It was only as you believed that you came into salvation. It wasn't automatic. Just so with this— 'count yourselves dead to sin' (Rom 6:11).

Liquorice all-sorts

Temptations are of various kinds. There is the temptation to do what you know to be wrong, and the temptation *not* to do what you know to be good and right (Jas 4:17). Satan uses various methods. As well as appealing *directly* to our appetites and selfish desires, he may use other people, as Potiphar's wife tempted Joseph (Gen 39:7), or as Peter tempted our Lord (Mt 16:21–23). Someone says something unkind, and you are tempted to give back in equal measure. He uses your success to tempt you to be proud, or someone else's success to tempt you to be jealous. He may use sickness, failure, disappointment, opposition, things going wrong to tempt you to discouragement, to accuse God of failing you. Like Peter when he denied Jesus, he may use your fears to prevent you from being true to Christ.

How to handle temptation

Here are six methods of handling temptation—and of making sure you come out on top:

1. Develop a right attitude. Recognize that temptation, though it comes from Satan, is one of the 'all things' that

God works for our good (Rom 8:28). 'Consider it pure joy' (Jas 1:2). Phillips renders this verse: 'When all kinds of trials and temptations crowd into your lives, my brothers, don't resent them as intruders, but welcome them as friends!' It is 'a time of need' that makes us call on God for his grace (Heb 4:16). There's nothing like temptation to teach us how weak we are and how strong God is.

2. *Always be alert.* The devil is a great deceiver and knows all the tricks of the trade. 'Watch and pray so that you will not fall into temptation' (Mt 26:41). To be proud, careless or cocksure of ourselves is to be heading for a fall (1 Cor 10:12)

3. *Keep your nose out* of what God says is forbidden territory, that is, where Satan holds sway. To get involved in things of the occult such as spiritism, witchcraft, fortune-telling, horoscopes, ouija-board is to wander into enemy territory and risk being taken prisoner. You don't have to learn Satan's 'deep secrets' (Rev 2:24) just as you don't need to roll in the mud to know it's dirty!

4. *Don't play with fire.* Some Christians play with temptation as children play with fire. Don't walk into temptation. Mum caught Joe sneaking in with a wet swim suit after being forbidden to swim in a dangerous pool. When asked why he had disobeyed he replied, 'Satan tempted me.' 'But why did you take your swim suit?' 'I took it—er—in case I was tempted!' Romans 13:14b says 'Do not think about how to gratify the desires of the sinful nature.' Pornographic movies, girlie magazines, video nasties, certain records and anything that you know stirs evil thoughts and desires will mean walking into the devil's trap. Jesus said that you must cut off anything in your life that makes you stumble and fall into sin (Mt 5:27–30). Gouging out an eye or amputating a hand means taking drastic action to stop looking at or doing something that causes you to sin.

5. *Stand up and fight.* This is how you deal with most

temptations, that is, 'Resist the devil' and he will do the fleeing (Jas 4:7). But first you have to 'Submit...to God', that is, place yourself afresh under God's control. That puts you on God's side and then he will fight for you. Resisting the devil is not done with human strength or determination, but with faith in God's power. The fight is one of faith (1 Tim 6:12). By faith you stand your ground and by faith you 'extinguish all the flaming arrows of the evil one' (Eph 6:13, 16). When under fierce attack always call on the name of the Lord, and he will intervene to save and deliver (Rom 10:12).

6. *Flee for your life.* This is the way to handle some temptations. Don't stop and argue with the devil when he tempts you to 'sexual immorality (1 Cor 6:18); see how Joseph reacted (Gen 39:11–12). Or with 'idolatry' (1 Cor 10:14). An idol is any person or thing that takes the place in your life that is rightfully God's. Or with 'love of money' (1 Tim 6:10–11). Or with 'the evil desires of youth' (2 Tim 2:22) such as are mentioned in Romans 13:13.

Memorize: *No temptation has seized you except what is common to man. And God is faithful; he will not let you be tempted beyond what you can bear. But when you are tempted, he will also provide a way out so that you can stand up under it* (1 Cor 10:13).

Home task

Make a list of all the areas of temptation in your life that you have experienced since you became a Christian. Then:

1. Read again *'Keep your nose out'* on page 111. Are there any 'no go' areas in which you have been trespassing? If so, confess them to God, and make up your mind to have nothing more to do with them. If you have had a lot of involvement with the occult in the past share this with your teacher.

2. Look at those areas of temptation you have listed in the light of *'4. Don't play with fire'* on page 111. Are there any situations where you are inviting temptation? Write down what your decision is about each one in the light of Matthew 5:27–30. Ask God to give you grace to carry through your decisions.

3. Start thanking God for all those areas of temptation in your life. Remind God in your prayer that they are teaching you to draw on his grace and prove to you that he is greater. Keep thanking God until you find joy welling up in your heart as it says in James 1:2.

Introducing Study 19

THE BIBLE AND SEX

One thing must now be clear. The Christian life is not merely something that affects you for an hour or so on Sunday morning; it changes you through and through and touches every area of your life. It is not surprising, therefore, that a disciple of Christ has a different attitude to sex from those who believe in what is called 'the new freedom' and whose only rule is, 'If it feels good, do it.' The Christian's attitude is regulated by what God says about it, and he knows that God gives him grace to live accordingly.

Many people think that God is against sex. Not a bit of it! He thought up the idea, and created us all with our sex characteristics and desires. He 'richly provides us with everything for our enjoyment', and that certainly includes sex.

But sex was not only for pleasure. It was also to be the means by which the human race was to be perpetuated, and this required that children should be born into a loving and caring family relationship. So God laid down strict rules for the practice of sex, rules that are designed to prevent men and women using it solely for pleasure, without the commitment of marriage, and the loving, caring family that marriage makes possible. Failure to obey these rules is one of the greatest causes of unhappiness in our unhappy world. And it not only affects those who break the rules, but also those who are the innocent victims of their sin, such as little children in broken homes, too young to understand what it's all about. Not only do we please God when we are careful to obey what he has said about this, but we ensure the fullest enjoyment of this wonderful gift.

The Bible and Sex

Read Genesis 2:19–25

Sex is pure

This century has seen a sex revolution. No longer do children grow up with the impression that sex is 'a smutty little secret' that nice people don't talk about. Instead sex is now a 'free for all'. People cry, 'Be liberated' and 'Whatever turns you on!' Nothing is honoured and nothing is barred. Neither view agrees with Scripture. The Bible speaks freely and frankly about sex. 'To the pure, all things are pure' (Tit 1:15). Sex within marriage is viewed as something honourable and beautiful, so much so that God used it to illustrate his union with his people. 'Marriage should be honoured by all, and the marriage bed kept pure, for God will judge the adulterer and all the sexually immoral' or (in other versions) 'fornicators' (Heb 13:4). In a word, *sex is for marriage and for marriage alone*. The Bible never weakens on this point.

God's word on adultery

Adultery means a married person going to bed with someone of the opposite sex to whom he (or she) is not married, whether the other person is single or married to someone else. God knew that this would be the greatest threat to marriage and family life, so he included it in the Ten Commandments (Ex 20:14). Under the law of Moses the punishment for breaking it was stoning (Jn 8:4–5). It involves the breaking of solemn marriage vows made before God and men.

God's word on fornication

Fornication (involving 'the sexually immoral', NIV) has the primary meaning of sexual intercourse between a man and a woman who are unmarried. 'Sleeping around' or indiscriminate sex among unmarried people is so common as to be generally acceptable in the world.

'Come on, don't be old-fashioned, everybody does it.' The fact that so many indulge in indiscriminate sex is actually a good reason for refusing. God says, 'Do not conform any longer to the pattern of this world' (Rom 12:2), or 'Don't let the world around you squeeze you into its own mould' (Phillips translation). Draw on God's grace to stand up and be counted. The man of the world may outwardly scoff yet inwardly admire Christians who have the courage to stand by their convictions.

God's word on homosexuality

We are talking about men having sexual relations with men, or women having such with women (called 'lesbianism'). It is expressed today in such organizations as 'The Gay Liberation Movement'. God hates all such forms of unnatural sex (Lev 18:22–23). We must hate them too, while having compassion towards those caught up in them. God overthrew the cities of Sodom and Gomorrah for the sin of homosexuality ('sodomy'). In the New Testament God had not changed his mind about this (Rom 1:26–27). Practising homosexuals are among those who will not inherit the kingdom of God (1 Cor 6:9–10), but there is no truth in the saying, 'Once a homosexual always a homosexual'. Some of the Corinthian believers had been set free from this practice (verse 11). God is still setting homosexuals free today.

A word about flirting

This means to 'play at courting or making love with no serious intention of marriage'. Even when this does not involve 'petting' (kissing and caressing) simply for kicks, it is still selfish and unworthy of a Christian. Flirting has been described as 'attention without intention'. Love is too serious for play-acting. One person may be play-acting and the other deadly serious. This can result in one being deeply wounded, if not scarred for life. Paul told Timothy how to treat the younger women in the church (1 Tim 5:2). If single, be wise and don't get locked into an exclusive friendship with a member of the opposite sex until you know you are meant for each other.

A word about courting

If you are unmarried God says, 'Do not be yoked together with unbelievers' (2 Cor 6:14), that is, don't marry someone not 'born again'. Marriage is 'a yoke' because it compels two to walk together. If you are already married God can use you to bless your unbelieving partner (1 Cor 7:14).

Courting develops the relationship in preparation for marriage. Petting obviously has a part to play, but the rule 'no sex outside of marriage' still applies. Going to bed together before marriage (pre-marital intercourse) is still fornication. So a couple determined to please God will refrain from 'heavy petting', that is, caressing the intimate parts of your partner's body, which is the build-up to sexual intercourse, for that would be walking into strong temptation. God's ideal is for the bride to present herself to her husband on the wedding day as a 'pure virgin' (2 Cor 11:2). If your relationship is in the will of God, you don't need a trial run to find out if you're 'sexually adjusted' to each other.

A word about self-control

Sex desire is like an inner fire (Prov 6:27–29). To have a log fire in the house may be beautiful if it's burning safely in the grate, but if it's burning merrily on the lounge floor the house could be burned down. Self-control keeps the fire in the grate, that is to say, keeps sex *in the right place for the right person at the right time*. Whether you are single, engaged, married, widowed or divorced you will always need the grace of self-control. The world says that to try to restrain your sex urges is to do yourself an injury. What nonsense! God commands us: 'Be self-controlled... be holy' (1 Pet 1:13–15).

One of the world's substitutes for self-control is masturbation. This means the stimulation of one's own sex organs to attain that climax of sexual excitement that God intended for the marriage act. This is not to say that masturbation is a sin like fornication, but it *is* sinful when accompanied, as is so often the case, by sexual fantasies and impure thoughts. It *is* sin when it masters you and you cannot 'kick' the habit (1 Cor 6:12), As a single young man Jesus had to face the same sex desires as we do. I cannot think that he chose the easy way of self-indulgence that some psychiatrists recommend, rather than drawing on the grace that teaches us to say no (Tit 2:11–12). Sex energies don't have to have a sexual outlet. They can be redeployed in the service of God and of others. You don't *have* to masturbate. Countless Christians have found that the grace of self-control is a better way. Having taken that

way, don't give up because of a failure. The grace of God
waits to restore you (Mic 7:8).

Memorize: *It is God's will that you should be holy; that*
you should avoid sexual immorality; that
each of you should learn to control his own
body in a way that is holy and honourable
(1 Thess 4:3–4).

Home task

The battle with sex temptation is really a battle in the
mind. If you win there, you end up a winner.

1. This battle is described in 2 Corinthians 10:3–5. It
speaks of 'strongholds' of the mind that must be demoli-
shed, and the 'weapons' that can do the job. Go over your
thought life and jot down what are the strongholds, the
places where pride, jealousy, uncleanness etc. hold sway.
Then take a look at your spiritual weapons, such as the
prayer of faith and speaking the word of God in faith. Aim
the weapon of prayer at these strongholds and start demo-
lishing them. Speak out in faith God's promises as you
pray—'Sin shall not be your master' (Rom 6:14). 'The one
who is in you is greater than the one who is in the world'
(1 Jn 4:4). 'Thanks be to God! He gives us the victory
through our Lord Jesus Christ' (1 Cor 15:57).

2. Access to the mind is through 'eyegate' and 'eargate'.
Take another careful look at the books and magazines
you read, the videos or television programmes you view
and the records you listen to. Get rid of whatever is being
used to set up strongholds. 'If in doubt, chuck it out!' Job
had a problem with 'eyegate'. If you have a similar problem
you can deal with it as he did (Job 31:1).

Introducing Study 20

THE GRAND FINALE

Rejected by the Jewish nation, condemned to crucifixion by the Roman authority, passing through the jeering crowds to a place of execution—that was the last the world saw of Jesus of Nazareth. He did rise again three days later, of course, but he only appeared to his followers. Then he went back to heaven. But he left his disciples a promise: 'I'll be back!'

The Saviour of the world, the Head of the church, the King of the nations has yet to be publicly owned and glorified by his Father before the whole universe.

> Look, he is coming with the clouds, and every eye will see him, even those who pierced him; and all the peoples of the earth will mourn because of him (Rev 1:7).

What a day! Both for him and for those who took his side when all the world was against him. The return of Jesus is the supreme hope of the Christian. It is mentioned 318 times in the 260 chapters of the New Testament, that is, an average of once in every twenty-five verses. In a world scared about the future, the Christian lifts up his head. If the outlook appears grim, the uplook is glorious! The best is yet to come. One day soon the world will acknowledge Jesus as King of kings and Lord of lords. What will his coming mean for the watching believer? For the careless Christian? For the Christ-rejector? For the world? For the future? That's the theme of our final study.

The Grand Finale

Read 2 Peter 3:3–13

The prophetic scriptures

A big proportion of the Bible is prophecy, teaching us about things to come, and helping us to understand God's future purposes. It is not 'history written in advance' but a series of future landmarks. Some we may only recognize as they happen (Mt 24:32–33). It's like looking for landmarks on a journey. You exclaim, 'There's the highrise flats. We're on course!' The prophetic scriptures are 'a light shining in a dark place, until the day dawns' (2 Pet 1:19). They give us guidance and assure us that everything is under control. The final goal of Bible prophecy is the *return of Christ*. Beyond all other expectations, this is the hope of the Christian (Tit 2:13).

The return of Christ

Before Jesus left his disciples to go back to heaven he said, 'I will come back and take you to be with me' (Jn 14:3). He was not referring to coming back to them in resurrection, or coming to them in the person of the Holy Spirit, or coming to them at death. The moment Jesus had gone back to heaven two angels informed his disciples, 'This same Jesus, who has been taken from you into heaven, will come back in the same way you have seen him go into heaven' (Acts 1:11), that is, personally, visibly, physically. Watch for references in Scripture to his 'coming', 'appearing', 'revelation'. Or to 'the day of God', 'the day of the Lord', 'the day of Christ', or simply 'the day'. All these expressions are used to describe the return of Christ.

A new age

The first coming of Jesus ended the age of law and brought in the age of grace (Jn 1:17). The second coming of Jesus will end the age of grace, with its opportunity to believe and be saved, and usher in a new age. Jesus spoke of 'this age' and of 'the age to come' (Mt 12:32). As we saw in our reading in 2 Peter 3, it will mean that this present world, once destroyed by water (The Flood), will be destroyed by fire. There will be new heavens and a new earth in which righteousness dwells. It will mean a new order of existence for which we will require new bodies.

A day of resurrection

At Christ's return those who have died as believers will rise from the dead with a resurrection body like that of Jesus (Phil 2:20–21). Believers still alive will be instantaneously changed (1 Cor 15:51–52) and with their resurrection bodies be 'caught up...to meet the Lord in the air' (1 Thess 4:17). This is sometimes called 'the rapture'. There will also be a resurrection of the ungodly. They will rise to be judged and condemned (Jn 5:28–29).

A day of judgement

All men are accountable to God. The accounting day is fixed for the return of Christ (Acts 17:31). (a) *For believers*.

Having received Christ, believers will not be judged on that issue of salvation, but will come before 'the judgement seat of Christ' to account for 'the things done while in the body, whether good or bad' (2 Cor 5:10). As a result we will receive rewards or suffer loss (1 Cor 3:12–15). (b) *For unbelievers.* Men will *not* be condemned for being in the dark, only for having refused God's way into the light (Jn 3:19). For this they will suffer eternal 'death' (Rom 6:23).

A royal display

Every bridegroom wants to show off his bride for she is his glory. At his return Jesus will be 'glorified in his holy people' (2 Thess 1:10). The kingdom will have finally come. He will reign supreme, with all his enemies subdued. Read Revelation 19:6–8, and begin to sense the jubilation of that coming hour of triumph for Jesus and for you.

The effect of this hope

Though Jesus gave us 'signs' or pointers to the nearness of his coming, he also stated that only God the Father knew exactly when he would return (Mt 24:36, 42). Scripture tells us his coming will be like that of a thief (1 Thess 5:2–3), requiring us to be continually alert lest we lose our spiritual valuables. The hope of Christ's coming requires us to live disciplined and holy lives and to purify ourselves from anything that could cause us shame when he comes (1 Jn 2:28, 3:2–3). To summarize, if you are gripped by this hope it will make you eager to serve Christ, ready to suffer for him and watchful to please him in everything.

Memorize: *What kind of people ought you to be? You ought to live holy and godly lives as you look forward to the day of God and speed its coming* (2 Pet 3:11–12).

Home task

Read the parable of the pounds (or minas) in Luke 19:11–26. Using the following questions interpret the parable, applying it to yourself.

1. Each of the servants received an equal portion of their master's wealth. As a servant of Christ, what would you consider is the pound (mina) that he has given you?

2. How are you now using your Master's pound so as to make it gain more?

3. Notice the three types of person whom the King dealt with on his return:

(a) the faithful servants (verses 16–19);

(b) the unfaithful servant (verses 20–26);

(c) the rebellious citizens (verses 14, 27).

Explain whom these three classes represent in terms of individuals whom Christ will deal with at his return.

4. The two classes that need to concern you are the first two. Write down where you find temptation to be unfaithful to Christ (e.g. laziness, unbelief, self-will, discouragement, 'I'm no good' attitude etc.), and claim in prayer God's promised 'grace to help us in our time of need' (Heb 4:16). Determine before God that you will be among those who receive Christ's 'Well done, good and faithful servant' when he returns.

Going On God's Way

ARTHUR WALLIS

KINGSWAY PUBLICATIONS
EASTBOURNE

Contents

SECTION 3—LIVING IN THE WORLD

A Word about the Course

As a sequel to *Living God's Way,* the study course for new Christians, *Going on God's Way,* is to take the believer into the next stage of spiritual development. You will need a New International Version edition of the Bible, a notebook and a pencil.

The ground covered here is not so broad as in the earlier course. The emphasis is on personal growth and living for Christ in an alien society.

Living God's Way was designed for use in a local church setting where the new Christian is being personally discipled. This is not so important with *Going on God's Way,* and although it would be ideal to have someone older in the faith to take you through, you will gain much through working on your own. But do seek the help of a leader or older Christian if you are stuck with a problem.

With each study there is a memory verse. May I encourage you to embrace this self-discipline. If your memory is poor, this exercise will work wonders. And developing the habit of memorizing key scriptures will prove over the years to be a great blessing in your life. The best method is to write the memory verse (including the scripture reference) on a small card that you can slip in your pocket. If there is another version of the Bible that you are more familiar with than the NIV, memorize from that. And keep refreshing your memory on the verses you have learned. Constant rehearsing is the secret of memorizing.

The 'Home Task' tends to be practical rather than theoretical. Often it will demand more than simply finding answers to questions, and so acquiring head knowledge. You will need to seek God over the issues that are presented.

At the end of each study is an item called 'For Further Study'. This is to meet the insatiable appetite of those Oliver Twist students who always 'come back for more'. It's an optional extra, which is a little more demanding than the 'Home Task', with fewer references to guide your thinking.

May God bless you as you go through this course, bringing you into that spiritual maturity that has always been God's purpose for you since you came to Christ.

Introducing the Theme

'Fred, put your toys away and get ready for supper.'

No reply. A little more loudly, 'Did you hear what I said, Fred?'

'Don't want any supper,' mumbled Fred, continuing to play with his Lego.

'Whether you want it or not,' replied mother, 'put your toys away.'

You may think this is a typical exchange between mother and child until you learn that Fred is not an eight-year-old, but a young man of twenty-five, who is only eight years old mentally.

Alan was above average intelligence and keen to go to university. But you would never think that he had seen eighteen summers. He was less than five feet tall, with a round boyish face that had never felt the touch of a razor. His parents told me how concerned they were to find the treatment that would enable their boy to develop physically. What a heartache it is to the parents when the growth of their child is arrested mentally or physically.

Susan was strong-willed and stubborn. Her school-friends found it hard to cope with her tantrums and her self-centredness. Three years ago she was converted to Christ. Now she goes to meetings instead of discos, but in lots of ways she's the same old Sue. She's had plenty of teaching, but is still an up-and-down type of Christian. Her friends still find her self-willed and lapsing into moodiness if she doesn't have her way. She's picked up the spiritual jargon very well, can pray quite nicely and talk about spiritual things, but her behaviour is not all that different from her unbelieving friends. If she is born into God's family she is certainly not growing up.

There are many children of God like this who are a heartache to their heavenly Father.

. Often there is nothing that medical science can do for the mentally and physically retarded. But what about those who are spiritually backward? Is this like a club foot—something that you're born with and have to live with? No, that is not what the Bible teaches. God is not a tyrant. He doesn't set us a standard that we cannot keep, or give us commands that we cannot obey. He gives us grace to grow, and expects us to do so. Whatever our background, upbringing or temperament, he holds us responsible for our immaturity.

If we are stunted believers we will lose out both in time and in eternity. We will deprive the church and the world of the blessing that we would have been, had we matured. But more importantly, we shall thwart God's purpose in saving us, and rob him of his portion in our lives.

In our opening study we shall take a close look at the symptoms of spiritual immaturity. That should help us to discover where we are. Then in Section 1 we will consider what the Christian is as *The New Person in Christ*, and how we may develop in every area of our renewed being. Section 2, *Growing Strong in God*, will touch a number of very practical areas that vitally affect our spiritual growth. Finally, in Section 3 *Living in the World*, we face the fact that the environment in which we are called to live for God is not 'home' to us. In fact it is antagonistic to the claims of Christ. But God has designed that this is the setting in which we are to fulfil our calling. Amazingly, he uses it to hone us, shape us and mature us for our heavenly destiny.

Facing our Immaturity

Read
Hebrews 5:11—6:3.

Signs of immaturity

God's simple plan for his children is that the crisis of *new birth* is followed by the process of *spiritual growth*, leading to a state of *spiritual maturity*. But it is possible for the process to be arrested. The Christians addressed in our reading, although truly born into God's family, had not grown up spiritually or become mature. They were behaving like spiritual babies. No one minds if a twelve-month-old toddler is constantly falling over, dribbling, spitting out his food, or bursting into tears. But what if a teenager behaved like this? The writer of the Hebrews epistle knew that these believers were not growing up in their spiritual understanding because he was finding it hard to teach them anything more than their spiritual ABC, which he calls 'elementary truths' (5:12). No wonder he was urging them: 'Go on to maturity' (6:1).

It is serious enough not to be growing, but even more serious when we do not recognize that this is so. It is possible to be gaining knowledge about the Bible, talking or even praying in spiritual language, and yet not be really growing. This passage gives us five marks of spiritual immaturity.

1. Having to lay again the foundation of repentance

The writer tells these Christians that not only are they not yet ready for more advanced teaching, but that they need to learn their ABC all over again (5:12).

A few verses later (6:1) he tells them that he wants them to be able to leave their ABC 'and go on to maturity, *not laying again the foundation of repentance*' (my italics). He was likening their Christian lives to a building under construction, with repentance as part of the foundation. It seems that they were constantly having to dig up the foundation and lay it again, so that after all this time the building had made little progress.

Let's take repentance. Do you find that the same old temptations are flooring you? That you are having to repent over and over again for the same sins? This could mean that your foundation of repentance has not been laid thoroughly; you may be using the right words as you confess your sins to God, but are you repenting from the heart and really turning away from that sin? This is a common mark of immaturity.

2. Unable to share the truth with others

'By this time you ought to be teachers' (5:12) says the writer. Was he being a bit tough on these Christians? No, he is not saying that they should all be able to teach a congregation. He is saying that part of growing up spiritually is that we become confident about what we have learned, and *able to share it* personally with others.

It is not just teachers, preachers or leaders who are called to share in this sense. It is something God wants all his children to be able to do. (See Hebrews 3:13 and 10:25.) The word 'encourage' in these scriptures may also mean 'exhort'. 1 Thessalonians 5:11 says the same thing, and teaches us that our sharing in this way will 'build each other up'.

Let's look at an example. Meeting a fellow Christian in the street who I know is going through a tough patch, I share with him the thought that God doesn't always or immediately change our circumstances, but he says, 'My grace is sufficient for you' (2 Cor 12:9). In other words, God's resources are available to give him victory in the situation. A very simple thought, but God speaks through it, and the Christian goes on his way strengthened and encouraged.

3. Unable to take solids

'You need milk, not solid food' (v.12) says the writer. He felt that these Christians had known the Lord long enough to be able to understand the more advanced teaching he was bringing them, but they were saying, 'It's too deep. We can't understand it. Please just give us the simple truths of the gospel.'

Here then is another test of whether you are growing spiritually. Do you only have an appetite for the simple truths that you learned when you first came to Christ—that Jesus died for your sins, that you have eternal life, that he has gone to prepare a home for you in heaven, etc.? Or do you find that you are able to manage a much more solid diet without suffering spiritual indigestion? If not, do believe that as you go through these studies, God will enable you to digest the solid food that it will contain.

4. Unable to use the word of righteousness

'Not acquainted with the teaching about righteousness' (v.13) is better rendered, 'Unskilled in the word of righteousness' (RSV). This has the thought of Scripture being a tool or a weapon that these believers should have

15

been trained to handle. The fact that this was not so was another mark of their immaturity.

They did not know how to use the word in meditation, and so feed themselves spiritually. They did not know how to use it to instruct and help others with their problems. They did not know how to use it to bring comfort to those who were sad, or counsel to those who were perplexed. They did not know how to use it in intercession, by pleading its promises with God. They did not know how to wield it as 'the sword of the Spirit' (Eph 6:17) to drive back the attacks of Satan.

Ability to handle the word of God practically is an important part of becoming mature. Pray that as you go through this course, God will make you skilful in using the word of righteousness.

5. Unable to distinguish good from evil

The Hebrew passage tells us that the mature 'by constant use have trained themselves to distinguish good from evil' (v.14). The one who is immature is not able to do this, and so may easily be influenced and led astray.

A business friend persuades a young Christian to join him in a business venture which looks very attractive, but is not fully honest. He falls for this temptation because he is not able to discern wrong. Someone comes to a believer's front door with what seems to be sound Bible teaching, and leaves him literature. It all seems right and reasonable, but he fails to detect the falsehood. Scripture warns us not to be led astray by 'false teachers' who will bring in 'destructive heresies' (2 Pet 2:1).

Paul teaches something very similar when he speaks of us all becoming mature: 'Then we will no longer be infants, tossed back and forth by the waves, and blown here and there by every wind of teaching and by the cunning and craftiness of men in their deceitful scheming' (Eph 4:14). When a young Christian is 'tossed back and forth' by various teachings he becomes unstable and insecure. In the early years of our Christian life, older Christians will be able to protect us and guide us in these areas, but we must not be satisfied to remain spiritual toddlers who need to be watched at every turn. We must grow up.

How you hear is the key

We have looked at the marks which showed that these Christians were not growing up, but what was the reason? The answer is found in the opening verse of our reading. It says that they were 'slow to learn'. Older versions translate this more literally as, 'dull of hearing'. That did not mean *that they needed a hearing aid!* It has to do with the spiritual ear which enables the heart (rather than the head) to hear and understand. Jesus often spoke of this kind of hearing (Mt 13:9; Rev 2:7). It did not mean *that they had not had the right teaching*. They had in fact been well taught the ABC of the Christian life, but had not properly taken it in. It did not mean *that they were lacking in human intelligence*. Natural wisdom is not the key to spiritual understanding. See what Jesus had to say about this (Mt 11:25–26).

Is your hearing of God's word sharp or dull? This decides whether or not you are really growing up. Let us look at the parable of the sower (Lk 8:5–15). Some of his seed fell along the path, some on rocky ground, some among thorns and some on good soil, all with differing results. This parable is not to teach us how to scatter the seed, but how to receive the seed, that is, *how to hear* the word of God. Jesus explained (vv.11–15) that the four different soils that received the seed picture how different people *hear* the word (vv.18–23).

The well-trodden path pictures the *hard heart* that doesn't respond to God's word. The rocky ground speaks of the *unbelieving heart*. The ground is so full of the rocks of unbelief that there is little room for the soil of faith. The thorny patch speaks of the *divided heart*, which is affected by life's worries, riches and pleasures. These smother or suffocate the good seed that tries to grow up. Of these, Jesus says, 'They do not mature' (v.14). Finally, the good soil speaks of the *noble and good heart* that produces a crop.

What we learn from this parable is that it is the state of our hearts that determines how we hear. If you have been listening to God's word but not growing, then it has something to do with your spiritual hearing. No wonder Jesus concluded the parable with these important words, 'Take heed then *how you hear*' (v.18 RSV). This is what we shall do in the second part of our home task.

Memorize

Therefore let us leave the elementary teachings about Christ and go on to maturity (Heb 6:1).

Home task

1. Look first at those five marks of immaturity. Write down in your notebook which of them you feel are true of you. If you believe God is going to use this course to help you to grow up, then confess that to him now. It is always important to confess what we believe. Now take these marks of immaturity to God one by one, asking him that before you have completed this course you will begin to change in each of these areas.

2. Turn again to the parable of the sower in Luke 8:5–15. Write down in your notebook what Jesus said about each kind of soil. It will not be so easy to recognize which soil (or soils) is a picture of your heart. The reason for this is given in Jeremiah 17:9. The heart is so deceitful it can even deceive its owner. But the way through is given in verse 10. Instead of trying to search your own heart, let God do it for you. Pray the prayer of David in Psalm 139:23–24, and believe for change.

For further study

'Unable to use the word of righteousness' was one sign of immaturity we noted in these Hebrew Christians. We saw that God's word was like a tool or weapon that could be used in several ways. Make a note of these. It is a good idea to have a notebook handy when you read the Bible, and to write out in full the scriptures you come across under headings like these. In this way you can build up a compendium of useful scriptures that will help you to be skilled, and not 'unskilled in the word of righteousness'. Let's make a start.

We can make valuable use of 'the word of righteousness' by pleading the prayer promises in our intercession. Read John 14—16 and then:

1. Note down all the asking promises Jesus gave.

2. Note how many times he said that we must ask 'in his name'.

3. What do you think this means? Give practical examples.

19

SECTION 1

The New Person

A Man in Christ

Read
John 14:15–21 and 15:1–10.

Introduction

'In Christ' was a favourite expression of Paul the apostle, and he was the only New Testament writer to use the expression 'Christ in you'. But what do these phrases really mean? 'In Christ' is another way of describing a Christian. Paul describes himself as 'a man in Christ' (2 Cor 12:2). Earlier in that same letter he had said, 'If anyone is in Christ, he is a new creation; the old has gone, the new has come' (2 Cor 5:17). But we will discover that these expressions tell us much more—something of what it really means to be a Christian.

Jesus said it first

It was not Paul, but Christ, who first spoke in this way, saying to his disciples, 'You are in me, and I am in you.' It was on that last night before he went to the cross. He was preparing his disciples for that moment when he would be forcibly taken from them. He promised that the Holy Spirit would come to them (Jn 14:16) and that he would more than fill the enormous gap left by his departure. He wanted them to know that the sacred relationship he now had with them was not about to end, but would shortly enter an even more wonderful phase.

It was at this point that Jesus made three mysterious statements that the disciples would have found difficult to understand. In the first he said, 'Before long, the world will not see me any more, but you will see me' (v.19). He was promising them *spiritual sight*. Then he said, 'Because I live, you also will live.' That meant a supply of *spiritual life*. And finally he said, 'On that day you will realise that I am in my Father, and you are in me, and I am in you.' That pointed to a *spiritual union*.

Before we look at these three statements of Jesus, did you notice how the last one commenced? 'On that day...'. What day was he referring to? Look back to verses 16–17, and you will see that he had been telling them about the coming of the Holy Spirit. So 'On that day' was the day of Pentecost, when the Holy Spirit would come on these disciples. Pentecost is not only a past event, but a present experience. Have you had that experience? Has the Holy Spirit come on you? If not, ask the friend who is taking you through this course, or someone else that you know, to help you and pray with you for this. Promises like Luke 11:13, John 7:37–39 and Acts 1:8 are there for you to claim. You cannot experience the full reality of what Jesus is saying here without that experience.

Spiritual sight

What Jesus was saying was that when he had gone they would still see him—with the eye of faith. This is one of the wonderful characteristics of our relationship with Christ. Though we do not see him physically, he is as real to us as if we did. It is by faith that we have this spiritual sight. Said Peter, 'Even though you do not see him now [physically], you *believe* in him and are filled with an inexpressible and glorious joy' (1 Pet 1:8). The world may say, 'Seeing is believing,' but the Christian declares, 'Believing is seeing.' If you lose sight of Jesus, or if your vision of him becomes dim, you are certainly suffering from defective faith, and you will need to enquire what the reason is. With renewed faith comes renewed vision. It's vision that makes Jesus real.

Spiritual life

'Because I live, you also will live.' How often he had warned these disciples of his coming death, and promised that he would rise again. But they had been too scared to take it in. Now he was telling them that this resurrection life would not be for him alone, but for them too. How important it was for them to know that fact when witnessing to a hostile world. It is equally important for us. Notice how Paul prayed for the believers of his day:

> That the eyes of your heart may be enlightened [that's spiritual sight] in order that you may know...his incomparably great power *for us who believe*. That power is like the working of his mighty strength, which he exerted in Christ when he raised him from the dead' (Eph 1:18–20, italics mine).

Notice that this power is 'for us who believe'. 'God... made us alive with Christ' by the same resurrection power (Eph 2:1–5). That was when we were born again.

Perhaps you say, 'Yes, I've had that experience, but it's keeping it up that bothers me.' It's here that the words of Jesus are so reassuring. He is telling them that they would continue to enjoy the flow of his resurrection life. In effect he is saying, 'Because I go on living, you will go on living too, by my resurrection life.' Perhaps the disciples were thinking to themselves, 'It sounds wonderful, but how will it work?' Jesus went on to explain.

Spiritual union

'On that day you will realise that I am in my Father, and you are in me, and I am in you.' On that day, when the Holy Spirit came to teach them, they would fully understand. One thing was clear; he was telling them, 'You will have the same relationship with me as I have had with my Father. Just as I have been in my Father, so you will be in me.' Wow! That relationship he enjoyed with his Father was something they had watched with envy all the time they had been with him. God seemed so close, so real to him. Just to think that they could now have that kind of relationship with him!

Jesus then, as he so often did, went on to make use of picture language. He used the wonderful parable of the vine and the branches (chapter 15) to explain this new relationship. It illustrates perfectly our union with Christ.

A vine-branch relationship

He had said, 'Because I live, you also will live.' Now he says, 'I am the vine; you are the branches' (v.5). Do the branches have any expectation of life apart from the vine? Could they continue to live if the vine died? Now we begin to see the truth that we share in Christ's resurrection (Col 3:1). No problem here of keeping it up. In the words of an old hymn:

> Moment by moment I'm kept in his love,
> Moment by moment I've life from above.

Notice that Jesus didn't say, 'I am the trunk,' but, 'I am the vine.' In fact a vine has very little trunk, it's nearly all branches. Jesus is the whole vine, and when we are born again we are united with him and become part of him. Is it not true that the branches are in the vine and that the vine is in the branches? It is equally true that we are in Christ and that he is in us.

Since we are part of Christ, 'we have come to share in Christ' (Heb 3:14). Just as all that there is in the vine is for the branches, so all that there is in Jesus is for us. Scripture says that all the fullness of God dwells in him (Col 1:19), and that that fullness is available to us (Col 2:9–10)—all that we shall ever need to live the Christian life. John the apostle spoke about it when he said, 'From the fullness of his grace we have all received one blessing after another' (Jn 1:16).

The one purpose

This wonderful relationship between vine and branch is not to make the branches feel good or get them 'all blessed up'. Jesus said that his Father was the gardener (v.1). Why does a gardener take so much trouble to cultivate his vine? He wants grapes. Count how many times 'fruit' occurs in verse 1–16. But what is fruit? All fruit is the product of life, and the fruit that God wants can only come from the life of Jesus flowing through us. God is looking for *the fruit of Christian character* (Gal 5:22–23)—what we *are* in Christ. He is also looking for *the fruit of Christian service* (Col 1:6, 10)—what we *do* for Christ.

Maintain the union

According to Jesus the one who *remains* in him bears fruit (v.4). That word remain (or abide) occurs again and again in the parable. It is the key to our part in the fruit-bearing process. If you as a Christian are not bearing fruit, what, according to this verse, are you failing to do?

To the command, 'Remain in me,' Jesus adds by way of explanation, 'No branch can bear fruit by itself.' For the first years of my Christian life I tried hard to prove that Jesus was mistaken. As a Christian surely I could now bear fruit. I must pray a little more, read the Bible more often, try a little harder. God had to use the discipline of failure to bring me to that cry of desperation, 'Oh, God, I can't.' Only then could I see that nothing but his life flowing through me, as the sap flows out to the branches, could produce fruit.

I began to understand what union with Christ really meant—a life of dependence on him for everything. 'Remain in me' could only mean maintain this living union by an attitude of trust. I saw how often an attitude of 'we've got what it takes', had replaced a childlike trust. I could see it was faith that released the 'life sap', and unbelief that cut it off. See how even Paul had to learn this lesson of his own weakness and of God's wonderful sufficiency (2 Cor 12:9).

Memorize

Remain in me, and I will remain in you. No branch can bear fruit by itself; it must remain in the vine. Neither can you bear fruit unless you remain in me (Jn 15:4).

Home task

1. John 15:2 speaks of God as the Gardener pruning fruitful branches. In what ways does he do this (Jn 15:3;

Eph 5:25–26; Heb 12:9–11)? Note down any experiences you have had of this pruning operation—and what you believe it has accomplished. Follow the psalmist and acknowledge God's goodness in this (Ps 119:66–68).

2. Read about two disciples of Christ in Luke 10: 38–42. Compare them with the two kinds of believer Jesus talked about in John 15: the one that remains in Christ and produces fruit, and the one who does not. Write down in your notebook the reasons why you think Jesus commended Mary, rather than Martha. Would you qualify for Mary's commendation?

3. We saw that the greatest hindrance to maintaining our union with Christ is an attitude of independence and self-sufficiency, and that God uses the discipline of failure to make us realize it. Write down what you think is the cause of this attitude in us, and how we should deal with it. (If, after a good think, you are without ideas, see if you find Proverbs 16:18 and 1 Peter 5:6 helpful.)

For further study

We saw that even Paul had to come to a place where he acknowledged his weakness and dependence on God. Turn to Romans 7:14–25 where he describes his struggle with indwelling sin. Note the verses in which he speaks of his perplexity as to why he behaved the way he did.

1. Write out the verse in which he acknowledges his total inability to live a life that pleases God. Compare this with two statements Jesus made in John 15:4–5.

2. Write out the verse that records his desperate cry for deliverance.

3. Turn on to chapter 8 verses 1–4 and describe in your own words the great deliverance he discovered.

The Mind Renewed

Read
Romans 12:1–3.

That think tank

There's a little verse that says of man, 'For as he thinks within himself, so he is' (Prov 23:7, New American Standard Bible).

Someone has put it this way:

> You are not what you think you are,
> But what you think—you are!

In other words, if we had some electrical device that could throw our thought lives on to a screen for all to see, everyone would know what kind of people we are. Ouch!

Our minds are the seedplot of our lives. 'Sow a thought, reap an act. Sow an act, reap a habit. Sow a habit, reap a character. Sow a character, reap a destiny.' No wonder that when Satan attacked Adam and Eve in the Garden of Eden, he aimed first at their minds, sowing distrust in their thinking about God (Gen 3:4–5). And he is still at the same game.

The mind needs converting

Since our minds, as well as every other part of us, were marred by sin, it is not surprising that salvation involves a complete turn about in our thinking. Scripture tells us that the mind of the unbeliever is:

(a) Defiled and corrupted (Tit 1:15).
(b) Blinded by Satan (2 Cor 4:4).
(c) Hostile towards God (Col 1:21).

Despite all this, through the gospel God appeals to men's intellect. He says, 'Come now, let us reason together' (Is 1:18). He wants men to know that 'the good news' is neither unreasonable nor illogical. Sometimes the seed falls on hard ground and the devil snatches it away. That's when men hear, but don't understand (Mt 13:19). Salvation doesn't call for blind faith, but reasoned faith.

In the change of mind that takes place at conversion man has his part to play and God has his. Man is required to *repent*, which means to rethink. It's more than saying 'sorry'. It's a change of mind leading to a change of course. He obeys the call, 'Let the wicked forsake his way and the evil man his thoughts (Is 55:7). God, for his part, promises, 'I will put my law in their minds and write it on their hearts' (Jer 31:33). So before we start living God's way we have to start thinking God's way.

This is the beginning of what the Bible calls 'the renewing of your mind' (Rom 12:2). New birth has to be followed by spiritual growth, and that includes our renewed minds. Paul tells us, 'Stop thinking like children ... but in your thinking be adults' (1 Cor 14:20). Think of your mind as a garden. Remember how neglected and out of hand it was when the Lord Jesus took possession of this property he had purchased. Things have changed, haven't they? But, I'm sure you will agree, there's still a lot more renewing needed. Both clearing and planting are called for.

Clear the ground

We are told to gird up our minds (1 Pet 1:13, RSV). In Bible lands the loose flowing robes of the Oriental had to be gathered at the waist with a girdle before he could walk, work or fight, otherwise he would trip. This was 'girding up the loins'. It means dealing with what hinders or impedes us. So the NIV rightly translates Peter's phrase, 'Prepare your minds for action.' Deal with the negative things that hinder right thinking. In gardening terms, we mean clear the ground for planting. Let's look at three poisonous weeds we need to tackle.

1. Impure thoughts

Do they matter? Yes, because thoughts produce actions, habits and character, as we have said. Jesus said, 'Anyone who looks at a woman lustfully has already committed adultery with her in his heart' (Mt 5:28). He wasn't implying that the thought is as bad as the act, but that the thought is where sin begins, so it must be nipped in the bud. This word of Jesus reminds us that Satan often uses our eyes to attack us with unclean thoughts. See how he did this with Potiphar's wife (Gen 39:7) and later with King David (2 Sam 11:2–4). Peter speaks of those who have 'eyes full of adultery' (2 Pet 2:14).

There is, of course, always forgiveness and cleansing when we confess impure thoughts, but prevention is better than cure. Job solved this problem by setting a guard on his eyes (Job 31:1). For us that would mean saying 'no' to certain paperbacks, glossy magazines and late-night movies—things that we know are calculated to stir up sexual desire.

Even when we avoid these, unclean thoughts may spring up unbidden in our minds. They are not sin if we reject them at once. Someone has said. 'You can't stop a bird alighting on your head, but you can stop it making a nest in your hair!'

2. Anxious thoughts

Worry is a form of fear, and Jesus dealt with fear on the cross, when he dealt with all our sins (Heb 2:14). So there is full deliverance from this destructive weed. We are not to make excuses: 'I take after Mum, and she's the worrying sort!' As believers we are under command: 'Do not be anxious!' 'Not even over something very important?' 'Do not be anxious *about anything*, but in *everything*...present your requests to God. And the peace of God...will guard your hearts and your minds in Christ Jesus' (Phil 4:6–7, italics mine).

We could summarize the above statement by saying, 'Turn your anxieties into prayer until the peace of God takes over.' Indulging in worry is indulging in unbelief. Handing over the situation to God in prayer is acting in faith. In this way we cultivate a steadfast faith. We can tell God with confidence, 'You will keep in perfect peace him whose mind is steadfast, because he trusts in you' (Is 26:3).

3. Earthbound thoughts

God knows that we are human beings with physical bodies that have to be clothed, fed and housed. We are not to be careless or unconcerned about material things. But nor are we to behave like unbelievers, whose minds are dominated by earthly things. 'For the pagans,' Jesus reminded us, 'run after all these things.' Instead we, who have a different set of values, are to 'seek first his kingdom' (Mt 6:32–33). Paul even stated that one mark of certain men, who were 'enemies of the cross', was that 'their mind is on earthly things' (Phil 3:18–19).

The Bible never suggests that material things are sinful. It is just our attitude to them that may be sinful. We are not to feel guilty about that which 'God...richly provides...for our enjoyment' (1 Tim 6:17). But since the cross has freed us from being bound to material possessions, and given us a heavenly goal, God's word exhorts us, 'Set your minds on things above, not on earthly things' (Col 3:2).

If our minds are to be renewed we must not only 'clear the ground', but also:

Plant the garden

'Nature abhors a vaccum.' If you clear the weeds but fail to plant out the beds, the weeds will reappear and grow even more vigorously. We spoke of not letting impure thoughts roost in the belfry of our minds, but Paul goes even further. He says, 'Whatever is true, whatever is noble, whatever is right, whatever is pure, whatever is lovely...think about such things (Phil 4:8). This is how we plant out the garden. But where is this 'food for thought' to be found? Primarily in God's word.

'Let the word of Christ dwell in you richly as you teach and admonish one another' (Col 3:16). So reading and meditating on the Bible is the way to fill your mind with 'God thoughts', and thus plant the garden.

Paul describes the minds of certain unbelievers that, 'their thinking became futile and their foolish hearts were darkened' (Rom 1:21). Futility and foolishness— that would have pretty well described the minds of all of us, till we were born again and made 'wise for salvation' (2 Tim 3:15). But that change from foolishness to wisdom when we received salvation is a process that goes on as we fill our minds with the truth.

This does not mean reading the Bible as if you were swotting for a Geography exam. It is not just filling your mind with biblical facts. Facts will teach you more *about* God, but that is not *knowing* God. How you plant the garden is vital. Letting the word dwell in you richly requires *faith*, that as you read, or listen to the word of God being read or explained, the Holy Spirit will give you that inner understanding that the Bible calls *revelation*. Do you remember that verse or truth that suddenly lit up for you? That was revelation. See how Paul prayed that the Ephesian Christians would have this (Eph 1:17–18). I pray for this continually, especially in connection with my Bible reading. You do the same, and the garden of your mind will surely be planted.

Memorize

> *Do not conform any longer to the pattern of this world, but be transformed by the renewing of your mind. Then you will be able to test and approve what God's will is—his good, pleasing and perfect will* (Rom 12:2).

Home task

1. Many Christians still have the mistaken notion that the thought life of the believer doesn't matter very much. Write down in your notebook the reasons why you think it is very important. Here are some more Scriptures that will help you to fill out your answer: Genesis 6:5; 1 Chronicles 28:9; Psalm 139:1–2; 1 Corinthians 13:11.

2. Let's have a ground-clearing exercise. We have only mentioned a few of the many poisonous weeds that

spring up in the garden of the mind. There may be others that you are conscious of. Pray David's prayer in Psalm 139:23–24. Ask God to show you all the weeds he sees. Confess them one by one, and be sure to receive by faith his promised forgiveness and cleansing (1 Jn 1:9). Then start the planting out. If it was proud thoughts you confessed, ask him to clothe you with the humility of Jesus. Make an entry in your notebook of these new plants. It will be useful to look over them later on and see how they have been growing.

For further study

1. 'You are not what you think you are.' What *do* you think of yourself? Consider two constrasting but accurate assessments Paul made of himself (2 Cor 11:5; 1 Tim 1:15) and his counsel to us (Rom 12:3).

2. Study the contrast between the spiritual mind and the unspiritual or fleshly mind (Rom 8:5–9; Col 2:18–19).

3. We are exhorted to have the attitude or mind-set of Christ (Phil 2:5–11). Consider what this attitude is, how you cultivate it and how it would affect your relationship with others (vv.2–4).

4. Loving God involves our minds as well as our hearts and our souls (Mt 22:37). What does that mean practically?

Controlled Emotions

Read
Isaiah 61:1–3.

Understanding emotions

An emotion is 'a mental feeling', so the theme is closely linked with our previous study. Note that:

1. *God has emotions*

Love is the very essence of his being (1 Jn 4:16), but he also hates (Prov 6:16). We read of God being joyful (Zeph 3:17), jealous (Ex 34:14) and angry (Deut 1:37). Since we are made in his image (Gen 1:27) it is not surprising that we are emotional creatures.

2. *People vary emotionally*

The measure in which we experience the same basic emotions, and the measure in which we express them vary greatly. This may be due to our sex (men being generally less emotional than women), nationality, culture and even experiences we have had in life.

3. *The Christian life is emotional*

Again, this varies with us all. From the time we first

experience conviction of sin, which pricks our consciences (Acts 26:14) and disturbs our peace, through the new birth experience where the love of God is poured into our hearts (Rom 5:5) to a 'believing' which Peter calls being 'filled with an inexpressible and glorious joy' (1 Pet 1:8)—all this could hardly be described as unemotional.

4. Our bodies are involved

In the first place emotional stress can bring on sickness or exhaustion. Doctors tell us that bitterness can bring on arthritis, tension can cause ulcers or back problems, and so on. But on the other side of the coin, mental and physical exhaustion can deeply affect our emotions. After his spectacular victory on Mount Carmel Elijah sank into deep depression, asking God to take away his life (1 Kings 19:4). This would not only have been due to a sense of failure (running for his life at the threat of Jezebel), but also to physical and mental exhaustion after the dramatic events recorded in the previous chapter (note verse 46). For emotional stability we should avoid over-taxing our bodies.

Emotions need to be released

God has not given us emotions to be repressed, but to be released. This is a real emotional need with many, especially in the West.

1. The example of Scripture

Orientals are much less inhibited. We even see this as we look at the believers in the New Testament. They were much freer than most of us in expressing their love for one another, their joys and their sorrows (Acts 20:36–38; 1 Thess 5:26). We see this in a character as manly and rugged as that of Paul (2 Cor 2:4; Phil 4:10).

2. Facing inhibitions

Emotions stifled or bottled up, especially in infancy or childhood, usually result in spritual inhibition. My wife used to be a bad sailor. Even before the boat left the quayside she would feel queasy. She was being prayed for by a friend who knew nothing of this. Suddenly she said, 'I see a little girl in a boat looking at the deep water. She is very afraid, but dare not tell anyone.' My wife did not know she had this repressed fear, and could not remember the incident, but from that moment she was released, and even a rough voyage was no problem. Natural emotions, such as sorrow at the loss of a loved one, need to find free expression. Tears help the healing process.

3. The Spirit-baptism factor

Most who have known the experience of the baptism in the Holy Spirit and the exercise of spiritual gifts testify to a real and valuable release in their emotional life. Some speak of being 'all screwed up inside' before they received the Holy Spirit. Others describe their receiving as 'falling in love with Jesus for the first time' (see Romans 5:5). This emotional factor that causes some to fear, or even reject this experience, is often the very thing they need.

Emotions must be controlled

If emotions are not to be repressed, as we have said, they are certainly to be controlled. God puts a high premium on this (Prov 16:32). It determines whether we are wise or foolish (Prov 29:11). Failure to control emotions could be more serious than repressing them.

41

1. The devil gets a foothold

If we give free rein to such emotions as temper, lust and jealousy, we may open the door to demonic activity in our lives. Paul warns us of this: 'In your anger do not sin. Do not let the sun go down while you are still angry.' In other words, bring it under control, and so, 'Do not give the devil a foothold' (Eph 4:26–27).

2. Some biblical examples

After David slew Goliath, the women, as they greeted the returning soldiers, praised David more than King Saul. Saul was angry and jealous (1 Sam 18:6–9). This opened the door yet further to demonic activity in his life and led to the first of many murderous attacks on David (vv.10–11).

Another case: Amnon, son of David, fell in love with Tamar, his half-sister. Lust took over, and he raped her. Immediatey love turned to hate—a characteristic mark of demonic activity (2 Sam 13:8–15). Later Amnon was murdered in revenge by Tamar's brother, Absalom.

These examples illustrate another kind of wisdom than that of the self-controlled man we noticed in Proverbs—a wisdom that is 'earthly, unspiritual, of the devil' (Jas 3:15).

Ruling our emotions

From a spiritual point of view emotions may be positive, negative or neutral. We need not concern ourselves here with the positive, such as love, joy and peace which are the fruit of the Spirit. Negative emotions, like the biblical examples we have just considered, are the reactions of our fallen nature, and must be handled very firmly. The neutral ones are human reactions, as with the sorrow of bereavement, the joy at some piece of good news, or depression through sickness or disappointment. Although these are not to be suppressed, they do need to be controlled.

1. Handling sinful emotions

In dealing with a whole range of behavioural patterns that belong to our old way of life, including emotions, Paul calls us to take radical action. He says, 'Get rid of all bitterness, rage and anger' (Eph 4:31). He says, 'Put to death, therefore, whatever belongs to your earthly nature: sexual immorality, impurity, lust' (Col 3:5). But how?

(a) Confess the source from which any ungodly emotion comes—that earthly sinful nature (see. above).

(b) Renounce it before God. Do it audibly.

(c) Then, acknowledging that Jesus dealt with this at the cross, confess by faith that you have now 'crucified the sinful nature with its passions and desires' (Gal 5:24).

(d) Since the Holy Spirit as well as nature 'abhors a vacuum', seal the whole transaction by putting on by faith those spiritual emotions which are the opposite of those that you have just put off: 'Clothe yourselves with compassion, kindness, humility...' (Col 3:12).

2. Controlling natural emotions

Although it is healthy and good for these to have a normal outlet, they may easily take over and so become a spiritual hindrance. For example, to be downcast for a while through difficult circumstances is natural, but if we don't snap out of it the way David did (Ps 42:5), we may sink into deep depression and our testimony will be affected. A time of joy and exuberance of spirits must not go off into an emotional 'high' because this is almost always followed by an emotional 'low'. Nor must sorrow be allowed to overwhelm us (2 Cor 2:7). This is where we are to stand out as different from the world. Our sorrow is hope-filled (1 Thess 4:13) while that of the world is death-filled (2 Cor 7:10). But if these are natural emotions that we are talking about, however will we manage to control them?

(a) We must recognize that we are no longer merely natural people but spiritual people (2 Cor 5:17) and have access to spiritual resources that natural people do not have.

(b) When we yield ourselves to God then our whole being, spirit, soul and body—and that must include our emotions—come under the rule of the Spirit. And 'the fruit of the Spirit is... self-control' (Gal 5:22–23).

(c) We must commit any uncontrolled emotion to God, and believe for the grace of the Holy Spirit to control it. If we cannot get through on this we may be in need of emotional healing. We will touch on this in our final section as we turn our eyes on—

Jesus—our pattern and our physician

The emotional life of Jesus provides us with:

1. Our perfect pattern

It was strong, rich and varied, but always under perfect control. Although it was predicted that he would be '*a man of sorrows*' (Is 53:3), we only read of two occasions where Jesus wept in public (Lk 19:41; Jn 11:35). However, it would seem that tears, even 'loud cries' characterized his private prayer life (Heb 5:7). But he never allowed his sorrows to bring heaviness to the company he was in. This must have been because of *the joy that always characterized him*, even when facing the cross (Heb 12:2). Paul spoke of being 'sorrowful, yet always rejoicing' (2 Cor 6:10), and Jesus demonstrated this perfectly. God had anointed him with 'the oil of joy' above his companions (Heb 1:9). When Jesus spoke to his disciples of his joy being in them, they knew he was promising them something very real and very wonderful (Jn 15:11).

Then there was *his amazing love and compassion*, not only for his own (Jn 13:1), but also for his enemies (see Lk 23:34). Compassion is that feeling of pity and deep sympathy towards those in need. Often we read of him being moved with compassion as he looked at the crowds in their need or the sick in their distress (Mt 9:36, 20:34). But note *the striking absence of negative emotions*. Though at times he displayed righteous anger at men's stubbornness, unbelief or hypocrisy, he never had an outburst of temper. He was without bitterness or jealousy, and he never gave way to self-pity, or discouragement, moodiness or irritability. The only fear he knew was the fear of the Lord. He has sent the Holy Spirit to make us like him.

2. Our divine physician

He did not come simply to leave us with an unattainable standard to follow, but also to touch us and make us whole, in our emotions as in everything else. He knows and understands our inner wounds and bruises, that 'crushed spirit' (Prov 17:22), or those feelings of inferiority or rejection. We may, indeed we *must*, open up these areas to him. Was he not sent to 'bind up the broken-hearted' (Is 61:1)? We may need the help of a mature Spirit-filled Christian here, but we must not settle for anything less than the wholeness Christ came to bring.

Memorize

*The Lord is close to the brokenhearted
and saves those who are crushed in spirit*
(Ps 34:18).

Home task

1. Read Ephesians 4:31–32 and Colossians 3:5–8, and jot down any of these characteristics of your earthly fallen nature that persist in showing up. Whether they are strictly emotions or not, you are told to put them to death and get rid of them. Do as Paul says. The four steps outlined under 'Handling Sinful Emotions' on page 43 will help you in doing this.

2. Emotions are powerful motivators. They move us to action. Read the first account in Scripture of sinful emotions and the action that resulted (Gen 4:1–12).

(a) What are the two emotions that moved Cain to murder his brother?

(b) God's questions to him (v.6) suggest a third emotion. What do you think it was?

(c) Do you see any similarity in the murder of Cain and the crucifixion of Christ (Mt 27:17–18)? Is there a lesson for us?

For further study

Psalms 42 and 43 were one Psalm in the original Hebrew. Study these two Psalms (only sixteen verses). You will find the writer is battling with an attack of depression. Try to find answers to the following:

(a) What do the two Psalms reveal of the causes of his depression?

(b) Though his sky is presently overcast, in some of the things he says shafts of sunlight break through. Pick these out, and use them to set out some spiritual remedies for being 'down in the dumps'.

A Sound Judgement

Read
1 Corinthians 4:1–5; 6:1–6.

To judge or not to judge

We have studied the renewing of the mind in general, but now we must focus on a very important function of the mind: the exercise of our judgement. It concerns the process by which we discern or evaluate, and so form opinions and make decisions. It is something we do naturally all the time. For example, I feel in urgent need of fresh air, but the weather outside is cold and it is threatening to rain. Shall I go out for a walk, or leave it till later? I decide to go. All right, shall I wear an overcoat for warmth, or a raincoat in case it rains? When I return, I shall know if my two judgements were sound!

When we come to the much more important business of judging the character or conduct of others we may find ourselves in difficulty. Should we do it at all? Sometimes the Bible seems to say 'No' and at other times 'Yes'. Since the Bible never contradicts itself, it is a challenge to look a little deeper. It usually means that the Scripture is referring to different things, as with the two passages in our reading.

What it means to judge

First, let us notice briefly a number of different ways in which the Bible refers to human judgement. Later, we will look at some of these more closely and the appropriate Bible references. There is *the judgement of condemnation*, which springs from a critical or condemning spirit. This 'playing the judge', or sitting in judgement on one another, is what Jesus told us we were *not* to do. Both our Lord and Paul taught that when we judge one another critically we are condemning ourselves, for we are guilty of the same sort of thing. What we need to do is to judge *ourselves* and bring correction to *ourselves*. Only then would we be in a position to concern ourselves with our brother's deficiencies. This is *the judgement of self-examination*.

We are often exhorted to turn away from what is evil and to imitate what is good. How can we do this unless we distinguish between the two? That calls for *the judgement of discernment*. Do you remember that we touched on this in our opening study? The ability 'to distinguish good from evil' is a very important aspect of maturing spiritually.

There is another aspect of this discerning judgement. For example, when a spiritual gift, such as prophecy, is operating in the church, we are not to accept everything that is uttered without discrimination. We are to 'weigh' and to 'test' what is said. You might call this *the judgement of evaluation*. Similarly, with a man's ministry, it needs to be 'proved' before he is publicly appointed.

The Christian's life is to be guided continually, and not just over the big decisions. Most of our guidance does not involve special prayer, and then waiting for 'a word from God'. It comes through our *judging rightly* what the will of God is through the influence of the Holy Spirit.

Finally, there is *the judgement of corrective discipline*. There are the civic authorities—the government, the judiciary and the police—who are appointed by God to judge and punish wrong doing, and decide disputes. Within the family this is the role parents have towards their children, and in the church it falls to the leaders to whom God gives the main responsibility of maintaining good order and discipline within the house of God.

Now let us look more closely at:

Judging to condemn

This is variously described in Scripture as *condemning* a brother (Lk 6:37), *looking down on* a brother (Rom 14:10), *slandering* or *speaking against* a brother (Jas 4:11). Although we are told not to do this, it is one of the most widespread and destructive sins in the professing church. Jesus said: 'Do not judge, or you too will be judged. For in the same way you judge others, you will be judged, and with the measure you use, it will be measured to you' (Mt 7:1–2). The one who spoke these strong words had been appointed by his Father as the Judge of the Universe (Jn 5:22–23). No one on earth was better qualified to sit in judement than he, but he did not do it (Jn 8:15). Get the full force of what Jesus was saying: 'You judge your brother like that, and one day I'll judge you in the same way.' James says something similar (Jas 2:12–13).

Two men on safari were attacked by a rhino. One shinned up a tree and the other dived into a great ant-heap. A few moments later, out came the man in the ant-heap. The rhino charged again, and again the man hid himself. When he came out a second time, his exasperated friend up in the tree called out, 'Get back in, you idiot!' 'Sssh,' hissed his friend putting his finger to his mouth, 'there's a sleeping lion in there!'

Don't judge your brother because you don't know all the facts, and cannot determine his motives. We must leave judging to God's time and to the One whom God has appointed (1 Cor 4:5).

Have you ever noticed that when you point that index finger of yours at your brother, you point three fingers at yourself? Notice what Romans 2:1 says about it. In the passage just considered, where Jesus told us not to judge, he went on to say that we were hypocrites if we tried to remove 'the speck of sawdust' in our brother's eye without first tackling 'the plank' in our own (Mt 7:3–5).

A hypocrite is one who pretends to be better than he really is. If I say, 'Joe appears to be a very enthusiastic Christian, but his motives are not pure,' it is time I examined my own motives. In the first place I am putting my brother down in order to lift myself up. I want everyone to understand that I would never be so unspiritual as to have impure motives! What Jesus would say to me is, 'Enough of that spiritual humbug! Take a long hard look at your own motives. Even if others don't know what they are like, I do.' The finest antidote to this sort of judging is to engage in the judging we call self-examination.

When we pass sentence on one another in this way without being in possession of the facts, and without ability to search into another's heart, our judgements are unrighteous. They are superficial because they are based on how things appear to us. Isaiah wrote about Jesus, 'He will not judge by what he sees with his eyes, or decide by what he hears with his ears; but with righteousness he will judge the needy, with justice he will give decisions for the poor of the earth' (Is 11:3–4). That's why he was in a strong position to say to his own critics and detractors, 'Stop judging by mere appearances, and make a right judgment' (Jn 7:24). What then is a right judgement?

A discerning judgement

Some people think that the judging we have been considering is wrong because it is judging *people*, while discernment has only to do with *facts*. No, this has also to do with people. When we distinguish good from evil (Heb 5:14), and the truth from the false (1 Cor 10:15), we are dealing with what people do and say. To imitate what is good (3 Jn 11), and to hold to the word that is true (1 Thess 5:21) means that I must exercise a discerning judgement as I look and listen. What makes this kind of judgement different from the other is *the purpose behind it*, and the spirit and attitude with which it is exercised.

Such spiritual judgement is very important when the gifts of the Holy Spirit are operating in the church, especially gifts of inspired utterance, such as speaking in tongues, interpretation of tongues and prophecy. We need to be sure that that the utterance is inspired by the Holy Spirit, and not by the human spirit or some other spirit. There is a gift called 'the ability to distinguish between spirits' (1 Cor 12:10). Those who receive that gift may know by revelation from God what spirit is operating. But this gift, given to the few, is not to let the rest of us off the hook. We *all* need to exercise our spiritual judgement. The command to test prophecy is not only given to the leaders or to certain gifted individuals, but to Christians in general (1 Thess 5:20–21). But how do we do it?

This is too big a question to answer fully here, but there are some simple tests that we may apply. An

utterance inspired by the Holy Spirit will never con-
tradict what that same Holy Spirit has said in his word (Is
8:20). That's why it's so important to get to know your
Bible. If the utterance fails this test it is to be rejected
forthwith. If it seems to accord with Scripture, ask, does
it do the three things that prophecy is given to do (1 Cor
14:3)? It could well contain a rebuke, bring conviction of
sin and humbling before God, but that would serve to
fulfil these three purposes. But if it brings condemnation
and confusion rather than edification, there is something
wrong. Prophecy should always be Christ-centred and
draw hearts to Christ (Rev 19:10), not to the personality
of the speaker or his gift.

Finally, you should have the peace of Christ ruling in
your heart as you listen (Col 3:15), bringing the assurance that the Holy Spirit is speaking.

Judging what the will of God is

Most Christians know that the Christian life should be a
life guided by God (Rom 8:14), and that we don't have
any in-built powers of self-direction (Jer 10:23). The Old
Testament picture of this is the children of Israel
journeying to the land of Canaan, being led by God,
through a pillar of cloud by day and a pillar of fire by
night (Ex 13:21). But many of us confine this idea of
guidance to the big decisions where we call on God for a
special 'word'. However, God was not only guiding
Israel when they came to an important crossroads, but
all the time. It should be so for us. The promise of Isaiah
58:11 still stands. But most of our guidance comes
through our human judgement—*influenced by the Holy
Spirit*.

Did you memorize that verse in the previous study?
Paul says that when your mind is renewed 'you will be

able *to test and approve what God's will is*—his good, pleasing and perfect will' (Rom 12:2, italics mine). Testing and approving is an action of your judgement. Elsewhere he speaks of every thought being taken captive 'to make it obedient to Christ' (2 Cor 10:5). When that happens God is guiding us by using our own thought processes.

Psalm 25:9 in the Authorized (King James) Version says, 'The meek will he guide in judgment: and the meek will he teach his way.' It has been said that 'meek' here means that we have a preference for God's will, and that 'judgement' refers to our own judgement. In other words, God guides those who really want his will—not necessarily through a visible sign, but by swaying their judgement, in the same way that a pair of balances are swayed by a finger on one side or the other. But if you want God to do this, you must keep your hand off. If you allow the finger of self-will to interfere you are not truly meek. We must seek God for grace to be 'humble' or 'meek' (Authorized Version) and thus free the Holy Spirit to guide us continually.

Summary

What then are the keys to possessing a sound and healthy judgement? We must take great care that we do not think and speak critically of others. And when we are aware of others' faults we need to examine our own hearts and make sure that we are not seeing a reflection of something in ourselves. We must have a mind that is well instructed in the truth of God's word. And we must have a meek spirit that desires God's will only and is continually sensitive to the Holy Spirit.

Memorize

Therefore judge nothing before the appointed time; wait till the Lord comes. He will bring to light what is hidden in darkness and will expose the motives of men's hearts. At that time each will receive his praise from God (1 Cor 4:5).

Home task

1. John talks to his friend George about a mutual friend and church member, Bill. He tells him: 'Bill's house-group leader has reported that Bill has not shown up at the group meeting for some weeks and that his church attendance generally has become very irregular. I phoned Bill to ask if we could meet for a chat, but he said he was too busy. When I put some pointed questions to him about his spiritual state he was very evasive. I am sure Bill is drifting spiritually and I am really concerned for him. Could you make contact with him, George, as he is an old friend of yours? And could we pray together for him?'

John has made a spiritual judgement about Bill. Would you think he is judging righteously or unrighteously? Record your answer in your notebook, giving reasons and, where possible, supportive scriptures.

2. 'The spiritual man makes judgments about all things' (1 Cor 2:15). Write down in your notebook:
(a) What is meant by 'the spiritual man'? Do all believers qualify? (1 Cor 3:1–4; Gal 5:13—6:3).
(b) What are the things that you would need to watch to make such a judgement? Some of them are negative—things you would need to avoid. Others are positive—things you would need to cultivate.

3. Put your notebook aside, and talk to your Father

about anything he has shown you that needs adjustment in the way you think and talk about others, and how you in general make judgements about things.

For further study

1. You saw the importance of *the judgement of self-examination* in connection with our tendency to judge others. Here are some other situations in which we are to examine ourselves:

(a) To make sure that we really are 'in the faith', and not self-deceived (2 Cor 13:5).

(b) Before we partake of the Lord's Supper, so that we do not eat and drink unworthily and so come under God's judgement (1 Cor 11:27–32).

(c) To make a sober assessment of ourselves and our ministry (Rom 12:3; Gal 6:1–5).

2. We mentioned that there was a place for the judgement of corrective discipline in the church.

(a) Study what Jesus said about this in the second of his two statements about the church (Mt 18:15–18).

(b) There was a serious case of immorality in the church at Corinth (1 Cor 5). Notice how the church was reacting and how, according to Paul, they should have reacted (vv. 1–2). What are the reasons Paul gives for the strong action he urges them to take? Note the teaching of verses 12 and 13 on this matter of corrective discipline.

(c) See also what Paul says about the handling of disagreements among Christians and what he thinks of one believer taking another believer to court (1 Cor 6:1–8).

(d) Notice how the church in Ephesus handled evil men, false apostles in their midst (Rev 2:1–3). Do you think that the head of the church was pleased or displeased with what they had done?

A Body for the Lord

Read
1 Cor 6:12–20.

Introduction

From ancient times there have been those who taught that everything material, including the body, is evil, and that man needed to be set free from this 'prison house of the soul' in order to be spiritual. This led to extremes of self-denial and 'harsh treatment of the body' (Col 2:21–23). In modern times the pendulum has swung the other way, with a tendency to pander to the body and satisfy its every demand. Men not only beautify it but glorify it, and almost worship it. Scripture does not support either of these attitudes, but shows us that the body is included in the plan of salvation (Rom 8:23) and teaches us how to honour God through our bodies.

God pronounced it very good

In the sixth and final day of creation, as his crowning wonder, God created man. The record says, 'The Lord God formed man from the dust of the ground' (Gen 2:7). That's all we know about how the man received his

59

physical body. At the end God said of all that he had made, man's body included, that 'it was very good' (Gen 1:31).

Though sin came in to mar the beautiful handiwork of the Creator, it did not alter God's original purpose. Through salvation man would be restored and God's intention for him would be fulfilled. By himself becoming flesh, Jesus has for ever stamped with purity and dignity what the Bible calls 'our lowly bodies' (Phil 3:21).

When Jesus had finished this work and returned to the Father, he did not leave his body behind. On the third day he was reunited with his body, and took it, glorified in resurrection, back to heaven. He is therefore 'the firstfruits of those who have fallen asleep' in death (1 Cor 15:20). Firstfruits are followed by harvest. If Jesus' resurrection is the firstfruits, the resurrection of his saints when he comes again will be the harvest (v.23). So the body of the believer has a glorious and eternal destiny.

For the present, God wants your body to be the means by which the life of God within you is expressed to men. Looking at our reading again, there is one *major* reason why you are to honour God with your body.

You are not your own

Notice how this is emphasized:

1. 'The body is...for the Lord' (v.13)

Not primarily for us, but for him. Just as he had a physical body prepared by God in which he did the will of God on earth (Heb 10:5–7), now the only physical body he has to continue his work on earth is that of the believer.

2. 'Your body is a temple of the Holy Spirit' (v.19)

This was fulfilling a wonderful promise that Jesus had made to his disciples when speaking of the coming of the Holy Spirit. He had said, 'If anyone loves me, he will obey my teaching. My Father will love him, and we will come to him and make our home with him' (Jn 14:23). So our bodies are a dwelling place for God by his Holy Spirit.

3. 'You are not your own; you were bought at a price' (vv.19–20)

When Jesus purchased you with his blood, he purchased your body as well as your soul. You have therefore relinquished your right to yourself. If you really believe that, it must affect what you do with your body. If you know that you have been bought—and at such a price—you will want to use that body to honour the One who has bought you. How do you do it?

Honour God

1. By keeping it holy

You might think that the questions Paul poses in verses 15–16 of our reading were very strange to put to a group of believers. But these Christians lived in Corinth, a city that was not only pagan, but renowned for its immorality—much of it in connection with the Aphrodite temple where the goddess of love was worshipped. In verses 9–11 he lists the sins that were common in Corinth and reminds the believers that that is what some of them were like before they were converted.

We have seen that God has purchased our bodies for his use. But how can a holy God live in a dirty temple? The heavenly surgeon wants to use us to perform

61

wonderful and delicate operations on the lives of others, but how can he operate with a dirty instrument (2 Tim 2:20–22)? This involves a work of cleansing (2 Cor 7:1). There is the cleansing through the blood as we confess (1 Jn 1:7,9), and there is cleansing through the word as we apply it by faith (Eph 5:26).

2. By presenting it to him

'I urge you, brothers,' says Paul, 'in view of God's mercy, to offer your bodies as living sacrifices, holy and pleasing to God—which is your spiritual worship' (Rom 12:1). What this means was made vivid to me by a childhood experience.

My brother and I had been dressed up in our Sunday best, kid gloves and all, as a lady and gentleman were expected. While our parents went to fetch them, we boys whiled away the time down near a stream. At length they arrived and our proud parents introduced their two little angels. We had been taught that gentlemen always take off their gloves to shake hands with a lady, so there was a palaver while fasteners were undone and kid gloves removed. Alas, the operation only served to reveal the dirtiest little hands you ever saw! The guffaws of our visitors saved the day and covered our parents' embarrassment.

When we try to offer ourselves to God without 'clean hands and a pure heart' (Ps 24:3–4), *he* certainly doesn't treat it as a joke. We must avail ourselves of the blood and the water, as we have just seen. Instead of the phrase '*offer* your bodies', the older versions have '*present* your bodies'. I prefer that, because 'present' is a bridal word. You are not to think of some terrible act of self-sacrifice, but one of loving and eager surrender, as a bride on her wedding day presents herself to her bridegroom, to be totally his. You are now to present yourself to God, place yourself at his disposal to serve him in whatever way he chooses.

By accepting it as it is

There are Christians who hold back from offering themselves to God, because of some physical blemish or deficiency, real or imaginary. 'If only I had Jack's athletic figure.' 'I really wish I could be medium height, like Sue; who wants a lanky girl?' 'Why did I have to be lumbered with such a long nose? At school they all call me Beaky.' Such thoughts are real, even it not expressed in words. How can you honour God with your body if you are rejecting that body?

The antidote to this wrong thinking is, first, to acknowledge that God has made you the way you are. You are not his first mistake! Moses had a problem with his natural limitations at the burning bush, because he was 'slow of speech'. He wanted to back off. What did God say to him? 'Who gave man his mouth?' (Ex 4:10–11). In other words, 'Moses, I take the responsibility for your lack of fluency, and I'm still calling you to serve me. Don't try to be wiser than Me.'

The second thing is to recognize that he made you thus for a wise and wonderful purpose. You are not the result of some mindless accident. Not only what he gives, but also what he withholds are expressions of his loving wisdom. When we recognize this, we can echo the words of David:

> For you created my inmost being;
> > you knit me together in my mother's womb.
> I praise you because I am fearfully and wonderfully made;
> > your works are wonderful, I know that full well.
> My frame was not hidden from you
> > when I was made in the secret place.
> When I was woven together in the depths of the earth...
> > > > > > > (Ps 139:13–15)

When you can look at your body with all its blemishes and say, 'Your works are wonderful,' you are honouring God with your body.

4. By keeping it healthy

The bodies of many believers are suffering from being worked too hard, exercised too little and fed too much. That's a sure recipe for breakdown. We are not to pamper our bodies, but we are to take care of them as the temples of the Holy Spirit.

My father, who was a preacher and a writer, used to say, 'I'd rather wear out in God's service than rust out.' He died at forty-nine, while at the height of his ministry. As a young fellow with the call of God on my life, I used to pray, 'God, let me burn out for you.' Then I noticed that God called Moses through a bush that burned, and was *not* consumed (Ex 3:3). I realized that God does not call us to wear out or burn out. He wants us to wear on and burn on! That means honouring God by taking care of our bodies and keeping them fit.

'Could I borrow your motor mower?' asked Vic.

'Sure,' replied Rob, 'but take good care of it. It's new.'

It was weeks later that Ron found a dirty mower in his shed. He hardly recognized it. The underneath of the machine was caked with matted grass, the grass box was dented and the engine wouldn't start. You could hardly blame Rob for being angry. 'That may be the way he looks after his own property,' he said, 'but that mower is mine!'

I think God wants to say to some of his children, 'The body you're treating like that belongs to me. It was bought with a price. Start honouring me with it, as though you really believed it was my dwelling place.'

Memorize

Do you not know that your body is a temple of the Holy Spirit, who is in you, whom you have received from God? You are not your own; you were bought at a price. Therefore honour God with your body (1 Cor 6:19–20).

Home task

You read in the notes: 'If you really believe that (you have been bought with a price and belong to God) it must affect what you do with your body.' We are going to work through a little practical application of that. The first task is more particularly for God's sons and the second for his daughters.

God' sons

We have seen that we honour God by keeping our bodies healthy, and that this may be undermined by working them too hard and feeding them too much.

(a) Overwork: Write down in your notebook the reasons why people overwork. The verses in brackets will give some biblical clues to help you to fill out your answers (Prov 19:2; 1 Cor 10:14 with Col 3:5; Prov 23: 4–5 with 1 Tim 6:9). If any of these scriptures apply to you write down the practical measures you plan to take to remedy this. Then talk to God about them.

(b) Overeating: The less polite word for this is 'gluttony', which means eating greedily or excessively. Write down in your notebook why this is dishonouring to the Lord (Prov 23:19–21; Acts 24:25 with Gal 5:22–23; Rom 8:12–14; 1 Cor 9:24–27). If this is an area where

you are not in God's victory, take the same steps as outlined under (a).

God's daughters

Your task concerns honouring God by the way you clothe and adorn your body.

1. Read 1 Timothy 2:9–10 and 1 Peter 3:3–4. Put down in your notebook:
(a) All that these verses teach about how a woman of God should dress.
(b) What they say you should avoid.
(c) What is the one thing that both passages are stressing?
2. Do you think these scriptures allow a woman of God to be careless or slapdash about her appearance? Write down your answer and give reasons. You will find answers in the description of the woman of noble character in Proverbs 31:10–31. If this study has shown you the need of adjusting your own outlook and practice, decide what change is needed, write it down in your notebook and then talk to God about it.

For further study

1. Hebrews 10:22 speaks of our drawing near to God, 'having our bodies washed with pure water'. Consider the spiritual meaning of this (cf Jn 15:3; Eph 5:25–27).
2. Romans 8:11–14 promises complete victory over sin when you:
(a) Offer yourselves to God as those brought from death to life.
(b) Offer the parts of your body to God as instruments of righteousness.
Work out what that means in practical terms.
3. In Matthew 5:29–30 Jesus spoke of an eye or a

hand causing us to sin. Consider the sort of temptation he was referring to (vv.27–28) and how one would practically carry out the instruction that he gave.

Taming the Tongue

Read
James 3:1–8.

Introduction

It is the tongue that brings the message of salvation, and the tongue by which the lie of the devil is spread. By the tongue men confess Christ and by the tongue they deny him. How much comfort and encouragement, illumination and enrichment have come to men through a tongue inspired by the Holy Spirit. But how much damage has been done in the church by an unrestrained tongue. It has 'the power of life and death' (Prov 18:21). A mature Christian is one who has every part of his being, especially his tongue, under the rule of Christ.

The power of the tongue

In our reading the tongue is likened to the bit in the horses' mouth and to the rudder of a great ship (vv.3–4). Each is small in size but great in influence. He who controls the bit controls the horse, and he who controls the rudder steers the ship. Even so, he who controls his tongue is able to bridle his whole body (v.2). This is not said of any other part of the body. Why does this small member play such a key role?

In Study 3 (The Mind Renewed) we learned that the way you think in your heart reveals your true character. So God never assesses us by outward appearance but what we are in our hearts (1 Sam 16:7). It is the heart that controls the tongue. 'Out of the overflow of the heart the mouth speaks' (Mt 12:34).

> The tongue also is a fire, a world of evil among the parts of the body. It corrupts the whole person, sets the whole course of his life on fire, and is itself set on fire by hell...no man can tame the tongue. It is a restless evil, full of deadly poison (vv.6, 8).

That's the human tongue—apart from the grace of God. Why such strong language? Because Scripture and experience teach us how totally corrupt is the human heart (Jer 17:9). It is because the heart is incurable that the tongue is untamable. But 'what is impossible with men is possible with God' (Lk 18:27). The One who can change our sinful hearts (and has he not begun this miraculous work?) can by the same means bring the unruly member under control.

We shall now look at four important areas where this needs to happen.

A lying tongue

With lying there must be *the intention to deceive*. To speak what is incorrect is not lying if the speaker believes it to be true. Satan is both 'the father of lies' (Jn 8:44) and 'the deceiver of the whole world' (Rev 12:9, RSV). 'Do not lie to each other,' says Paul, 'since you have taken off your old self with its practices and have put on the new self, which is being renewed in knowledge in the image of its Creator' (Col 3:9–10). To do so is to sin against the body, for we are all fellow members of that one body (Eph 4:25). Loving and practising any form of falsehood is the characteristic of those whose final destiny is exclusion for ever from the City of God (Rev 22:15).

Worldly people may disapprove of 'black lies' but justify 'white lies', when they deem the motive of the untruth to be good. For example, a doctor may lie to a patient who is terminally ill with cancer, because he doesn't want to upset his patient. The fact is that every person, believer or unbeliever, has a right to know that he is approaching the great terminus of life, where all passengers have to change. He may need to make his peace with God, or put things right with his fellow men. No, all lies are black.

Perhaps you never tell a barefaced lie, but are there *grey areas* where you skirt the truth?

'What is the purpose of your visit to the USA?' asked the immigration officer. I had been warned that to say I had come to preach could lead to further questions about payments for preaching, and create difficulties. I was advised: 'Just say that you are visiting friends.' This was true, but was not 'the truth' for it would have misled the officer. I told him the truth, and the warning proved true. I did get asked further questions, but in five minutes I was through—with a clear conscience.

Another grey area is *exaggeration*. Pride is normally the motive. We want to impress, and the plain unvarnished truth is not all that impressive so we enlarge, embellish and fill in imaginary details from the storehouse of our own wishful thinking. This is a form of 'unwholesome talk' which grieves the Holy Spirit (Eph 4:29–30). One kind of exaggeration that smacks of insincerity and hypocrisy is *flattery*, or false praise. It is buttering someone up for our own advantage (Jude 16). Scripture equates this kind of speech with lying (Prov 26:28). Because it is something that God hates (Job 32:22) we must hate it too.

A backbiting tongue

Backbiting, gossipping and criticizing are forms of evil speaking which have wrought terrible havoc in the church of Jesus Christ. The devil is the father of this activity also. 'A whisperer separates close friends' (Prov 16:28, RSV), and in the Garden Satan whispered things in the heart of Eve, which blackened God's good character, and resulted in the break up of a beautiful friendship between God and man (Gen 3:4–5).

We noticed in Study 5 (A Sound Judgement) that speech which puts others down is designed to exalt the speaker. Often there is a spirit of jealousy and competitiveness behind it. Miriam and Aaron criticized Moses for marrying a Cushite wife but they were simply jealous of Moses' position (Num 12:1–2). We see the humility of Moses in his refusal to defend himself (v.3) and how God showed his anger when he intervened to defend his servant (v.9). It is specially grievous to God when there is this kind of criticism against his appointed leaders. He says, 'Do not touch my anointed ones; do my prophets no harm' (Ps 105:15).

Persistent backbiting and criticism had broken the spirit of a servant of God. When he became gravely ill one of the chief culprits became conscience-stricken and went to him to confess and ask forgiveness. 'I forgive you, but I want you to take this pillow to the window and shake out the feathers,' said the sick man. He did so. 'Now go collect up the feathers,' was the next request. 'That I cannot do,' was the reply. 'Nor can you undo the false things you have said about me,' replied the other;

72

'they will be put right at the judgment seat of Christ' (2 Cor 5:10; Col 3:25).

A grumbling tongue

From the moment God's people were redeemed they began to grumble. Whenever they were discontented with their lot they looked for a scapegoat. Usually they picked on Moses and Aaron. So often grumbling among God's people is directed against leaders. This is not to say that leaders never make mistakes. If they do, there are ways to rectify the situation, but grumbling is not one of them. In fact, Moses pointed out that the Israelites were really grumbling against God (Ex 16:8). They were rebelling against his ordering of their lives. We read of God's anger being aroused when he heard them complaining (Num 11:1). What do you think he feels when he hears our grumbling?

Perhaps we may feel that Paul and Silas had an excuse for complaining, when in the midst of their campaign in Philippi they were wrongfully arrested, beaten and flung into prison. No prospect of any sleep at that midnight hour with their backs bleeding and their feet fastened in the stocks. But read what they did, and then what God did in response (Acts 16:25–30). That is the way to face situations that seem to go wrong.

A talkative tongue

There is a time to be silent as well as a time to speak (Eccles 3:7). Some believers are silent when they should speak, some speak when they should be silent, and others seem to talk all the time.

A wife was suing for divorce on the grounds that her husband hadn't spoken to her in years. 'Is that really true?' asked the incredulous judge. 'Well, 'er,' replied the husband, 'I, 'er just didn't like to interrupt!'

We are told that 'a chattering fool comes to ruin' (Prov 10:8), but that 'a man of knowledge uses words with restraint' (Prov 17:27). Similarly the New Testament warns us to 'avoid godless chatter' (2 Tim 2:16). Why is this so important? Firstly, self-control which is one segment of the fruit of the Spirit (Gal 5:23), is essential in every aspect of our lives, but especially in our speech. In a great flow of words we can boast, exaggerate, misrepresent, confuse and, before we realize it, say things that we may later regret. 'When words are many, sin is not absent' (Prov 10:19).

The New Testament is equally clear: 'Everyone should be quick to listen, slow to speak and slow to become angry' (Jas 1:19). If an unrestrained and undisciplined tongue exposes you to the temptation of the devil, it is equally true that by guarding your lips you guard your soul (Prov 13:3).

How to tame it

1. You must be convinced that it can be tamed

This is by the grace of God. 'No *man* can tame the tongue' means that you are closed off to Christ. Read about the power that enables him to bring everything under his control (Phil 3:21). A few verses later comes that tremendous confession, 'I can do everything through [Christ] who gives me strength' (4:13). Make that confession your very own. Confess it until you fully believe it. What follows will only be effective if you hold fast to this confession.

2. Acknowledge where it needs to be tamed

Wherever the Holy Spirit has brought conviction you need to acknowledge that to God. In fact, we have only

74

dealt with four of the more common sins of the tongue. There are many others. God may want to put his finger on speech that is unwholesome (i.e. unclean or suggestive), boastful, unkind, bitter, derisive or whatever. What the Holy Spirit pinpoints take to God in humble confession.

3. Bring every area of failure under the rule of Christ

'Lord, I have confessed that power which enables you to bring everything under your control. I now hand over my tongue to you. Take control over it. Subdue those words that are critical, unkind [or whatever the Holy Spirit has brought to your attention]. So cleanse my heart that I will not even want to speak such words. Make my lips instead to show forth your praise. Amen.'

Memorize

Set a guard over my mouth, O Lord;
Keep watch over the door of my lips.
(Ps 141:3)

Home task

1. Under 'How to tame it' above, go through the three steps with your notebook. *In the first place* ask yourself whether you really believe that your tongue can be tamed. Meditate on Philippians 3:21; 4:13 and John 8:36, until with real conviction you can write in your notebook, 'I believe that this tongue of mine can be brought under Christ's rule.'

Secondly, pinpoint by confession to God the sins of the tongue that you know you need to deal with. Don't be discouraged if you feel, 'I sin so much here I don't know where to begin.' Let the Holy Spirit focus on those that he sees are urgent. Write them down in your notebook.

Finally, use the prayer suggested—or better still, one of your own—to bring each area of failure under Christ's rule. Believe he is responding as you pray. Thank him for doing so. As he shows you other areas, tackle them in the same way.

2. Now look at a tongue that was always under perfect control—that of our Lord Jesus. Notice the impression created by his first public utterance (Lk 4:22). 'Gracious words' fulfilled a prophecy made about him hundreds of years earlier (Ps 45:2). However, we are not to put him on a pedestal; rather we are to imitate him (Col 4:6). If our conversation is to be 'always full of grace' write down what that means. List first the kind of language we would need to avoid, and then the kind we would need to cultivate. Claim the promise of 2 Corinthians 12:9.

For further study

1. As we become more knowledgeable as Christians there is the temptation to become quarrelsome and argumentative. In our witnessing we can win the argument and lose the man. But Paul strongly discourages argumentativeness, especially among Christians (Phil 2:14; 1 Tim 1:4; 2:8; 6:4–5; 2 Tim 2:14, 23–25). It could disqualify a man from being an elder (1 Tim 3:3). List the reasons why we need to avoid this. What do you think lies behind an argumentative spirit?

2. Read Matthew 12:33–37. Why did Jesus teach that men would be acquitted or condemned on the day of judgement on the basis of their words? He also said that we would be held accountable for 'every careless [idle, ineffective, worthless] word'. What words would come into this category?

SECTION 2

Growing Strong

Knowing the Fear of the Lord

Read
Isaiah 8:11–17.

What is the fear of the Lord?

We must distinguish three kinds of fear in human experience.

Natural fear

For example, reacting to a situation of physical danger. Driving home one winter's day, I was travelling too fast for the icy road conditions. The car began to swing to the wrong side just as another car appeared, coming towards me. Gripped with the fear of a head-on smash I wrestled to correct the skid. Still out of control, it swung back as the approaching car shot past. This instinctive fear which we have all felt—the fear that motivates us to act to preserve our lives—is not sinful, it is natural.

Sinful fear

This may prevent us from doing the will of God, for example, not owning up to some wrong doing; or compel us to do what is not God's will, like Peter denying the Lord. This may come as a sudden attack, as with Elijah

(1 Kings 19:1–4), or it may be an habitual thing, a slavery of the devil to a certain kind of fear (Heb 2:15). How prone we are to fear is apparent from the fact that there are 366 occasions in the Bible where God tells us, 'Fear not.'

Godly fear, or the fear of the Lord

The fact that Scripture sometimes links this kind of fear with trembling (Phil 2:12) proves that we are talking about the same basic human emotion as the other two. Modern translations that replace the word 'fear' with 'reverance' or 'respect' are weakening it. There is a good reason why the Holy Spirit, with many alternatives at his disposal, has used the word 'fear' in both the Old and New Testaments. If the emotion is the same with the three different kinds of fear, the source and the motivation are very different with godly fear.

The fear of the Lord depends on a right understanding of God's character. You could have a wrong view of God, thinking him to be unjust, unmerciful or even tyrannical, and that might make you frightened of him. That would be sinful fear, *not* the fear of the Lord (see Lk 19:21). Sinful fear is always self-centred, while godly fear is always God-centred.

Why do we need it?

Scriptures on this neglected theme are so numerous, especially in the Old Testament, that we shall only be able to touch on the more important aspects. The fear of the Lord is one of the great motivating factors of the Christian life. It is a corrective when we are tempted to deviate from the centre of God's will and follow some by-path meadow, and it is an antidote to so much that may be dubbed 'Christian', but which is shallow and superficial. It will ensure:

1. A right attitude to God

There was a holy intimacy with God that marked the lives of men like Abraham (Jas 2:23) and Moses (Deut 34:10). That is something we should all seek. But there is a wrong kind of familiarity that addresses this awesome and majestic God as though he were one of our buddies, and that tries to bring him down to our level. What is lacking here is godly fear. None of us will ever attain to God's friendship unless we retain a sense of awe and wonder in our approach. This will affect us in all our dealings with him. It will make our worship acceptable because we recognize that 'our God [not just the God of the unbeliever] is a consuming fire' (Heb 12:28-29).

2. A needful repugnance for sin

'To fear the Lord is to hate evil' (Prov 8:13). Sin is repugnant to us. We may occasionally be deceived by the enemy, or tempted by the devil, but we will never flirt with sin. If we are tripped and fall into the mire, we will never wallow in it. Instead we respond in the words of Micah 7:8 as we pick ourselves up. The fear of the Lord will cause us to take avoiding action when we see sin looming ahead (Prov 16:6). There are particular temptations that are defeated by showing the enemy a clean pair of heels (1 Cor 6:18; 10:14; 2 Tim 2:22).

3. A prayer life that prevails

You will find that the great recorded prayers of the Bible were saturated with the fear of God, especially those offered for the restoration of God's people and of God's house. See how Daniel addresses God (Dan 9:4), and the true humility that characterized his praying (v.7). We sense the same tone with the praying of our Lord,

'Father...Holy Father...O righteous Father' (Jn 17:1, 11, 25). We are told, 'In the days of his flesh, Jesus offered up prayers and supplications, with loud cries and tears, to him who was able to save him from death, and *he was heard for his godly fear*' (Heb 5:7, RSV, italics mine). Notice that Jesus didn't get any head start in prayer because he was God's Son. He prevailed because he prayed with a true appreciation of God's character. If we have godly fear we shall also prevail.

4. A pure motivation for service

As Christians we don't need to be told more things to do. We have been exhorted to do so much, and the list gets longer with every message we hear, or every Bible study we go through. We need to be *motivated* to start doing the things we know to do. There is no more effective motivation for service than the fear of God. Fearing the Lord and serving him go together in Scripture (Deut 6:13; 10:12; Josh 24:14). Onlookers must have thought Noah's building of the ark was crazy, but the motivation for his obedience was 'holy fear' (Heb 11:7). Do you find reluctance to speak to people about Christ? Paul knew that too, but note what it was that overcame his reluctance (2 Cor 5:11).

5. A means to make holiness perfect

Says Paul, 'Let us cleanse ourselves from every defilement of body and spirit, and make holiness perfect in the fear of God' (2 Cor 7:1, RSV). To make holiness perfect does not mean to reach sinless perfection (1 Jn 1:8–10). Only Jesus ever lived on earth a completely sinless life (1 Pet 2:22). It means 'perfect' in the sense of coming to full growth or maturity. This would mean that we live in Christ's promised victory, display the fruit of the Spirit (Gal 5:22–23), and that failure is the exception rather than the rule. Cleansing ourselves is the negative side of perfecting holiness, becoming like Jesus in our character is the positive. Why do we need the fear of the Lord? It creates within us a longing to be God-like, and it provides within us the motivation and faith to make it happen.

6. A release from sinful fear

'Do not call conspiracy everything that these people call conspiracy; do not fear what they fear, and do not dread it. The Lord Almighty...he is the one you are to fear' (Is 8:12–13). Are we gripped by the fears that haunt the world—fear of sickness, of unemployment, of violence, of nuclear war, etc? Only if the fear of the Lord has not taken over.

A member of a bomber crew whose plane has been hit and set on fire may be fearful at the thought of ejecting and committing himself to his parachute. But he does so because of the greater fear of staying in a blazing plane. The greater fear overcomes the lesser.

It was a fearful thing for Abraham to raise the knife to slay his son. But the moment he did God stayed his hand saying, 'Now I know that *you fear God*' (Gen 22:12). An epitaph to Sir John Lawrence of India in Westminster Abbey says, 'He feared man so little because he feared God so much.' There is no antidote to the fears that plague the human heart as effective as the fear of the Lord.

How do you get it?

The fear of God and the knowledge of God go together (Prov 2:5). It was said of the coming Messiah, 'The Spirit of the Lord will rest on him...the Spirit of knowledge and of the fear of the Lord—and he will delight in the fear of the Lord' (Is 11:2–3). Notice that there was nothing fearsome about this fear. Jesus didn't have to steel himself to practice it. He delighted in it, and so shall we. This passage shows us that it is the work of the Spirit, and that it is linked with knowledge. What kind of knowledge does the Holy Spirit bring?

First and foremost the knowlege of God. This is the revelation of God that Paul prayed the Ephesian church might have (Eph 1:17). The more we have of this the more we shall know of the fear of the Lord.

This work of the Holy Spirit doesn't happen automatically, or we wouldn't need to be answering this question. Those who experience the fear of the Lord are those who desire it deeply. It is a result of seeking the Lord—not just praying. There is a difference (2 Chron 7:14). When you pray you expect to get answers. When you seek God you expect to make a new discovery. Read Jeremiah 29:11–13. Verse 13 gives the key:

It tells me that I will seek God and find him. When I seek him _____

Memorize

Continue to work out your salvation with fear and trembling, for it is God who works in you to will and to act according to his good pleasure (Phil 2:12–13).

Home task

1. Ephesians 6:5 says, 'Slaves, obey your earthly masters with respect and fear, and with sincerity of heart, just as you would obey Christ.' This applies equally to the employer/employee relationship today. The fear is not primarily fear of the boss, but the fear of the Lord (cf Col 3:22 'fearing the Lord'). List the kinds

of things that a Christian employee, with the fear of the Lord in his heart, might do that others would probably not do, and that he would not do that others probably would. Is this an attitude you need only adopt if the boss is nice (1 Pet 2:18)?

2. The fear of the Lord is not only to characterize the individual believer, but the whole church. In the first reference in Scripture to 'the house of God' (Gen 28:16–17), note down what it says about Jacob (v.17). Then turn to Acts 9:31. Write down what you think would be the difference between a church 'living in the fear of the Lord', and one that was not.

For further study

Read Philippians 2:12–13. Paul says 'work out your salvation'. Write down:

1. What you think Paul meant by this, in practical terms.

2. Where you think the Philippian Christians were failing to do this. The following references will give you some clues (1:27; 2:2–4, 14–15; 4:2).

3. Why he says that they were to do it 'with fear and trembling'. How would this influence the spiritual problem considered in question 2?

Finding God's Will

Read
Colossians 1:9–14.

Introduction

We have touched on one aspect of this theme in Study 5 (A Sound Judgement). It would be good to re-read the section 'Judging what the will of God is'. But Spirit-directed judgement is only one way in which we come to know God's will. The whole theme is one of paramount importance. We saw in that earlier study that we don't have any inbuilt powers of self-direction (Jer 10:23). We need to be guided by God—especially over important decisions, such as career, life partner, what church to join, where to live, the friends we make. Then we need to know God's will on many other wider issues. It concerns the whole way God wants us to live and behave, work and witness. This is essential to our becoming mature. See how Epaphras prayed for his fellow Christians (Col 4:12).

Think first of relationship

Knowing God's will is so much more than learning some technique of guidance, or applying certain principles.

We need to think less about method and more about relationship. I had been ministering at a church in a distant city. Before leaving I asked one of the leaders if he could put me on the right road for my return journey. I was expecting instructions, but he gave me a guide. 'Neil will pilot you. He takes that route home anyway.' Instead of trying to decipher some scribbled directions as I drove, I had only to keep in touch with Neil in the blue Datsun.

God didn't give the Israelites a route to follow. He himself went ahead of them to guide them on their way (Ex 13:21).

Whether it is guidance in specific decisions or just understanding the will of God in important matters of life, relationship is the key. If we are living in disobedience and therefore out of touch with God we cannot expect to receive God's guidance, even though we may pray earnestly for it (1 Sam 28:5–6, 15; Ps 66:18–19). We must be in right relationship with the Guide.

Learn from Paul's prayer

Paul's prayer in our reading confirms what we have been saying.

> We have not stopped...asking God to fill you with the knowledge of his will through all spiritual wisdom and understanding...that you may live a life worthy of the Lord and may please him in every way: bearing fruit in every good work, growing in the knowledge of God.

Note:

For whom Paul prays

Not simply for the leaders of the church, but for *all* the believers. Paul could pray like this with confidence,

because when he was newly converted he was told that
God had chosen him 'to know his will' (Acts 22:14). You
too have been chosen to know God's will.

For what Paul prays

Not simply that the Colossians may be informed as to
what the will of God is, but to be *filled* with the knowledge of it. To be filled with the Spirit is to be possessed
and ruled by the Spirit. To be filled with the knowledge
of God's will means that you are so ruled by that will that
you carry it out. That's what Paul wanted for the
Colossians, and that's what God wants for us.

With these results, we are firstly to '*live a life worthy of
the Lord*'. How can we live such a life if we have never
troubled to find out what pleases and what displeases
God, or what his particular will is for our lives?

Secondly, '*bearing fruit in every good work*'. If we
know the will of God and are doing it by the power of the
Holy Spirit we cannot help being fruitful.

Lastly, and most wonderful of all, '*growing in the
knowledge of God*'. This means that the relationship
with our divine Guide that we spoke about earlier is
continually deepening. Knowing God's will and knowing
God are closely related.

A young man was trying to persuade his friend to go
with him to a certain questionable establishment in town.

'No thanks,' said the other.

'Why not?'

'It would upset my dad,'

'Oh I see. He's told you not to go there?'

'No, he hasn't—but I know my dad.'

Not only is it true—getting to know God's will you get
to know God, but getting to know God you get to know
his will, especially over many 'Is it right?—Is it wrong?'
issues.

Importance of heart attitude

If anyone finds the business of ascertaining God's will difficult, it is usually because the heart attitude is not right. Here are four requirements:

1. Dependence

Any sense of self-sufficiency must be broken down if we are to trust God with all our heart and not lean on our own understanding (Prov 3:5–6). Common sense and human wisdom will prove totally inadequate. We are required to understand what the will of the Lord is. Not to do so is 'foolish' (Eph 5:17). We will not discover God's will by trying to fathom it with our human intellect (Job 11:7), but by God revealing it in answer to prayer (Eph 1:17–19).

2. Obedience

This is never a problem—till you discover that God's will crosses yours! After the fall of Jerusalem to the Babylonians, the leaders of the Israelites who were not carried away into captivity asked the prophet Jeremiah to enquire from God where they should go and what they should do. God was their witness that they would do whatever the Lord said (Jer 42:1–6). But see how they responded when God did speak (Jer 43:1–2). More often than not God will not trouble to reveal his will to us if we are not disposed to obey it. Jesus once said that his teaching was not his own but God's, and that if anyone chose to do God's will they would know that this was the case (Jn 7:16–17). In the same way, if we have hearts truly set to do God's will, we shall know assuredly what God's will is.

3. Patience

When we enquire of the Lord it is not often we get a reply by return of post. This is where our determination to obey is put to the test. We must learn to wait for God. While we wait he is acting for us (Is 64:4). How often Christians ask God for direction, and when he doesn't answer as quickly as they would like they do whatever they think best. That is, they 'lean on [their] understanding' (see above). Often God's zero hour is just after ours. We must wait for God. Failure to do this was King Saul's first major blunder, and it cost him his throne (1 Sam 13:7–14). If our hearts are right God will always guide in time.

4. Sensitivity

One of the great Bible promises for knowing God's will is Psalm 32:8–9. Instead of 'I will counsel you and watch over you' most versions read, 'I will counsel you with my eye upon you.' The eye is a very sensitive but effective method of counselling. I recall occasions when we had visitors to tea, and my brother and I were tucking into the cream cakes before anyone else had a look in—until we caught Father's eye! That was enough. No words were needed.

As Christians that means keeping our eye on the Lord to pick up the signals, just as one serving at table would watch the master or mistress (Ps 123:1–2). After promising to counsel us with his eye (Ps 32:8), the Lord tells us, 'Do not be like the horse or the mule.' Does God have to tug you first this way and then that to get you where he wants you? That's the only way he can deal with some. Pray for sensitivity to those gentle checks or nudges of the Holy Spirit.

How God communicates

Finally we must consider briefly the practical ways by which God communicates his will to us. First, there are the *Scriptures*. As well as using these in general to teach us, God often lights up a phrase or passage to give us special direction.

When I received my first invitation to minister God's word overseas there seemed no way that I could say 'Yes'. Then this scripture came strongly to me, 'Go; I will help you speak and will teach you what to say' (Ex 4:12). I took it as God's word, and amazingly the obstacles were removed one by one.

Then there is the *inward voice* of the Holy Spirit (Acts 10:19–20). We often read of God speaking to the Old Testament saints, but seldom it would seem with an audible voice; rather with that 'still small voice' within. We have the inward sensing that we have heard from God.

There is also the *ordering of our circumstances*. God has a way of cutting off finance and of releasing it; of shutting doors and opening them (1 Cor 16:8–9), and he uses these to move us, or keep us where we are.

We must include here the *counsel of others*, especially our leaders. We are not loners serving God. We are members that belong to each other and have a concern for each other in the body of Christ (1 Cor 12:25–26). It should not surprise us that God may give or confirm his direction to us through fellow-members of the body.

God also uses *the gifts of the Holy Spirit*. The first missionary movement was set in motion by a direct word from the Holy Spirit, probably through one of the prophets present (Acts 13:1–3). Note that this word was a confirmation, setting two men apart for the work to which God had already called them. If such an utterance

is not a confirmation, it will need to be tested and
confirmed (1 Thess 5:20–21). God may also use *dreams*,
as in Bible times, to enlighten us, warn us, or give us
special direction (Mt 2:12–13).

Invariably God uses two or more means in a given
situation to communicate his will. If you are not sure,
stay put until you are. There is one final indication that
should be present every time you think you discern the
will of God—*the peace of God* ruling in your heart (Col
3:15). The word 'rule' here means to arbitrate, or act as
referee. When your peace is disturbed, the referee has
blown his whistle to stop the game. Never move if the
peace of God is not ruling in your heart.

Memorize

*I will instruct you and teach you in the way you should
go; I will counsel you and watch over you. Do not be
like the horse or the mule, which have no understanding but must be controlled by bit and bridle or
they will not come to you (Ps 32:8–9).*

Home task

1. Write in your notebook your honest answer to the
following personal questions. Write out in full any
scripture with its reference that confirms your answer.
(a) Do you believe that God has a plan for your future
which is good, well-pleasing and perfect?
(b) Are you expecting him to unfold, or to continue to
unfold, that plan to you?
(c) Are you willing to forego any plan of yours if it
should clash with God's revealed plan?
(d) For you to know God's will, God has his part to play
and you have yours. What is your part?

For further study

1. Study the track record of Saul over this question of seeking God's will (often called 'enquiring of the Lord'), and then that of David. Write down all you can learn from these incidents of the characters of these two men.

Saul: 1 Samuel 14:16–20 (the ark was used for consulting God); 36–37; 28:6; 1 Chronicles 10:13–14; 13:3.

David: 1 Samuel 23:2, 4; 30:8; 2 Samuel 2:1; 5:19, 23; 21:1.

2. Isaiah 30:21 is a promise that if we mistake God's path for us he will correct us. The voice *behind us* tells us our Shepherd is no longer leading us, and turning to right or left means deviating from the right path (Num 20:17; Deut 5:32). See what you can learn from two examples of God's corrective guidance in the life of David, and two from the life of Paul:

David: 1 Samuel 25:1–34; 2 Samuel 7:1–16.

Paul: Acts 16:6–7.

Resisting the Tempter

Read
1 Peter 5:5–11.

Who is the tempter?

Satan was a very high angelic dignitary, one of the
cherubim, until he and his angels rebelled and were
expelled from heaven (Is 14:12–14; Ezek 28:14–16). It is
these powers of darkness, not human beings, who are
now our real enemy (Eph 6:12). Satan (meaning adversary) is committed to opposing God and all those who
belong to God's kingdom.

Satan's objective

Since his ambition was to make himself 'like the Most
High' (Is 14:14) he sought to tempt that first pair to
transfer their allegiance to him. He first seduced Eve
into disobeying God, then through her Adam (Gen 3:1–
6). The attack was on Eve's mind, and Satan came in the
guise of a serpent, which suggests cunning and deceit (2
Cor 11:3). In this way he succeeded in injecting the germ
of rebellion into the human race, so that death came on
all (Rom 5:12). The measure of Satan's success is that he

is acknowledged in Scripture as 'the prince of this world' (Jn 12:31) and 'the god of this age' (2 Cor 4:4). He has 'blinded the minds of unbelievers' to keep them from seeing the light and knowing who it is they are serving. Now 'the whole world is under the control of the evil one' (1 Jn 5:19).

God's intervention

Now for the bright side. Satan's success caused no panic in heaven. Nothing took God by surprise. His plan of salvation was prepared before the need for it came into existence (Rev 13:8). The coming of Jesus was like D-day in Europe, a strategic attack by the kingdom of heaven to recapture lost territory. His preaching the kingdom, healing the sick and casting out demons was stage one of this heavenly invasion (Mt 12:28). Stage two was to be accomplished through that army of redeemed men and women called the church, formed at Pentecost. And the final victory will be when the last trumpet sounds heralding Christ's return in glory, and a mighty cry is heard from heaven: 'The kingdom of the world has become the kingdom of our Lord and of his Christ, and he will reign for ever and ever' (Rev 11:15). Not only does the believer have the assurance of ultimate victory, but even Satan himself knows that his days are numbered (Rev 12:12).

Don't underestimate your enemy...

This is a common mistake of believers. They think that 'the roaring lion' is toothless, all bark and no bite. Or they think that deception is his only weapon, that he can only pull the wool over your eyes. We must take the devil seriously. He is a spirit being with supernatural power. He brought down fire from the sky and a storm from the desert that dealt death and destruction to Job's household and possessions (Job 1:12, 16, 18–19). He was able to transport the Son of God from the desert and set him on the highest point of the temple in Jerusalem (Mt 4:5). Then from a high place he was able to show him all the kingdoms of the world in the flash of a second (Lk 4:5). If we have the fear of the Lord we shall maintain a healthy respect for the authority God has given Satan. If the great archangel was not free to slander him, we must be careful how we speak about him or address him (Jude 8—9).

... but don't see him too big

It is just as serious a mistake to think that Satan has a free hand to do what he wants. Far from it. Since 'the world, and all who live in it' belong to the Lord (Ps 24:1), the devil is God's devil, and owes his existence and authority to the Most High. He is only 'ruler of the world' and 'God of this age' by divine permission, and until God decides to settle accounts (Rev 20:10). He cannot lift a little finger against God's children without God's approval. He launched two fierce attacks on Job, but observe how they were monitored and controlled by God (Job 1:12; 2:6), and permitted for Job's ultimate good and blessing (Job 42:12; Jas 5:11). Our temptations too are controlled by God (1 Cor 10:13).

God meant it for good

Though God may lead us into temptation (Mt 4:1; Acts 20:22–23), or permit us to be tempted, he himself never tempts us to do evil (Jas 1:13). If God can control our temptations we may wonder why he doesn't intervene to

97

stop them altogether. It is because they accomplish a valuable purpose in our lives. What is God doing through temptation?

1. Strengthening your faith by putting it to the test

Faith is like muscle. The athlete is subjected to greater and greater tests in order to reach his peak performance. Strong winds that cause the trees to bend also drive their roots deeper into the soil. Without temptation faith would be flabby (Jas 1:2–4; 1 Pet 1:6–7).

2. Purifying your character as gold in a crucible

Before he went through the fire of trial Job was *'righteous'*. That had more to do with his outward acts. *After* the fire Job was *holy*, for God had dealt with inner attitudes. He had said himself, 'When he has tested me, I shall come forth as gold' (Job 23:10).

3. Maturing you for God's approval

It is only having 'stood the test' under trial that we qualify for 'the crown of life' (Jas 1:12).

Two pocket watches in a jeweller's appeared to be absolutely identical except that one was twice the price of the other. The reason? The more expensive one had undergone stringent tests, such as being subjected to enormous pressure, great extremes of temperature, immersed in water for days, and suchlike, and had come through unaffected. But God intends that we shall not ony come through unscathed, but made 'strong, firm and steadfast' (1 Pet 5:10).

An old Puritan was watching a blacksmith tempering metal. With the rod in his hand he pointed to different parts of the red-hot iron, and wherever he pointed, his assistant brought down the sledge hammer with a great thud. The Puritan saw how God points out where we

need tempering, and there the devil brings down the
hammer of temptation. 'Thus I perceived,' he said, 'how
God makes the devil sweat for the saints' good!' The
devil meant it for harm, but God meant it for good.

How to resist

1. Take a positive attitude

This means believing what has just been said about
temptation: that God means it for good.

I was lying immobilized on a hospital bed 12,000 miles
from home. An accident had terminated my preaching
tour in that country before I had fulfilled the main
engagements I had come for. It seemed that every
bone in my body was aching, as well as my injured head.
And the verse God gave me was James 1:2! How do you
respond to a word like that? Only by declaring in faith
there and then, 'Great good will come out of this.' And,
of course, it did.

Have you shuddered when you read the catalogue of
Paul's hardships? He could refer to them as 'light and
momentary troubles' only because he saw them in the
light of what they would achieve (2 Cor 4:17–18).

2. Recognize the attack

That means being constantly alert. Jesus told a bunch of
drowsy disciples, 'Watch and pray so that you will not
fall into temptation' (Mt 26:41). How would you behave
if you were in the bush, and you knew that there was a
lion prowling around? Well, that's exactly the situation
you are in, and Peter gives you the answer (1 Pet 5:8). To
be proud or cocksure of ourselves is to be riding for a fall
(1 Cor 10:12). Often the enemy disguises his attack. We
may not be aware that that strange bout of depression or

that feeling of deep discouragement could be an attack of the devil. Let us trust the Holy Spirit to alert us.

3. Don't court temptation or walk into danger

We are *not* to 'think about how to gratify the desires of the sinful nature' (Rom 13:14b). The world about us will provide endless scope for this, but the grace of God teaches us to say 'No' (Tit 2:11–12). The sinful nature is to be crucified, not pampered and nourished (Gal 5:24). There are certain 'no go' areas where the child of God trespasses at his peril. We are to have nothing to do with anything occult, however harmless it may seem. Spiritism (usually called spiritualism), witchcraft, fortune-telling, horoscopes, ouija board and suchlike are forbidden because powers of evil are operating there (Deut 18:9–13). Any soldier who strolls into enemy territory is liable to be taken prisoner (Acts 8:9–11, 18–23).

4. Submit to God—resist the devil (Jas 4:7)

If you do not first submit to God you have no power to resist the devil. Submission brings God's power to your aid. How do you resist? Not by taking a deep breath and gritting your teeth. Our fight is one of faith (1 Tim 6:12). So Peter tells us how to resist the roaring lion—'by standing firm in the faith' (1 Pet 5:9). It is not even enough to think about God's superior strength or his promise to deliver you, you must give voice to your faith. Confess with your mouth what you are believing in your heart. If you memorize some of the great victory promises you will be able to quote them in the heat of the battle. For example:

Sin shall not be your master (Rom 6:14).

Thanks be to God! He gives us the victory through our Lord Jesus Christ (1 Cor 15:57).

We are more than conquerors through him who loved us (Rom 8:37).

Those temptations that come from within, rather than the outside attacks of the devil, will be dealt with in our next study.

Memorize

Consider it pure joy, my brothers, whenever you face trials of many kinds, because you know that the testing of your faith develops perseverance. Perseverance must finish its work so that you may be mature and complete, not lacking in anything (Jas 1:2–4).

Home task

1. Temptation is a learning time. Look back over your own experience of temptation. Note down what you have learned:
(a) about yourself
(b) about God and his word
(c) about your need of fellow Christians.
    2. Now make a note of what you believe temptation has done in making you a better Christian. Thank God for each thing you write down. And if you are still going through some temptation, start thanking God for this and confessing that you believe his purpose in it will be fulfilled, and that he is giving you the victory.

Further study

1. Jesus referred to the devil when he said, 'The thief comes only to steal and kill and destroy' (Jn 10:10). In what ways is this generally true of mankind? And in what ways does he try to rob the believer? How are we to guard against this?

2. Jesus also referred to the devil as 'a strong man' guarding the valuables in his house (Mt 12:29; Lk 11:21–22). What is his house? What are these valuables? How in practical terms are we to enter his house, tie him up and make off with his goods? Find scriptures to support your answer.

Embracing the Cross

Read
Romans 6:1–14.

Salvation past, present and future

The Bible teaches that through the cross the believer
has been saved from the *penalty* of sin (Jn 5:24), that he *is
being saved* from the *power* of sin (Rom 5:10) and one
day, when Christ returns, he *will be saved* from the
presence of sin (Rev 21:23, 27). But many Christians
only seem to know about salvation in the past tense.
They know that the cross has cleared their past account,
that they have been forgiven and accepted by God
because of what Jesus did on the cross. But they seem to
think that they can now leave the cross behind and press
on into the more positive blessings of the Christian life.
'No,' said Jesus. 'If you really want to be a true disciple
you must take the cross along with you' (see Luke 14:27).
Salvation is so much more than a free pardon for the
past. It deals with those temptations that come from
within, mentioned at the close of the last study.

What the cross signifies

Because it adorns a church building, or may be worn around the neck, we forget that the cross is no pretty emblem. Today we would talk of a hangman's noose or an electric chair, for the cross has to do with the execution of a criminal. Note three things that the cross signifies:

1. Shame

All that accompanied crucifixion, as well as the execution itself, was shameful as well as painful. The condemned man was scourged, mocked and spat upon (Mt 27:26–31). There was the procession to the place of execution through the hooting, jeering crowd, the prisoner carrying his cross (Jn 19:17). Finally he was stripped and nailed naked to the stake for all to see (Ps 22:17b). The wonder is not that the Son of God 'became obedient to death'—but that it was 'even death on a cross!' (Phil 2:8). Was there ever a death more shameful? Embracing the cross means coming to terms with 'the offence of the cross' (Gal 5:11).

2. Weakness

Again Psalm 22 puts these words prophetically into the lips of Christ:

> I am poured out like water, and all my bones are out of joint. My heart has turned to wax; it has melted away within me. My strength is dried up like a potsherd, and my tongue sticks to the roof of my mouth' (vv. 14–15).

The cross puts a man into a place of appalling weakness and helplessness. Paul, speaking of the risen Christ to the Corinthians, says, 'He is not weak in dealing with you, but is powerful among you. For to be sure, *he was*

crucified in weakness, yet he lives by God's power'
(2 Cor 13:3–4, italics mine). The cross is designed to
bring us to an end of our own resources and to a place of
total dependence on God.

3. Death

When Jesus spoke of bearing the cross, he wasn't talking
about playing a game of 'let's pretend'. His hearers
would know exactly what he meant. A man with ashen
face, struggling down the street with the cross on his
shoulder, goaded and kicked by a squad of Roman
soldiers, was a *man sentenced to death*. He was on his
way to execution. In that last scripture Paul said, 'We
felt the sentence of death.' Clearly they had the cross on
their shoulders. That this ugly emblem lies at the heart of
the Christian message should remind you that the gospel
was never intended to give you a mere spring-clean,
brighten you up, or make you a little more acceptable to
your Creator. It was designed to *finish you off*—so that
there could be 'a new creation' (2 Cor 5:17). The cross is
not to titivate, but to terminate. It offers a radical final
solution to the problem of on-going sin, and so opens the
way to bring us into all the blessings that lie on the
resurrection side of the cross.

Looking beyond

When we hear about being crucified with Christ, it all
sounds dark and forbidding. Who wants to tread such a
path? Christ is here our inspiration. 'Let us fix our eyes
on Jesus...who *for the joy set before him* endured the
cross, scorning its shame, and sat down at the right hand
of the throne of God' (Heb 12:2, italics mine). But
however could the prospect of the cross inspire any joy?
Because Jesus was *looking beyond the cross*, and seeing

what it was to accomplish. It was this that filled him with joy and took him triumphantly through the suffering and the shame. It will do exactly the same for us. Notice four tremendous things that the cross accomplishes for us.

1. It breaks the dominion of sin

To be falling into sin continually, having to confess it to God, and then draw on the grace of his forgiveness, is not the picture of the normal Christian life we find in the New Testament. It is sub-standard and we must not settle for it. 'Shall we go on sinning so that grace may increase? By no means!' says Paul. What then is the answer? Read on: 'We died to sin; how can we live in it any longer?' (Rom 6:1–2). The cross means death, and death is the only solution to the problem of recurring sin.

Note that Paul does *not* say: '*If* we die to sin we would not live in it.' He tells us straight—we *did* die to sin, so that continuing in it is not an option. Perhaps you respond, 'But I don't feel as though that old sinful self is dead, or if it's dead it won't lie down!' But God has not invited us to consult our feelings on the matter. He has not even suggested that we consider our track record or our past experience. He is telling us what happened when we were united by faith to Christ crucified: 'We died to sin.' In verse 6 of this same passage he says, 'We *know* that our old self was crucified with him.' How do we know? Only by the Holy Spirit revealing it to us.

A young woman, having asked Christ to be her Saviour, was told that she was now forgiven and accepted by God. But she said, 'I don't feel forgiven. How can I know it's true?' She was told, 'You will only know as you believe God's word. The Bible says, "Call on him and you will be saved. Confess your sins and you will be forgiven."' As she believed what God had said, she came into the good of what God had promised. It is just the same with dying to sin. We must believe what God says and not our own feelings.

2. *It brings power out of weakness*

We have already seen that the cross spells appalling weakness, but Jesus showed that it was the pathway to power. Only as he submitted to the way of the cross could he experience the power of the resurrection. It is that same resurrection power that we need to overcome the world. It is only ours as we tread the path he trod. So when Paul tells us about Jesus, that 'he was crucified in weakness, yet he lives by God's power', he then adds, 'Likewise, we are weak in him, yet by God's power we will live with him to serve you' (2 Cor 13:4).

The way to know this power is to take a positive attitude to everything that God permits in our lives to make us weak. We may not know for certain what was 'the thorn in the flesh' that Paul had to endure. We do know, however, why God did not remove it in answer to prayer. It was sent to keep him humble and to keep him weak (2 Cor 12:7–9). But the thorn was just one of the many things God used to strip Paul of his self-sufficiency and throw him back upon God (v.10). Things that we would have avoided were Paul's glad boast. To him they were the pathway to power and effectiveness.

Therefore, thank him for thy helplessness, beloved,
And if thou needst must long,
Let it be for the rest of utter weakness
In the arms for ever strong.
Long only that he make thee bare and empty,
Take all that is thine own,
Thy prowess and thy strength and thine endeavour,
And leave thee God alone.

3. It makes us fruitful

And which of us does not want to be fruitful? During the last week of his earthly life some Greeks requested an interview with Jesus. It seems he did not grant this request. Did he sense that they would present him with some attractive proposition to turn him from the path of the cross? 'The hour has come,' he said, 'for the Son of Man to be glorified'—but not the way that these men were in all probability proposing. He knew that the path to glory was via the cross, so he continued: 'I tell you the truth, unless an ear of wheat falls to the ground and dies, it remains only a single seed. But *if it dies*, it produces many seeds' (Jn 12:22–25, italics mine). What was Jesus saying?

Firstly, he was pointing to himself. He was the ear of wheat that had to fall into the ground and die. Centuries before it had been prophesied of him: 'Though the Lord makes his life a guilt offering, he will see his offspring' (Is 53:10). Here it was being fulfilled. It was looking beyond the cross and seeing the great harvest that would spring from his death. If Jesus had been unwilling to 'fall into the ground and die', he would have remained a single seed. By consenting to the cross, he would produce the harvest—'a great multitude that no-one could count' (Rev 7:9).

Jesus was also pointing out the path of fruitfulness for us. We too must be willing to be seen to fall into the ground and die if we are to bear much fruit. Strictly speaking, it is not the seed but the outer husk that dies in the process of germination. So Paul says, 'We always carry around *in our body* the death of Jesus, so that the life of Jesus may also be revealed in our body' (2 Cor 4:10, italics mine). It is by the Spirit that we must learn to 'put to death the misdeeds of the body' (Rom 8:13). As 'death is at work in us...life is at work' in others (2 Cor 4:12).

4. It is the pathway to glory

This is not something we may only experience when we get to heaven. We may know it in measure now if we have embraced the cross. Says Peter, 'If you are insulted because of the name of Christ...the Spirit of glory and of God rests on you' (1 Pet 4:14). Christians who have suffered much for Christ's sake usually have a joy, a radiance and a beauty in their faces that is not of this world. They seem to carry with them a sense of God. This is only a foretaste of the glory which we are to enjoy when we enter God's presence.

Probably the greatest temptation Jesus had to face in his earthly life was to take a path to glory that bypassed the cross. In the wilderness temptation the devil offered him all the kingdoms of the world and their glory if he would worship him (Lk 4:5–7). Jesus knew that one day they would all be his, but first he must 'face death for everyone'. It was because of his obedience to death that God has exalted him to the highest place (Phil 2:9). There was no short cut for him (Lk 24:26), and there is none for us (2 Tim 2:11–12a). The cross is still the only path to glory.

Conclusion

So if you would know—

> *Abiding victory over sin*
> *God's power made perfect in weakness*
> *A life of abundant fruitfulness*
> *And the hope of glory*

—you must come to terms with the cross as a present experience. If you have already been baptized in water this will not require you doing something that has not been done, but recognizing something that Christ has already done for you.

Memorize

For we know that our old self was crucified with him so that the body of sin might be rendered powerless, that we should no longer be slaves to sin (Rom 6:6).

Home task

1. 'Sin shall not be your master' (Rom 6:14). That is both a command and a promise. If there are temptations that regularly floor you, you have not yet fully embraced the cross. Read again your memory verse. It says, 'We *know . . . .*' That is more than a mental knowing, it comes by the revelation of the Holy Spirit. Call on God to give you that revelation. You will know that you have it when you can say boldly and with conviction, 'I *know* that my old self was crucified with Christ.' Don't move on to the next point until you can do this.

2. Read Romans 6:12–14. Says Paul, 'Do not offer the parts of your body to sin . . .' (v.13). Instead do two things:

a) 'Offer yourselves to God.' But how? 'As those who have been brought from death to life.' Do that right now. Surrender yourself totally to God, in the faith that the old self is dead, and that you are a new person in Christ (see Romans 12:1).

b) 'Offer the parts of your body to him.' Think of what part of your body is involved in each area of temptation. 'Here is my mind, Lord, that used to think wrong thoughts. I present it to you as an instrument of righteousness.' Go through them all one by one, and

remember, you are not under law—you keeping it up—
but under grace—God keeping you up (v.14).

For further study

1. This will help you to discover the secret of spiritual
power through the cross. Read again 2 Corinthians
12:7–10. Note Paul's list of the hard things he had to face
(v.10). They were not sins, but weaknesses and testing
situations. Compile your own list of the things that you
find hard, like shyness and self-consciousness, difficulty
in expressing yourself, being ridiculed at work, opposition at home, and all the things that make it hard to
follow Jesus. Under the list write what God says about
them all (v.9). Ask God to help you believe what he
says. The proof will be when you can:
(a) Boast about your weaknesses instead of moaning
about them (v.9).
(b) Delight in them instead of shrinking from them
(v.10).
(c) Know that Christ's power has been made perfect in
your weakness (v.9).
2. The cross is the path to glory. See how this is
illustrated in the life of Joseph (Gen 37, 39—40). Make
a note of the events in these chapters that you think
would have worked the cross into Joseph's life. What
particular weaknesses do you think God was dealing
with in Joseph in order to fit him for the throne (Gen
37:2, 5–11)?

Understanding God's Ways

Read
Hebrews 12:4–11.

Something very important

Though God redeemed Israel out of Egypt and made them his people, they did not understand his ways. They saw him do great things for them in deliverance and miraculous provision. They also saw him act towards them in judgement and discipline. Moses understood what lay behind these deeds—God's *ways*—but the people didn't: 'He made known his *ways* to Moses, his *deeds* to the people of Israel' (Ps 103:7, italics mine). That speaks of two very different levels of understanding. Knowing the ways of God is how we come to know God. See how Moses reached out for that deeper understanding in Exodus 33:13.

At the end of the wilderness wanderings, Moses said to the people: 'Remember how the Lord your God led you all the way in the desert....He humbled you, causing you to hunger and then feeding you with manna' (Deut 8:2–3). Causing them to hunger and feeding them with manna were both acts of God, but it was much easier to understand God's 'deeds' in feeding them than to understand why he suffered them to hunger. In this study we are going to focus on the ways of God that we find difficult, the disciplining of our lives. This is something vital if we are to mature.

God is sovereign

This means that God not only governs the affairs of men, but that he possesses absolute authority. He acts, he intervenes, he permits, he promotes, he forbids and he overrules—in order to accomplish his purpose. He doesn't do all this—circumstances permitting, or human beings permitting, or Satan permitting. He does it all regardless (Is 14:27). That's what we mean by absolute authority. He may use men, even wicked men (Acts 2:23). He may even use Satan (see under 'But don't see him too big', Study 10). The fact is, 'He does as he pleases with the powers of heaven and the peoples of the earth. No-one can hold back his hand or say to him: "What have you done?"' (Dan 4:35).

The New Testament bears equal witness to this truth of the sovereignty of God. We are introduced to one 'who works out everything in conformity with the purpose of his will' (Eph 1:11). And the circumstances of a believer's life are so perfectly controlled by God that 'in all things God works for the good for those who love him' (Rom 8:28). We have no problem in believing this when God's ways obviously work out for our happiness and prosperity. But what do we feel when they bring disappointment and adversity? This is where we must learn to sing the song of Moses and the song of the Lamb: not only, 'Great and marvellous are your deeds, Lord God Almighty,' but also, *'Just and true are your ways*, King of the Ages' (Rev 15:3, italics mine). To have full faith in God's sovereignty is essential for a proper understanding of God's ways.

God, Satan or chance?

How do you react when unforseen events overtake you? If it was a legacy for £10,000 left you by Aunt Fanny, you would no doubt bless God and bless Aunt Fanny. But if, as in the case of a friend of mine, you learn that you have lost £10,000 as a result of a business failure you may find there are conflicting reactions. Do you simply dismiss it as 'bad luck', one of those misfortunes that could happen to anyone?

The fact is you are not 'anyone', but someone very special to God, one of his children for whom he takes a fatherly responsibility. If we have grasped the truth of God's sovereignty we will know that our affairs are not subject to luck, fate or chance, whether good or bad (Rom 8:28).

Of course you might feel it was your own silly fault for agreeing hastily to invest in that firm, or in not seeking the advice of others. But the fact is, you were still in the hands of One who is willing and able to intervene and over-rule your foolish decisions—and often does. Why did he not do it this time?

Was it Satan? If you grasped the lesson of Job's misfortunes (Study 10) you will know that though Satan possesses supernatural power and is our sworn enemy, he is only permitted to operate within certain clearly-defined boundaries. These are laid down by God, and *God has purposes of blessing in all that he permits.* In Job 1:6–12 and 2:1–6 we are told about the argument between God and Satan as to whether Job was the good man that God said he was. After that Satan is never mentioned again in the book. Job came right through into victory, and his health and fortunes were restored, and so far as we know he never knew that Satan had any part in the attacks on his possessions, his family and his health. When God shows us that we are under satanic attack, then we resist him by faith. At other times we deal with God, as Job did, and whether or not Satan is involved need not concern us.

Does God punish us?

The answer to this is 'Yes' and 'No'. If we are thinking of punishment as divine condemnation for sins committed, the answer is 'No'. The ungodly will suffer this on the day of judgement (Mt 25:41, 46), but the true believer 'has eternal life and will not be condemned; he has crossed over from death to life' (Jn 5:24; cf Rom 8:1).

But if we mean, 'Does God punish us by corrective discipline?' the answer is 'Yes'. Scripture teaches us that just as surely as a human father who truly loves his son will not spare the rod (Prov 13:24), so our heavenly Father uses his rod with his children (Deut 8:5). You will have seen from the reading that this is a New Testament as much as an Old Testament concept.

A man noticed that some of his choice desert apples were disappearing from his orchard at the bottom of the garden. That evening he saw a figure among the trees, and when the young culprit was apprehended, it was his own boy. Had the thief been a stranger, he would have rung the police, but since it was his son, he said, 'Go to your bedroom and wait for me there.' In due course 'the board of education' came into painful contact with the 'seat of learning'.

When we sin we are not handed over to the law to face the Judge of all the earth. Christ's death on the cross has fully satisfied the demands of the law on our behalf. But that doesn't mean we can sin with impunity because we are believers. There is still the discipline and correction of our heavenly Father (1 Cor 11:32).

The discipline of the Lord

There are some things in our reading that we must understand if we are to respond aright to God's dealings with us.

1. Expression of love

Look at Hebrews 12:8: 'If you are not disciplined (and everyone undergoes discipline), then you are illegitimate children and not true sons.' From the beginning of Scripture through to the end that's the way discipline is viewed (Rev 3:19). If we ever speak of God 'punishing' his children we must understand that his action is a proof of his loving commitment to bring us through into maturity. This verse 8 is teaching us that it is *the absence* of God's fatherly discipline and correction in our lives that should give us cause for concern. We should have to ask ourselves, 'Am I a true son?' God doesn't discipline the unsaved and the ungodly, any more than the man with the orchard would have felt free to apply the stick to someone else's son. Discipline is the mark of God's special concern.

2. No exceptions

Did you notice those three words in verse 8, 'Everyone undergoes discipline'? Certainly not every one of the Father's children are worldly, wayward or backslidden, but all are disciplined. So not all discipline is because of unrighteous acts. Job's friends made the mistake of thinking this about Job, though God had expressed the very opposite when he spoke to Satan. But there was still a purifying of his character which God had to accomplish. Even when we are generally living in victory and walking in the Spirit, thoughts, motives and attitudes need to be purified (2 Cor 10:5).

3. It hurts!

The closing verse of our reading says: 'No discipline seems pleasant at the time, but painful.' Our older versions generally use the old-fashioned word 'chastisement' instead of discipline. This is the word that describes the fatherly 'laying on of hands' in the case of the son caught stealing his father's apples. It is not meant to be pleasant, it's meant to hurt. Sometimes the pain is mental, sometimes physical. With Job it was both. But far more painful than the physical afflictions of being covered with sores was the mental pain of being wrongfully accused by 'the friends' who had apparently come to comfort him. One thing is certain. Whatever affliction God orders or permits, it is always an expression of his unfailing love, and always for our ultimate blessing (Lam 3:33).

4. For our profit

That is what verse 11 in our reading goes on to say: 'Later on, however, it produces a harvest of righteousness and peace for those who have been trained by it.' Not just a little fruit, but a *harvest*. Take Job. God had blessed the early part of Job's life. According to Satan that was the only reason why Job served God (1:9–11). Satan, the accuser, implied that it was cupboard love. But 'The Lord blessed the latter part of Job's life more than the first' (Job 42:12). That doesn't only mean that God increased his possessions. He had had a conviction, even in the midst of his trial, that God was refining him, and that he would come forth as gold (Job 23:10), and that's exactly what happened. God changed a man who was outwardly righteous into one who was inwardly holy. 'God disciplines us for our good, that we may share in his holiness' (Heb 12:10).

Handling it aright

'You intended to harm me, but God intended it for good' (Gen 50:20). That's what Joseph said years after to his brothers who had sold him into slavery. Whether our misfortunes come to us through the malice of the devil or the evil intentions of men, it is always true— 'God intended it for good.' That is another way of expressing Romans 8:28. But whether God's intention is fulfilled depends on our reacting aright. Would Joseph have ever qualified for the throne—would he have ever become the instrument of blessing and salvation that God intended, if he had allowed his brothers' cruel injustice to fill him with bitterness and resentment? In verses 5 and 6 of our reading we have two negative commands which teach us how to respond aright to the Lord's discipline:

1. Do not make light of it

This is how we may be tempted to react. We shrug it off. We explain it away. 'Surely this couldn't be God saying anything to me.' It is humbling to acknowledge that God is disciplining us and adjusting us, so we dismiss the thought and look for natural explanations. This verse is saying, 'Take God's discipline seriously. Things don't happen in your life accidentally.' The right response, as our reading reminds us, is one of submission (v.9). See how positively and believingly the psalmist responded to his trials (Ps 119:71, 75).

2. Do not lose heart

This is the other, opposite temptation. We don't shrug it off or deny that it is God, but we take it badly. We feel that God is being harsh and unloving. 'Doesn't he understand all that I've been through already?' We let feelings of resentment lodge in our hearts. If our trial has come through God's people, we may have resentment towards them, but it's really against God that we have these feelings. This is what happened to Job. His 'friends' with their false accusations stirred him up, and then out came his words about God being unjust (Job 9:15–18). In the midst of his fiery affliction poor Job lost heart altogether. He wished he had never been born, and only wanted to die (Job 3:11, 20–21).

Job felt the way he did because he couldn't see the purpose of grace that God had in mind for him. He could only hear the devil's whisper, 'You are going through this because God hates you and has abandoned you.' Have you ever heard Satan whisper that? God says, 'No, you are going through this because I love you and accept you as my son [see Hebrews 12:6–7]. And because you are my son, I want you to bear the family likeness, that is, share my holiness [see verse 10]. What you have had before has been firstfruits, but I want to give you a harvest' [see verse 11].

Memorize

No discipline seems pleasant at the time, but painful. Later on, however, it produces a harvest of righteousness and peace for those who have been trained by it (Heb 12:11).

Home task

1. Note some of the ways in which God changes us through trials and testings. What are the changes described by the following scriptures? Jot them down. Are you able to identify with some of them from your own experience?

(a) Psalm 107:17–20.

(b) 1 Peter 1:6–7.

(c) 1 Peter 5:10.

(d) Hebrews 12:10.

(e) 2 Corinthians 1:3–4.

(f) 2 Corinthians 4:17.

2. Are you going through some discipline of the Lord right now?

(a) Make sure that you are not falling into either of the two traps mentioned in Hebrews 12:5–6.

(b) Do you understand what God is wanting to do in you through this testing? If not, ask him to show you, and then call on him for grace to respond aright to his working in you.

For further study

In 1 Corinthians 11:17–34 Paul speaks of the way the Corinthians had been misbehaving when they celebrated the Lord's Supper in church.

(a) Write down the things for which Paul reprimanded them (vv.20–22).

(b) How is their behaviour described in verse 27, and then in verse 29?

(c) This had serious physical consequences for the believers concerned. What were they (v.30)? The last phrase in this verse becomes clear by its use in 15:6 of this same epistle.

(d) These consequences are described as being 'disciplined' by the Lord (v.32). How else are they described in this verse and in the previous verse?

(e) What does all this teach us about how we should celebrate the Lord's Supper?

Enjoying Spiritual Nourishment

Read
Psalm 1.

The art of meditation

This is the theme of our study, but it has nothing to do with TM (transcendental meditation). TM claims to be a scientific method of exploring into the deepest levels of your own being, and so finding freedom from stress and peace of mind. But it is a deception. Though it claims to be non-religious, the mantras that are recited are prayers to Hindu gods and the practice involves opening up one's self to spirits other than the Holy Spirit. The meditation advocated in the Bible does not focus on ourselves, but on God and his word. Most of the teaching on this theme is in the Old Testament, but it is equally a New Testament practice. Our handling of scriptures may involve hearing, reading, memorizing, studying and even singing, but meditation is the major means of our spiritual nourishment.

An Old Testament picture

As soon as God had delivered Israel from Egypt he spoke to them about their daily food, 'bread from heaven', that he promised to supply. They were to gather it each day, and this was to be a discipline, a test of obedience (Ex 16:4). Gathering the manna was not simply something for leaders or a special squad to do. Each redeemed Israelite had to gather it. Nor was it an annual, monthly, or even weekly event. It was to be gathered *daily*, for it could not be kept (vv.19–20). This 'bread from heaven' is a picture of Christ (Jn 6:32–35). It is equally a picture of God's word, for feeding on God's word is feeding on Christ. So no one who has been redeemed is too young in the faith to start gathering his daily manna. If this was an important discipline for the Israelites (Deut 8:3–5), it is equally so for us.

A farming picture

1. Chewing the cud

We have all watched cows grazing. Most of the time they are not nibbling, but lying down endlessly munching. This is called 'chewing the cud' or ruminating. They chew the grass over and over to get all the nourishment out of it. The Oxford dictionary tells us that to ruminate also means 'to revolve, to turn over and over in the mind, to meditate deeply upon, to consider with a view to subsequent action'. Biblical meditation, however, is more than a mental exercise. It includes the human spirit, and requires the aid of the Holy Spirit.

2. Mind or spirit

Bible study and Bible meditation often overlap, but there is distinction. Study puts the emphasis on the mind. It is an intellectual activity, also needing the aid of the Holy Spirit. But not all believers have the mental equipment to cope with Bible study. In meditation, though the mind is used, the focus is more on the human spirit, and *all believers* must learn this art. Intellectual ability, yielded to God, is valuable, but we don't need it to hear God speak to us through his word. When that happens the simple become wise in the estimate of heaven (Ps 19:7).

3. *The secret of its effectiveness*

Sitting on the conference platform was a big man wearing a rough suit, his head on one side and his mouth half open. 'Who is that?' asked a young man in the congregation, turning to his friend.

'He's the speaker,' came the surprising answer. 'He's a farm labourer who left school at the age of twelve.'

The young man groaned, and then settled down to endure what was to come!

The speaker commenced by quoting a verse of that old hymn 'O Christ what burdens bowed thy head'. Suddenly the place was filled with the presence of God. Then he opened his Bible and gave the assembled company 'honey out of the rock'. So impressed was the young man that he asked the preacher afterwards where he got such great truths. He told him that he rose early in the morning, lit a candle, got dressed, and then read one or two verses over and over again. Then he put his coat on and walked the country lanes, trusting the Holy Spirit to put the truth that was in his head into his heart. 'That's where I get it all' he concluded. Oh yes, he had been educated all right—in the school of meditation— personally tutored by the Holy Spirit.

The process of meditation

This consists of three phases which God uses to impart truth:

1. Apprehension

This initial phase involves spiritual understanding or insight (Ps 119:99). Remember in the parable of the sower, Jesus spoke first of how the seed fell on the path. He said that this spoke of those who heard the message and did not *understand* it (Mt 13:4, 19). He was speaking of spiritual understanding that comes by the revelation of the Holy Spirit. Notice the contrast with what Paul says about us believers who *have* the Spirit (1 Cor 2:12), with what he says a moment later about the unbeliever who *has not* the Spirit (v.14).

2. Assimilation

This is more than spiritual understanding. To feed the spirit it is not enough to take in spiritual food, it must be digested. This is the heart of the meditation process. You can eat a lot, so the medics tell us, and still be undernourished if the body fails to assimilate food. If we are reading the Bible regularly, receiving much teaching, but not growing or maturing, it is because our spiritual digestive system is undeveloped or out of order. 'You are what you eat' is the provocative title of a book on health foods. It is a reminder that your food becomes you in terms of bone, blood cells, tissue, etc. Equally our spiritual food forms our spiritual character when we assimilate it. Good spiritual digestion gives soul satisfaction (Ps 63:5–6). Paul is talking about this in Colossians 3:16.

3. Application

Finally there is a practical outworking of the process of meditation. As well as building up our characters and nourishing our faith, there is an adjustment of our lives. On the positive side, we assimilate the word that we may conform our lives to it. We meditate on it with a view to obeying it (Josh 1:8). To put it differently, we become doers as well as feeders (Jas 1:23–25).

On the negative side we let the word of God convict and purge us where we have failed to obey it. David records how he kept quiet about something that he should have confessed to God, but as he meditated the fire of conviction burned (Ps 39:2–3). He later confessed to God (vv.7–11).

Some of the benefits

There are five that came in our reading of Psalm 1. These should be sufficient to motivate us.

1. Enjoyment

'His delight is in the law of the Lord' (v.2). Though there is a discipline involved in getting down to meditation, when you do it, there are delightful surprises in store. To the psalmist, discovering God's promises was like tasting honey or finding treasure (Ps 119:103, 162). This same psalmist has no fear that he will neglect God's word, because it is his delight (v.16). No wonder he bursts out, 'Oh, how I love your law! I meditate on it all day long' (v.97).

2. Nourishment

'He is like a tree planted by streams of water' (v.3), so that the roots are well nourished. A sickly Christian is almost always undernourished. He has not learned, or has neglected to feed his soul on, God's word. This was one of the first lessons the Old Testament prophets had to learn. Ezekiel was told to eat the scroll which had words from God on it before he could go and speak to the house of Israel (Ezek 3:1–4). Similarly Jeremiah records: 'When your words came ['were found' in AV and RSV], I ate them' (Jer 15:16). God's words 'being found' suggests that Jeremiah had made a discovery, one that comes by the revelation of the Spirit. Only when the truth reaches the heart is it assimilated and we are nourished.

3. Fruit bearing

'A tree...which yields its fruit in season' (v.3). We saw that feeding on the manna was a picture both of feeding on Christ and feeding on his word. The parable of the vine emphasizes abiding or remaining in Christ, and Christ remaining in you. The result? Fruit! But Jesus linked this with his word when he said, 'If you remain in me, and *my words* remain in you' (Jn 15:7, italics mine)—you will be very fruitful, for you will always get your prayers answered. Christ is the source of our life (Jn 14:19) and the word is also the source of our life (Jn 6:63). If we try hard to remain in Christ while neglecting to dwell in his word, we will court failure and frustration. If we meditate in his word we shall be truly fruitful.

4. Healing

'Whose leaf does not whither' (v.3). What has that to do with healing? In Ezekiel's vision of the river flowing from the sanctuary he saw fruit trees on the banks, and was told, 'Their fruit will serve for food and their leaves for healing' (Ezek 47:12; also Rev 22:2).

Jesus said, 'These signs will accompany those who believe...they will place their hands on sick people, and they will get well' (Mt 16:17–18). Note, this was not said of leaders or those with special gifts. It is a promise to all believing believers. Sharing in a ministry of healing whether spiritual, emotional, mental or physical is open to us all.

5. Success

Finally, 'Whatever he does prospers' (v.3). What does that mean? 'The Lord was with Joseph and he prospered...the Lord gave him success in everything he did'—even though he was a slave (Gen 39:2–3).

To prosper in the estimate of heaven is to have God with you so that everything you do is successful. What Christian does not want that?

Notice how God promised exactly this to Joshua, that God would be with him, and that he would prosper, but with exactly the same condition as the man in Psalm 1 who meditated on God's word day and night, and obeyed it implicitly (Josh 1:5, 8).

Getting down to the job

1. Reading and meditating

If you cannot give time to meditate separately from your daily reading, you can quite successfully combine the two. It is a good way to start. First, ask God where in the Scripture he wants you to read and meditate. Try to avoid flitting from one passage to another. Instead, meditate consecutively. Read your passage slowly, looking to God to speak. Soon a phrase or thought will arrest you. Stop your reading and start to meditate. Turn it over and over in your mind. It may take you to other verses or incidents in the Bible.

2. Uttering and muttering

The two main words in Hebrew for 'meditate' also mean 'to speak, commune, or even to mutter or talk to yourself'. This is not the first sign of madness! David often did it (Ps 42:5). God said to Joshua, 'Do not let this

Book of the Law depart from your mouth [that is, don't stop uttering it]; meditate on it day and night' (Josh 1:8).

Mouthing and meditating go together (Ps 19:14). Uttering and muttering are not simply to fix truth in your mind. They are part of the digestive process; you are assimilating the truth. Often it develops into confession, prayer or praise.

3. Record your findings

Even when it reaches your heart, there is no guarantee that your mind will retain it, so use a notebook to record the fruit of your meditation. Writing will also help to clarify your thinking and it will order your thoughts so that you can better share these good things with others.

Memorize

> *Do not let this Book of the Law depart from your mouth; meditate on it day and night, so that you may be careful to do everything written in it. Then you will be prosperous and successful* (Josh 1:8).

Home task

Choose a portion of Scripture for meditation. Ask God to guide you to the right passage. If nothing springs readily to mind, turn to your last Scripture reading and follow the instructions I have given under 'Getting down to the job'. When you have fixed on a verse or sentence, read it over and over again, but don't bite off more than you can chew. One verse should give you plenty of scope.

Pray continually, 'Lord speak to me the truths I need to hear. Feed me with the food you see I need.' As thoughts come, write them down in your notebook—and don't forget to utter or mutter! You will need to allow twenty to thirty minutes for this. Your meditations may well lead to confessions of failure, to thanksgiving, or to supplication for yourself and others. It may help you to record the gist of these too in your notebook.

For further study

1. What are the main things that God has taught you in this study on meditation? When you have noted them down, write underneath what action you have determined to take to carry out this teaching.

2. Psalm 119, as we have already noted, has much to teach us on meditation. If you are using the NIV you will find 'meditate' occurs eight times. Note down each verse and what it teaches:

(a) The situations and circumstances in which the Psalmist meditates.

(b) His testimony as to what meditation does for him.

(c) The conditions that make for successful meditating.

Maintaining the Fullness

Read
Acts 6:1–8.

Introduction

This study is written for those who know that they have received the Baptism in the Holy Spirit. If you have not yet come into that experience I would commend to you Study 6 in the earlier course, *Living God's Way*. If necessary, seek help from a mature Christian you trust who has been baptized in the Spirit, who will counsel and help you. You are not yet ready for this study, because you cannot learn to maintain a fullness that you have never received.

Fullness must be maintained

Experiencing 'baptism in the Spirit' doesn't immediately lock us into a place of spirituality and effectiveness from which we can never lapse. On the contrary, because we have been endued with power, we have become a greater threat to the enemy, and he will redouble his efforts to bring us down. Notice what happened to our Lord after

the Holy Spirit came upon him at the Jordan (Mt 3:16—
4:3).

It is sad but true that believers *can*, and in some cases
do, lose the blessing of the anointing of the Holy Spirit.
David had a real fear of this after his grievous sin over
Bathsheba, as we see from what he says in his prayer of
repentance (Ps 51:11). He would have remembered what
happened to Samson, one of Israel's judges, on whom
the Spirit came in power (Judg 14:6; 16:20–21). Or even
more vividly, what happened to his predecessor, King
Saul. David always acknowledged him as 'the Lord's
anointed', for he had had a powerful enduement of the
Spirit (1 Sam 10:9–10; 16:14).

Charisma or character?

Charisma (meaning 'gift of grace') emphasizes what we
do. *Character* emphasizes what we *are*. When you look
at what the Bible teaches about the baptism of the Holy
Spirit, that it is an enduement of power (Lk 24:49; Acts
1:8), and that it brings spiritual gifts, the emphasis is
clearly upon charisma and what we do. Notice that it was
normally received by new converts. They were not
required to reach a special standard of holiness, become
mature or knowledgeable before they received the Holy
Spirit (Acts 2:38–39; 8:14–17). Jesus had promised that
his heavenly Father would give the Holy Spirit to those
who asked him (Lk 11:13), provided, as always that they
asked in faith (Gal 3:14). It was as simple as that.
However, though the Galatians and the Corinthians had
received the Spirit by faith, the Galatians lapsed into
legalism, and the Corinthians into carnality (worldliness).

What we must understand clearly is that how the
blessing is *obtained* is one thing, how it is *maintained* is
something else. As we go on living the Christian life we

receive more light (understanding of truth). God then requires us to walk (conduct our daily lives) in that greater light that we have received (1 Jn 1:6–7). The crisis of receiving must be followed by the process of maintaining and increasing. The renewal of the Spirit is not a once-for-all experience. It must be renewed day by day (2 Cor 4:16). There is no doubt that the Ephesian church had had the crisis. They had been marked with the Spirit's seal (Eph 1:13). We are actually told how the twelve foundation members of that church had had this experience through the laying on of Paul's hands, and immediately following their water baptism (Acts 19: 4–7). So when he exhorts them to be 'filled with the Spirit' (Eph 5:18), he is not emphasizing the crisis but the process. It could be translated 'be being filled' or 'go on being filled with the Spirit'. In other words, let your experience of 'being filled' become a state of 'being full'.

Understanding 'Spirit-filled'

When Scripture uses 'filled' in connection with the Holy Spirit, it is emphasizing quality rather than quantity. When we say, 'That man is Spirit-filled,' we are not describing *measure*—how much he has of the Spirit—so much as *influence*—how much the Spirit has of him.

When Jesus spoke in the Nazareth synagogue, the hearers were 'filled with fury' (Lk 6:11, RSV). That is to say, they lost all self-control, anger took over and they behaved like men 'possessed'. Anger characterized their words and actions.

To be Spirit-filled is to be Spirit-possessed. Your speech and behaviour take on the characteristics of the Holy Spirit, who is both holy and spiritual. Let us ask ourselves some questions about someone who has received the Holy Spirit and even come into an experience of spiritual gifts.

1. If he is not walking with God any more, is he Spirit-filled?

2. Though he may attend church, participate in meetings, etc, if he is not a witness for Christ, and his life lacks power and effectiveness (Acts 1:8) is he Spirit-filled?

3. If he engages in many forms of Christian service but there is little or no lasting fruit, is he Spirit-filled?

4. If his fellow believers find him as difficult to get on with as they did before he received 'the baptism' is he Spirit-filled?

5. If he has the gifts of the Spirit, but little of the fruit of the Spirit, is he Spirit-filled?

The Corinthian church had received the power of the Holy Spirit and were moving strongly in spiritual gifts. Paul thanked God for this (1 Cor 1:4–7), and encouraged them to press on into greater gifts (1 Cor 12:31; 14:1, 12), but he says reprovingly, 'I could not address you as spiritual but as worldly—mere infants...acting like mere men' (1 Cor 3:1, 3). Hardly the description of a Spirit-filled company! They had not maintained what they had obtained. The crisis had not been followed by the process. They had received the Spirit but were not walking in the Spirit. They were strong in charisma, but weak in character.

Christ is our model

The marks of a Spirit-filled person are seen first in our Lord Jesus.

1. Spirit-led

At his baptism the Spirit came upon him. Then we read, 'Jesus, *full of the Holy Spirit*, returned from the Jordan and was *led by the Spirit* into the desert' (Lk 4:1, italics mine). So a Spirit-filled man is led by the Spirit. He does not initiate a lot of Christian activity, and then ask God to bless it. He lets God do the initiating and he does the responding. This marked the whole of Jesus' earthly ministry (Jn 5:19).

2. *Spirit-empowered*

After the wilderness temptation, this Spirit-filled man 'returned to Galilee in *the power of the Spirit*' (Lk 4:14, italics mine). There is no evidence in Scripture that he displayed this power before the Holy Spirit came on him. We know that all his life he was 'holy, blameless, pure, set apart from sinners' (Heb 7:26), but for those first thirty years, we do not read of one sermon being preached, one disciple being made, or one miracle being performed. After the Jordan experience, however, what a change! Wherever he went, the power of the Spirit accompanied his ministry and made it effective. So after Pentecost, Peter could even address a foreigner like the Roman Centurion, and say, 'You know what has happened throughout Judea... how God anointed Jesus of Nazareth with the Holy Spirit and power, and how he went around doing good and healing all who are under the power of the devil' (Acts 10:37–38). Had not Jesus told the disciples himself that the evidence that the Holy Spirit had come upon them would be *power* (Acts 1:8)? Power which would make their witness and their ministry effective.

A man was pushing his cycle to the top of a steep hill. A motorcycle zoomed past him to the top, and when he arrived there, puffing and panting, the motorcycle was parked and the owner, looking cool and relaxed, was enjoying the view. Said the push-cyclist, ruefully eyeing the Suzuki, 'The difference between your machine and mine is yours is "spirit-filled"!'

Power is an indispensible mark of being Spirit-filled. But as the fullness is maintained, we should expect the power to be increased, as it was with Saul of Tarsus (Acts 9:18, 20–22).

3. Grace and truth

Jesus was not only full of power, he was also 'full of grace and truth' (Jn 1:14). This was the 'character' aspect of his fullness, the perfect balance to the 'charisma' aspect. Power unrelated to godliness may produce results, but no lasting blessing. How unacceptable would have been the miracles of Jesus if they had been devoid of grace. How dubious would his healings have been if we never read, 'Jesus moved with compassion' healed the sick. He wept at Lazarus' tomb before he called him back to life. Grace and power are essential ingredients of the Spirit-filled life.

There was a man who turned up in a Christian circle I know and dazzled everyone with his charisma. When he laid hands on people for the Holy Spirit, they were filled and spoke in tongues. When he prayed for the sick, they were healed. He had remarkable words of knowledge about people's situations. Soon everyone was deferring to him as the leader. But he was a phoney. He was a married man, and when his colleagues heard about the women in his life, his lying and dishonesty over money, they could not believe it. Charisma is dangerous without character.

Balaam was a prophet. He had a reputation for predicting things that came to pass (Num 22:6). He certainly heard God and spoke words from God. He was so at home in the supernatural that when the Lord opened the donkey's mouth to speak to him, he answered him back without batting an eyelid (Num

22:29)! But his character was crooked, and in the end he was slain by the Israelites and branded as an occultist (Josh 13:22).

Christ shows the way

Even as Jesus demonstrates the perfect Spirit-filled life, he also reveals the open secret of how it is to be maintained.

1. Righteousness and wickedness

'You have loved righteousness and hated wickedness; therefore God . . . has set you above your companions by anointing you with the oil of joy' (Heb 1:9). Back of this unique and remarkable fullness that Jesus enjoyed was a passion for what pleased God and a loathing for the things God hated. When his Father anointed him at the Jordan, God declard audibly, 'You are my Son, whom I love; with you I am well pleased' (Lk 3:22). And because all through his earthly course he never deviated from this, and never compromised his convictions, the Spirit continued to rest on him in power. But there was also the element of faith:

2. Drinking from the brook

Did you know that the Son of Man had to live by faith just as we are required to do? It is said of the coming Messiah, 'He will drink from a brook beside the way; therefore he will lift up his head' (Ps 110:7). Alongside the God-directed path that followed was the brook, 'the supply of the Spirit', needed for living as well as for serving. Had he strayed from the way, he would have been out of touch with the brook. Of course he never did, because of what we have already observed in (1). Whenever he grew weary, or was assaulted by the devil, or tempted to discouragement, or challenged by the need or opportunity, he simply drank from the brook, and pressed on with head held high. Jesus was living out what he had taught the woman by the well, that the Holy Spirit would be 'a spring of water welling up to eternal life' (Jn 4:14), continually renewing, refreshing and invigorating the inner man. Drinking is receiving the Spirit by faith, and it is not something you do once-for-all. 'There is no such thing as a once-for-all fullness. It is a moment-by-moment faith in a moment-by-moment Saviour, for a moment-by-moment cleansing and a moment-by-moment filling' (Dr Charles Inwood). That's how the fullness is maintained.

Memorize

If a man is thirsty, let him come to me and drink. Whoever believes [present continuous tense] *in me, as the Scripture has said, streams of living water will flow from within him* (Jn 7:37–38).

Home task

1. If you believe you have been filled with the Spirit, check yourself out to know whether you are still full of the Holy Spirit, or have become a leaky vessel. Go over the three points under 'Christ is our model' and see how your own Christian life measures up to these three marks of being Spirit-filled. Where you sense that you come short, seek God for a renewing, or a fresh infilling, of the Spirit by means of repentance (for sin and failure) and faith to lay hold of God's grace which is abundantly available.

   2. Note that the blessing of the Spirit is maintained

and increased by the same principles as it was initially received. Pick out from the following scriptures, the two main conditions for receiving:

(a) Acts 5:32, cf John 14:15–16

(b) Galatians 3:14, cf John 7:38

Consider carefully whether there has been failure on your part to continue to fulfil these two key principles. Talk to God freely and frankly over these areas of your life. Here is a simple resolution that you may like to use:

'I resolve by the grace of God and his enabling that I will continue day by day to _____ and to _____ _____ [the two key conditions] in every area of my Christian life.

For further study

1. Jesus promised his followers power. It has been said, 'Power is dangerous stuff in the hands of those not qualified to handle it.' Write down in your notebook:

(a) Whether you think this is a valid and important statement in relation to the power of the Holy Spirit, and if so why.

(b) What do you think the safeguards are? Try to support your statements from Scripture.

2. King Saul is one of the saddest cases in Scripture of a man who lost his spiritual anointing. The following scriptures tell the story of how his decline began: 1 Samuel 13:5–14; 14:24–28, 36–45; 15:1–35. Pick out the places where he went wrong, and note down any lessons or warnings that you believe God has for you in the story.

SECTION 3

Living in the World

In it — But not of it

Read
John 15:18–21; 17:13–19.

Introduction

We are taking a look at 'the world' in this study. It is important to understand what Scripture means by 'the world', as the term is used in different ways. Also what it means to be 'in it, but not of it'.

Defining 'the world'

Scripture speaks of the world in at least three distinct ways:

1. The world of nature

This demonstrates God's wisdom and power. It should always move us, as it did the psalmist, to recognize God's greatness and our nothingness (Ps 8:3–4), and so to worship him as the great Creator (Ps 104). Here we have to watch that we do not worship the creation rather than the Creator. From antiquity this has been the curse of heathenism (Job 31:26–28). God warned Israel against idolatry (Deut 4:15–19).

2. The world of men

This is 'the world' that 'God so loved' and for which 'he gave his one and only Son' (Jn 3:16). This is the world that we must learn to love too, even in all its sinfulness, if we are to play any part in winning it (2 Cor 5:14, 20). It comes down to loving individual men and women who are lost.

3. The world order

This is the system that controls the thinking and behaviour of mankind. Satan masterminds it, and he is therefore called 'the prince of this world' (Jn 12:31; 14:30). His lieutenants in that spirit world are fallen angels, described as 'the rulers...the authorities...the powers of this dark world' (Eph 6:12). In contrast to 'the world of men', this is 'the world' that we are commanded *not* to love. If we do love it we do not have the love of God (1 Jn 2:15). It is the world that hated Christ and eventually crucified him, because he testified against its evil (Jn 7:7). It will likewise hate us because we side with Christ, and not with it (Jn 15:18–19).

In it—but not of it

1. Why are we here?

You will have noticed in our first reading that Jesus told his disciples, 'You do not belong to the world, but I have chosen you out of the world. That is why the world hates you' (v.19). We are like members of the Resistance in France during the Nazi occupation. Living under an alien rule, they felt at times like strangers in their own land. Perhaps you wonder, 'If, as Jesus says, the world hates us because we don't belong to the world, why doesn't God take us straight to heaven when we are born again?' One reason is that this very situation of conflict in which we are called to live is designed to shape us and make us what God wants us to be.

2. Conformed or transformed?

The very thing God would use to make us, the devil can also use to mar us. The question is how we handle the conflict. Paul puts the issues squarely: 'Do not conform any longer to the pattern of this world, but be transformed by the renewing of your mind' (Rom 12:2). The believer in the world is either being conformed or transformed. Phillips translates this verse well: 'Don't let the world around you squeeze you into its own mould, but let God re-make you so that *your whole attitude of mind is changed*.' Whether we are conformed or transformed depends on our attitude of mind. The French Resistance fighter must have often been tempted in his mind to give in and conform. That was the easy way of escaping from the conflict. This is the greatest danger we face. We do not escape the temptation because we have been filled with the Spirit. We must heed fully what God says about our attitude and relationship with the world.

Two opposing kingdoms

That is, the world's and God's. Jesus said, 'My kingdom is not of this world' (Jn 18:36):

1. The kingdom of this world

This is the world order that we have just been describing, which is totally antagonistic to the rule of God. Although energized and controlled by Satan, he has made rebel man—man without God—the centre of his empire. It is ruled by human wisdom and human reason (1 Cor 1:17–20). A characteristic of this kingdom is its *impermanence*.

147

It is passing away (1 Jn 2:17). Its rulers are coming to nothing (1 Cor 2:6). Those who live for it are tragically short-sighted. One day it will be destroyed for ever and the reign of Christ will take over (Dan 2:44; Rev 11:15).

2. The kingdom of God

In this sphere God is of course the centre. His revealed will, not human reason, is the rule and measure of all things. Men may only see and enter this kingdom by means of the new birth (Jn 3:3, 5). As we know, that involves changing sides, coming under God's rule and submitting to his new order. Before this we were motivated by 'the spirit of the world' in all our thinking, but now we have received 'the Spirit who is from God' (1 Cor 2:12), so that our lives have been radically re-orientated.

What is worldliness?

1. An inadequate concept

Christian tradition sometimes presents us with a view of worldliness that is not strictly biblical. It deals with externals but fails to touch the root of the matter. How a believer dresses, whether or not he indulges certain habits, engages in certain entertainments or pleasures, what he drinks, and what he permits himself to do on Sunday, will—according to this view—determine whether or not he is worldly. Such a believer *may* of course be worldly. But those who criticize him may be worldly in more serious areas. These externals are not the true criteria.

The scribes and the Pharisees had a similar list of rules by which they judged the piety of others. They were so careful about the trivial but overlooked the vital. They looked at the outside but neglected the inside. Jesus told them, 'You strain out a gnat but swallow a camel' (Mt 23:23–26). Those who are quick to judge their fellow Christians today by such external standards would do well to study a little more carefully what the Bible says.

2. The biblical concept

As we know, it is sadly possible to be born into God's kingdom, and yet behave as though we still belong to the world. 'You are still worldly. For since there is jealousy and quarrelling among you, are you not worldly? Are you not acting like mere men?' (1 Cor 3:3). This gives us the biblical concept of worldliness, *'acting like mere men'* instead of men who belong to God. Paul is not here speaking of how the Corinthian believers dress, or spend their leisure time, but of the more important matter of their relationships together, which were more characterized by 'the spirit of the world' than 'the Spirit who is from God'. In other versions of this passage you may find the word 'worldly' more literally rendered 'carnal' or 'fleshly', but it makes no difference because, as we shall now see, *carnality is worldliness*.

The Bible definition

'For everything in the world—the cravings of sinful man, the lust of his eyes and the boasting of what he has and does—comes not from the Father but from the world' (1 Jn 2:16). Scripture contains no definition of worldliness more comprehensive than this. It may touch body, mind or spirit.

1. Your body

If it is not under the rule of the Holy Spirit it will be ruled by 'the cravings of sinful man' ('the lust of the flesh',

RSV). This refers to the appetites of the body. They are God-given and good, but we must learn to rule them. If they rule us we are 'acting like mere men'—we are worldly. This word 'craving' (lust, desire) which occurs three times in 1 John 2:16–17, is the main characteristic of the world (note verse 17 especially). It is not confined to mere bodily appetites. Paul speaks of 'worldly passions' (Tit 2:12). It is the major motivation for all that the worldly man does.

2. Your mind

This finds its main satisfaction through 'the lust of the eyes'. The eyes are the main avenue to the mind. Consider the modern man's insatiable appetite for 'viewing' and spectating, and the massive industry that exists to satisfy it. It dominates his leisure time. He finds momentary satisfaction by being transported into an artificial and unreal world, which leaves him empty, and dissatisfied with his humble lot. Then his mind is bombarded with commercials to try to persuade him to buy on easy terms what he can't afford. He is ruled by the false philosophy that wealth is the secret of happiness, and that acquiring more and more of this world's goods will bring satisfaction. And so he craves. See what God says to him in Isaiah 55:1–2.

3. Your spirit

We are speaking here of the human spirit which, if it is not ruled by the Spirit of Christ will be ruled by 'the pride of life' (RSV) or 'the boasting of what he has and does' (NIV). This pride of life may also cause the worldly man to crave for money, not only to acquire material things, but for the popularity, prestige and worldly influence he believes it will bring. All this is the spirit of the world. Not only are many in the kingdom of God subtly influenced by it, but it even invades the work of God's kingdom. All competitiveness and rivalry has this spirit behind it. It lay behind the 'jealousy and quarrelling' of the Corinthian Christians that Paul said was worldly.

As you consider the above characteristics notice that they are all self-centred. We saw that that was the mark of the kingdom of this world. The man who truly lives for God's kingdom, however, is always Christ-centred (Phil 1:21).

The answer to worldliness

We have already seen that the New Testament is very clear in its commands. It says:

> Don't love the world (1 Jn 2:15).
> Don't be a friend of the world (Jas 4:4).
> Don't be conformed to the world (Rom 12:2).

But how can you live in the world without doing any of these?

1. Negatively

You can't do it by *rules and regulations*. This is the way of the scribes and Pharisees.

You can't do it by *escaping from the world*, so Jesus did not pray this for his followers, but that in a hostile world they would be protected (Jn 17:11–15). We are not called to a cloistered life, but to let our light shine before men (Mt 5:16).

You can't do it by *dealing with the externals*. 'O God, sweep away the cobwebs of pride, or jealousy, of selfishness in my life.' A brother used to weary everyone by praying after this fashion every week in the prayer meeting. One day someone cried out in the middle of his prayer, 'God, please kill the spider!' We must get to the root.

2. Positively

The only remedy for the spirit of the world in the life of the believer is the cross. We must view the world as a man would view it when nailed to the stake. That's what Paul says: 'May I never boast except in the cross of our Lord Jesus Christ, *through which the world has been crucified to me, and I to the world*' (Gal 6:14, italics mine). Though it may take on a thousand forms, worldliness is self-centredness instead of Christ-centredness. That's why the cross has to be the answer. We have dealt with this in Study 11, but we may now see new areas in which that teaching needs to be applied.

Memorize

Do not love the world or anything in the world. If anyone loves the world, the love of the Father is not in him. For everything in the world—the cravings of sinful man, the lust of his eyes and the boasting of what he has and does—comes not from the Father but from the world (1 Jn 2:15–16).

Home task

1. Israel's deliverance from Egypt (a type of the world) by the blood of the Passover lamb is a parable of our salvation. It has been said, 'It was one thing to get Israel out of Egypt, but quite another to get Egypt out of Israel.'

(a) Note the different forms that their worldliness took on (1 Cor 10:1–10).

(b) How did God react? Note the things that happened to them.

(c) Could believers today who behave similarly experience the chastening of their heavenly Father? (10:11; 11:17–34).

2. In Scripture, worldliness is pollution. Believers are called upon:

(a) To come out and be separate (2 Cor 6:17–18).

(b) To keep themselves from being polluted (Jas 1:27; Rev 3:4).

Write down what you think these mean. Also what they do *not* mean (see notes under 'The answer to worldliness'). If there are areas in your life where you know that you have compromised with the world, confess this to God now, receive his cleansing and declare in faith that, through the cross, you are dead to the world and the world is dead to you.

For further study

1. Compare the three-fold definition of worldliness (memory verse) with:

(a) Eve's temptation in the garden (Gen 3:6).

(b) Our Lord's temptation in the wilderness (Lk 4:3–13).

Do you see a correspondence? What lessons should we learn from the woman's defeat and Christ's victory?

2. In Luke 17:26–36 Jesus likens the period preceding his return to 'the days of Noah' and the 'days of Lot'.

(a) Make a list of the characteristics of those days from the Genesis account.

(b) What is Jesus mainly emphasizing in verses 30–36 in

making this comparison? Can you find other scriptures where Jesus gives the same warning?

(c) What is the lesson for us from Lot's wife (v.32)?

Salt and Light

Read
Matthew 5:13–16.

Introduction

In our last study we viewed the believer in the world from a negative viewpoint. The world was an alien society that could overwhelm and absorb him. He needed to watch lest he be corrupted and seduced by the love of the world. He must know that he belongs to another kingdom, and preserve his spiritual identity.

Now we must look at the positive and beneficial influence he may exert to affect the world around him. In Christ's words, his followers are 'the salt of the earth' and 'the light of the world'.

Significance of salt

To the oriental salt had two main uses:

1. For seasoning

'Is tasteless food eaten without salt, or is there flavour in the white of an egg?' (Job 6:6). So even Job liked salt with his egg! Salt gives flavour to what is otherwise insipid. Our conversation is tasteless if it is without spiritual seasoning (Col 4:6). Humanity is morally insipid. We cannot say to God, 'O taste and see that mankind is good,' for mankind is not only tasteless, but rotten.

2. For preserving

Salt is rubbed in to meat and fish to prevent them from going bad. In the days of Noah we read, 'Now *the earth* was corrupt in God's sight and was full of violence (Gen 6:11, italics mine). This could well be used to describe the twentieth century, but it was describing the days of Noah in the dawn of human history. This was the world that God visited with the judgement of the Flood. Noah and his family alone were righteous. They were the salt in their day. Had they been present in the earth in greater numbers they would no doubt have saved the earth from destruction. It was the same with Sodom. Had God found a righteous remnant of only ten people he would have saved the city (Gen 18:32). All this gives force to Jesus' statement here. He is saying that though the earth is corrupt, 'You are the salt [or preservative] of *the earth*.'

What God's salt is to do

1. It's not a permanent remedy

Salt is no final solution to decay. At best it can only delay the process. As salt we are not called to bring complete healing to human society. Christ's church is not a Human Improvement Society. We are to evangelize the world, but not to try to Christianize it. Scripture does not give us the expectation that evangelism will win over the whole of society, but rather that it will result in 'taking from [the world] a people' for God (Acts 15:13). It is important to be clear on this. The world is under judgement. 'Babylon the Great' is doomed to fall, never to rise again (Rev 17:18—18:3), and nothing will happen to change this. We are not looking for a paradise on earth, for it is destined to be destroyed by fire (2 Pet 3:10–13). Our citizenship and our inheritance are not earthly but heavenly (Phil 3:20; Heb 11:13–16).

2. It must oppose sin

We live in a world full of violence, greed, materialism, dishonesty and immorality. We are to be God's antiseptic in this putrifying carcase. Our standards are to be totally different. If the presence of a Christian has a restraining influence on profanity and smut in the place where he works, that Christian is salt.

'You're wanted on the phone,' said a Christian to his boss.

'Tell him I'm out,' was the reply.

The Christian picked up the phone. 'I'm sorry, sir, but the boss says he's out!'

Surprisingly, he wasn't fired, but nor was he ever asked to do it again. That man was salt. To God 'white lies' are black lies. With salt there is no compromise.

3. It must be society's conscience

Even in the 'enlightened' West there is injustice, inequality and selfishness. We are loud in our condemnation of apartheid, but within our own society there is discrimination on the ground of colour, lack of respect for the sanctity of life, the legalizing of abortion (a human life is slaughtered every three minutes in this country), a lobby for euthanasia and great pressure to permit the use of human embryos for scientific experimentation. Looking further afield, there are the prisoners of conscience, especially believers, behind the iron and bamboo curtains, and the starving millions of the Third World, and so much else.

Are Christians to try to influence society in these areas? A Spirit-filled church *will* inevitably do just that. Far-reaching social change has always come, even if not immediately, in the wake of spiritual revival. But there have always been the labours of individual Christians. Dedicated men and women like Shaftesbury, Wilberforce and Elizabeth Fry have changed the face of society. However, social action as such is not part of Christ's Great Commission to the church (Mt 28:18–20). That is confined to evangelism (which includes healing and deliverance, [Mt 10:8]) and the discipling of those who believe.

Social action is an individual matter. Some are particularly called to this, and they must know what part of this massive need they are to address. The church must always watch that it is not deflected from its major task of evangelism by the vast needs of suffering humanity. This has happened in the past with serious spiritual loss. Involvement in social action by believers does reflect the compassion of Christ, who fed the multitude as well as preached the good news to them, and may often pave the way for the reception of the gospel. 'You can't expect a man with no food in his stomach and no shirt on his back to listen to the gospel.' Jesus told his disciples to let the world see their good deeds (Mt 5:16), and Paul made reference to them in Titus 3:8, 14. The RSV renders verse 14, 'And let our people learn to apply themselves to good deeds, so as to help cases of urgent need, and not to be unfruitful.' Note that this is an appeal to the individual.

How salt works

1. It must be different

How could salt have any beneficial effect if it were the same in its nature as the meat, that is, subject to corruption? Salt and meat are in character diametrically opposed. This points to the nature of the new birth experience. Believers and unbelievers are as different as chalk from cheese. They are a different order of being (2 Cor 5:17). This is why we are told not to conform to the world (Rom 12:2). There is always pressure to do just that, and so be accepted. God calls his people 'holy' (1 Pet 2:9), which means set apart or different. But he also tells them, 'Be holy' (1 Pet 1:16), in other words, 'Be what you are.'

Jesus didn't say, 'Try to be the salt;' he said, 'You *are* the salt.' But he warned that it was possible for the salt to lose its saltiness, that is, for the Christian to lose his influence. The scientist would tell us that salt does not normally lose its saltiness. It is not affected, for example, by exposure to the elements. Probably it is only by excessive dilution that this can happen. For us, who are spiritual salt, the world is the diluting element. See how closely this theme is related to our last study. If we do not take heed to the things said there, worldliness will rob us of our distinctiveness, and so of our influence.

The American writer, Tom Sine, refers to this when he says, 'We have been remarkably effective at diluting Christ's extremist teaching and truncating his radical gospel.' Then speaking of America he goes on, 'That explains why we can have a nation of 200 million people, 60 million of whom profess to be Christian, and yet make such an embarrassingly little difference in the morality of our society.'

Here in Britain, though we do not have such a big proportion of professing Christians, the situation is the same. Our influence is minimal. Jesus told us to evangelize, and then to disciple (Mt 28:19–20; Mk 16:15). We have many converts but too few disciples. The disciple is always different. He is salty salt.

2. It must make contact

To be the conscience of society we must permeate society. To be the preservative of mankind we must mingle with mankind. 'You can't preserve fish by putting the fish in one barrel and the salt in the other.' In this, as in all else, our Lord Jesus is our perfect model. He lived no cloistered life. He could talk freely with Nicodemus the theologian, with Zacchaeus the tax collector or with the woman of 'easy virtue' that he met by a well. But in his mingling he never compromised his standards. Two statements concerning him, one by his critics and the other by the Holy Spirit, give us the perfect balance: the one said that he was 'a friend of...sinners' (Mt 11:19), the other that he was 'set apart from sinners' (Heb 7:26). If we are to be salt, like Jesus, we shall not allow ourselves to be *segregated from the world nor assimilated by the world*.

Significance of light

'You are the light of world' (Mt 5:14). Salt emphasizes more the believer's negative influence on the world, that is, counteracting corruption, while light emphasizes the positive.

A picture from creation

Many have seen that the creation account in Genesis 1 is a parable of salvation. It shows a world in chaos and darkness, like man without God. Then God said, 'Let there be light,' and the situation began to change. In verse 16 we read, 'God made two great lights,' referring to the sun and the moon: 'The greater light to govern the day and the lesser light to govern the night.' This corresponds to the two statements of Jesus, '*I am* the light of the world' (Jn 8:12)—he is the sun—and, '*You are* are the light of the world'—we are the moon. In the darkness of this age the church is to govern by being God's moon, and the only light we emit is the reflected light of the unseen 'Sun', who is at God's right hand. The New Testament confirms that ours is a borrowed light. We are not light in ourselves, we are only 'light in the Lord', because Christ has given us light (Eph 5:8, 14).

2. What the light is to do

It is only because God has imparted to us his life that we are the light of the world (Jn 1:4). Jesus goes on to speak of how the light is to be manifested in the life of his disciples: 'Let your light shine before men, that they may see your *good deeds* and praise your Father in heaven.' The Bible teaches us that we are not saved *by* good works but we are saved *for* good works, that is, we are saved to do them (Eph 2:8–10). They are the visible expression of the life God has put within us. They are the output of Christian character. They are not confined to doing good turns to neighbours. They are rather a demonstration of a totally different lifestyle. Such good deeds will mean at times our confessing Christ before men (Rom 10:9–10), witnessing to what he has done for us (Mk 5:19), giving a ready answer to those who ask us about our hope (1 Pet 3:15). Letting our light shine means influencing others by our lives and by our words.

3. Light is uncompromising

Just as salt reacts to corruption, light reacts to darkness. It has no truck with darkness except to expose it (Eph 5:12–13). God is like that (1 Jn 1:5), and we are to be like that too. 'For you were once darkness, but now you are light in the Lord. Live as children of light (for the fruit of the light consists in all goodness, righteousness and truth)' (Eph 5:8–9). Almost every day we see and hear things which are the fruit of darkness. They are the normal fare on our TV screen. Have they become acceptable practice to us? Paul warns us, 'Have nothing to do with the fruitless deeds of darkness, but rather expose them' (Eph 5:11). Turn over a stone, and all the insects that live in the dark will scurry for their holes. That's the effect that we are to have. We can seize the initiative and put the enemy on the defensive.

4. It must be in the right place

The danger facing salt is to lose its saltiness, but the danger facing light is to be put in a concealed place (Mt 5:15). There were secret disciples in Christ's day who for fear of the authorities would not confess him (Jn 12:42–43). They are still around. By failing to shine they rob God of his due (Mt 5:16). They also rob the church, the world and themselves. See what Christ says of them (Mt 10:32–33).

Memorize

Let your light shine before men, that they may see your good deeds and praise your Father in heaven (Mt 5:16).

Home task

1. In what ways might a believer lose his saltiness? Don't merely quote scriptures like Romans 12:2 or Ephesians 5:11, but give practical examples of what these verses could refer to today.

2. In what ways might a believer hide his light instead of letting it shine? What might be the main reasons for doing this? What is the remedy?

3. Take time to examine your own life in the presence of God, and ensure that neither (1) nor (2) are true of you.

For further study

1. Consider the following statement: 'When believers understand their true function as salt and light, they will be preserved from a wrong view of what the Bible teaches about separation from the world' (see 2 Corinthians 6:17).

(a) What does that mean?

(b) Can you give scriptural examples of this wrong separation?

(c) Can you think of examples of it in the history of the church?

2. Jesus was speaking to a bunch of very ordinary men, most of them fishermen. He did *not* tell these humble disciples of his, 'You have some part to play in influencing the world for good and lighting its darkness.' He said, 'You are salt of the earth... you are the light of the world.'

(a) What does this teach us about the nature of Christianity in relation to other religions and philosophies of the world?

(b) Have these other religions any answers to a world in decay and darkness?

(c) Do they provide an alternative way to God? Quote scriptures for your answers.

On the Job

Read
1 Peter 2:13–21.

Introduction

Most people spend the bulk of their waking moments in secular employment. For some this is a drudgery and a bore. For many it is the constant scene of strife, with disputes and strikes over pay and working conditions. Growing numbers have been made redundant, or face the fear of it. Does the Bible give us 'a work ethic'? What has it to say about how we should perform our daily task?

God is our model

1. At work in creation

This is how the Bible story opens. After six days of activity '[God] rested from all his work' (Gen 2:2). Thus God has given to 'work' the concept of dignity, significance and value. He has taught us that seasons of labour need to be followed by times of rest. God pronounced his work 'very good' (Gen 1:31). So the first

Worker enjoyed 'job satisfaction', and his work was stamped with excellence. God did not sentence man to work because he fell into sin. He created man in his own image to be a worker too, to 'subdue' the earth (Gen 1:28), and then in the Garden of Eden, 'to work it and take care of it' (Gen 2:15).

2. Continuing to work

Having launched the universe on its course and placed man at the helm, God did not then leave him to get on with it. God continued to work. Jesus said, 'My Father is always at his work to this very day,' and then he added, 'And I, too, am working' (Jn 5:17). Jesus was implying that he took his cue from his Father. We must do the same. In the fourth Commandment God tells us to work as well as to rest, and pointed to himself as the model (Ex 20:9–11).

Importance of right attitudes

This is where the believer should stand out in sharp contrast to his unbelieving colleague. His whole attitude to his secular employment should be totally different. He is to have a kingdom 'workstyle', and this will be a powerful witness to Christ.

1. The unbelievers are watching

And if we are in secular employment, there is no place where they see more of us than at our place of work. So Peter exhorts us, 'Live such good lives among the pagans that, though they accuse you of doing wrong, they may see your good deeds and glorify God on the day he visits us' (1 Pet 2:12).

It was in an army barrack room that I was often accused. The men picked me up for anything I said or did that didn't measure up to their concept of a Christian. It kept me on my toes, and before long I saw that, despite my faults and failings, my lifestyle was making an impact.

2. Our attitude to the boss

Those watching us fasten on this at once. If it is negative, or if we fail to give 'full respect', all that we stand for may be compromised, for God's name and our teaching may be slandered (1 Tim 6:1). On the other hand, a right attitude of fidelity and trustworthiness towards those over us 'will make the teaching about God our Saviour attractive' (Tit 2:9–10). We will have more to say about this as we look at three very important areas where we need to watch our attitudes:

A right attitude to work itself

1. The attitude of society

The vast majority cannot think of work except in terms of money. Work is a necessary evil to be endured in order to earn enough to maintain a desired standard of living. Those who work hard and conscientiously, and who find enjoyment and fulfilment in their work are a diminishing segment of the work force. Those agitating for more pay for less work are on the increase.

On the wall of a business establishment I once read the following notice:

> Sometime between starting and quitting time, without infringing on lunch periods, coffee breaks, rest periods, story-telling time, holiday planning and the rehashing of yesterday's television programmes, we ask that each employee try to find some time for a work break!

2. The true motivation

That the average worker is joyless and unfulfilled is not primarily because his work is boring, but because his attitude to work is not right. It is the spirit of 'get' rather than 'give'. The Christian's primary motivation must be *serving*. This will dramatically change a person's whole approach to his work. He will no longer do his job half-heartedly with one eye on the clock and the other on the wage packet. This serving spirit within him will make him faithful, conscientious and hard-working.

3. Serving which 'boss'?

Does this concept of serving seem rather unreal in our modern society? 'I don't mind you telling me to serve Christ, but serving that so-and-so I work for...' In fact it *is* Christ we are talking about. Paul is telling believing slaves how they should obey their earthly masters, working with all their heart, and then he drops the bombshell to blow their resistance to smithereens: 'It is the Lord Christ you are serving' (Col 3:24). And if that was true in relation to working for an unscrupulous slave-owner of the first century, it is certainly true in relation to a twentieth-century employer.

A right attitude to money

1. The worker and his wage

Like every other member of society, the Christian must work to live. Jesus taught that 'the worker deserves his wages' (Lk 10:7). He is also responsible to support his dependents (1 Tim 5:8). What a worker should look for is 'a fair day's pay for a fair day's work'. But as we have been saying, money is not to be his primary motivation for working. What is commanded of an elder should be true of the believer in his secular job: 'Not greedy for money, but eager to serve' (1 Pet 5:2). The 'get rich quick' philosophy of modern man should have no place in the heart of the follower of Christ (1 Tim 6:9), and if, as often happens, God does prosper him, he is neither to set his heart on it (Ps 62:10), not to put his hope in it (1 Tim 6:17).

2. *The contented spirit*

Solomon tells us that 'all labour and all achievement spring from man's envy of his neighbour' (Eccles 4:4). He looks at what the other man has and becomes discontented. He's for ever trying to 'keep up with the Jones's'. John the Baptist told the soldiers who came to his baptism and professed repentance, 'Be content with your pay' (Lk 3:14).

God commands us, 'Keep your lives free from the love of money and be content with what you have' (Heb 13:5). This is an increasingly difficult command to keep in a world where we are bombarded with commercial propaganda designed to effect the very opposite in our thinking. There is, however, a legitimate money motive in working hard. It is to help the weak and give to the needy, as Jesus himself commanded us (Acts 20:35; Eph 4:28).

A right attitude to authority

In this the Christian's attitude will be as different from that of the world as in the two attitudes already discussed, for everywhere authority is being attacked and undermined.

1. *God delegates authority to men*

This is not only in the church but in the secular world. For example, governing authorities are established by

God, and we are commanded to submit to them—not because they always act rightly or justly, but because they are 'God's servants' to rule in the secular realm Rom 13:1–5).

2. God delegates authority to employers

What the New Testament teaches about the master-slave relationship applies now to the boss-worker relationship in our modern society. It is clear that 'masters' (employers) are viewed as acting for God, because we are told to 'be subject' to them, and to 'try to please them' (Tit 2:9). We are further told to do this 'with all respect' (1 Pet 2:18).

3. Obey them as you obey Christ

This is exactly what Paul says (Eph 6:5). You will have noticed that in our reading Peter does not confine this submission to masters 'who are good and considerate, but also to those who are harsh' (v.18). That's heavy stuff, but read on and see what he says about the spiritual value of 'unjust suffering' (vv.19–21). You will find nothing in these passages about 'workers' rights', but everything about how the Christian worker is to respond to authority.

Does God then have no concern that employers should be just and considerate? Yes, and we shall see what he says to them in a moment. They are dealt with at another level. All that he says to the Christian worker points away from his taking action against an unjust boss. Sarah, overtaken with jealousy, mistreated her slave girl Hagar so that she ran away. But see what God said to Hagar (Gen 16:8–9). This teaching is not nullified because slavery is abolished in our society. This is the only teaching in Scripture on how a worker is to relate to an employer.

The marks of a Christian worker

Fulfilling the command to obey your earthly master 'just as you would obey Christ', and to serve him 'as if you were serving the Lord' (Eph 6:5, 7), will radically affect how you work, and whether you are fulfilled. It will not be difficult to work as the Bible exhorts us to:

1. With heart and soul

Solomon, a great and successful worker, said, 'Whatever your hand finds to do, do it with all your might' (Eccles 9:10). Paul says the same thing, but notice the motivation he gives for doing so (Col 3:23-24).

2. With fidelity

By our trustworthiness in material things we are qualifying to handle the 'true riches' (Lk 16:10–11). Christians are told 'not to steal from [their masters], but to show that they can be fully trusted' (Tit 2:10). But would a true believer steal? I have met those who seem to have no conscience about using office stamps or stationery for their own use, or stealing the boss's time by not giving him a fair day's work for their pay. Any unrighteousness may go unnoticed by our earthly boss, but not by our heavenly one (Col 3:25).

3. Without complaining or arguing

That's a tough one, but it's there, and it's an important aspect of our witness before a 'crooked and depraved generation' (Phil 2:14–15). It's an expression of true respect for authority, as is also the command 'not to talk back' (Tit 2:9).

4. Not to curry favour (to gain promotion)

You are to do what they want, 'not only when their eye

is on you and to win their favour, but with sincerity of heart and reverence for the Lord' (Col 3:22). So you work just as conscientiously when the boss is not around as when he is, because you are really working for another Boss—and he's always around (Gen 16:13; Phil 4:5).

A word to employers

1. The Judge stands at the door

He watches to see if there is fair play (Jas 5:9). James pronounces 'woe' on the rich in verses 1–6, men who have hoarded ill-gotten wealth at the expense of the poor. See what God said of a king who was unscrupulous towards his workers (Jer 22:13, 18–19). The cries of the oppressed always reach God's ears (Jas 5:4). He may bide his time, but he will act.

> Though the mills of God grind slowly, yet they grind exceedingly small;
> Though with patience he stands waiting, with exactness grinds he all.
>
> (Friedrich von Logau)

2. Be a do-gooder

Having told slaves, 'The Lord will reward everyone for whatever good he does,' Paul goes on to tell their masters, 'Treat your slaves in the same way' (Eph 6:8–9). The law even commanded a master to give a 'golden handshake' to a slave being freed (Deut 15:12–15). So the Lord carefully watches boss-worker relationships to reward each as they do good to the other.

3. Don't threaten

Ephesians 6:9 tells masters not to threaten their slaves as the rulers of the Jews threatened the apostles (Acts

4:21). A fair warning is justified, but threatening is a wrong use of authority. He who had all authority in heaven and on earth did not do this (1 Pet 2:23).

4. Give a square deal

'Provide your slaves with what is right and fair' (Col 4:1). This covers the whole area of pay and conditions. Note, the Christian employer is to act in the knowledge that his own 'Boss' in heaven is watching.

Memorize

> *Whatever you do, work at it with all your heart, as working for the Lord, not for men, since you know that you will receive an inheritance from the Lord as a reward. It is the Lord Christ you are serving* (Col 3:23–24).

Home task

'When it comes to work, some turn up their sleeves, and some turn up their noses.' The Bible calls the latter laziness. We are not speaking here of genuine unemployment, but of those who could work but don't, or who are lazy in their work.

1. Read the following scriptures and list all the things that characterize and accompany slothfulness: Proverbs 10:5; 24:30–31; 26:13, 16; Matthew 25:24–25; 2 Thessalonians 3:6–8, 11–12.

2. Read the following scriptures and make a list of all the encouragements to diligence and all the discouragements to slothfulness: Proverbs 6:9–11; 10:26; 12:24; 13:4; Ecclesiastes 10:18; Ephesians 6:7–8.

For further study

1. 'I'd rather have a man of the world as my employer than a Christian.' I have had believers say this to me. What do you think could be wrong with the attitudes of employer and/or worker to call forth such a remark? As well as the scriptures in the notes, look at 1 Timothy 6:2.

2. Matthew 20:1–16 is a parable about unemployment and work. Why did some of the workers think the boss was unfair? What factors could have caused him to pay the later workers the way he did, and still fulfil his promise to pay them what was right (v.4)? What may we learn from this?

Pressing on Towards the Goal

Read
Hebrews 11:8–10, 13–16.

Introduction

In this final study we shall see that the only way to be living in this world as a mature Christian is to live for the next! Our goal must be heavenly, not earthly. We need to understand that we are 'strangers in the world' (1 Pet 1:1), impelled by a heavenly vision.

The world is passing

We have seen that salt is no permanent solution to decay. It only delays the process. As 'the salt of the earth' we can only delay corruption until God's purposes have been fulfilled. For the world, the sands of time are running out.

1. The natural world

It's like an old garment wearing out, soon to be changed and discarded (Ps 102:25–26). Men are tempted to think that 'nothing changes here', or in the words of Peter, 'Everything goes on as it has since the beginning of creation.' But they deliberately forget, Peter tells us, that the world has once been destroyed by water, and is finally to be destroyed by fire (2 Pet 3:4–7).

2. The world of men

This is also under judgement. The knowledge of this should be a great incentive to us to persuade men to believe on Christ, and thus escape from God's wrath (Jn 3:36). Noah was 'a preacher of righteousness' (2 Pet 2:5) who warned men of coming judgement, but they did not heed his warnings. As it was in the days of Noah, so it will be at the time of Christ's return (see Luke 17:26), only this time it will be a judgement of fire, not water (2 Thess 1:6–10).

3. The world system

It is obvious that this must also be doomed: 'The world and its desires pass away, but the man who does the will of God lives for ever' (1 Jn 2:17; see also 1 Corinthians 7:31). This puts mankind into two classes: those who live to fulfil their own desires, who are thus identified with the world system, and those who live to fulfil the will of God. The future of the one is grim, but the future of the other is glorious (Mt 25:46; 2 Thess 1:6–10).

How should this affect us?

'Since everything will be destroyed in this way, what kind of people ought you to be?' (2 Pet 3:11). A good question! Peter answers it along three lines:

1. Our living

'You ought to live holy and godly lives.' The knowledge that the world is to come to a fiery end should compel us to live lives that are pleasing to God. If we are different in our nature from the world, and with a totally different destiny, surely we should be different in our lifestyle. That was a powerful statement when Peter wrote those words. How much more powerful now that we are nearly two thousand years nearer the event.

2. Our outlook

'Looking forward to the day of God.' We must be a forward-looking people. The future prospect of the world is one of 'doom and gloom', but ours is thrilling. We are looking forward to 'the glorious appearing of our great God and Saviour, Jesus Christ', when he will be finally vindicated. It is 'the blessed hope' of the Christian (Tit 2:13). And it should make us perpetual optimists.

3. Our aim

'To speed [or 'hasten' RSV] its coming.' We are not to wait passively for zero hour to strike. We have our part to play to bring that day nearer. Only God knows the full number of his chosen (2 Tim 2:19) whom he has given to his Son as his inheritance (Ps 2:8; Jn 6:37), but every conversion to Christ brings that final harvest nearer. As we play our part in the world as salt and light we inevitably 'speed its coming'.

Our status in the world

1. A heavenly people

Having been rescued from the dominion of darkness, we have entered the kingdom of heaven. We are therefore a colony of heaven, living on earth. Our thinking is now to be dominated by this unseen heavenly world, not by the seen world (2 Cor 4:18). We have received:
   (a) A heavenly vision. For Paul this happened on the

road to Damascus. A light brighter than the midday sun blinded him (Acts 22:11). It was symbolic of the glory that burst upon him, and left him blind to the dazzling sights of earth.

A business man saw a little child sucking a dirty stick of toffee. The child could not be persuaded to part with this until, presently, the man emerged from a sweet shop with a large slab of milk chocolate. There was no problem now in making him let go of the toffee. This has been called, 'The expulsive power of a new affection.'

Said Paul, 'Whatever was to my profit I now consider loss for the sake of Christ' (Phil 3:7). Paul 'was not disobedient to the vision from heaven' (Acts 26:19).

(b) A heavenly calling (Heb 3:1). Conversion is a right about turn, when we start moving in a new direction, propelled by a heavenly calling. Paul speaks of this as though he were an athlete, with a powerful motivation to go for gold: 'I press on towards the goal to win the prize *for which God has called me heavenwards in Christ Jesus*' (Phil 3:14, italics mine). What we experience here and now is but a foretaste of our heavenly inheritance. What starters is to the banquet.

Being a heavenly people means that we are:

2. *Strangers on earth*

Many young Christians have been distressed to find that their conversion has alienated them from their own family. That's how Christ felt (Jn 1:10–11, RSV). Conversion means a change of citizenship, from one that is earthly to one that is heavenly (Phil 3:20), and this inevitably brings a sense of alienation. The secular world has an increasing number of *displaced persons*, who for military, political or economic reasons have been uprooted, and are now without a homeland. The Christian is like that. The only difference is that he has no sense of loss, convinced that he has another and far better homeland awaiting him—and he's on his way.

3. The continuing conflict

The world is seeking to draw us. It wants to break down this sense of alienation and get us to conform (Rom 12:2). The world is uncomfortable with us as we are, and wants to assimilate us. Here is the conflict for the Christian, having to resist this perpetual influence. Jesus said, 'In this world you will have trouble. But take heart! I have overcome the world' (Jn 16:33). God could have evacuated us when we were converted. He could have airlifted us to our true homeland, as he will do one day (1 Thess 4:15–18). But this conflict is itself preparing us to reign with Christ in his coming kingdom (2 Tim 2:11–13; Rev 20:6).

Two contrasting characters

Abraham and his nephew Lot were citizens of Ur of the Chaldees. They turned their backs on its idolatry in response to a call of God, lured by the promise of an eternal city. Though they were wealthy, they became tent-dwellers in the land of Canaan.

1. Abraham

It is Stephen who gives us the key to this man's astonishing career: 'The God of Glory appeared to our father Abraham' (Acts 7:2). Abraham was sick and tired of Ur, and that day he caught a vision of a 'city with foundations'—which he knew Ur didn't have—'whose architect and builder is God' (Heb 11:10). That heavenly vision didn't simply spoil him for Ur, it spoiled him for earth. It turned him from a city-dweller into a tent-dweller (Heb 11:9). Of course there is no special virtue in being a tent-dweller, but Abraham was called to demonstrate something which should be true for every Christian, that 'here we do not have an enduring city, but we are looking for the city that is to come' (Heb 13:14). In pursuing this heavenly goal Abraham not only became a giant of faith, 'the father of us all' (Rom 4:16), but he had also the supreme honour of being the man in Scripture whom God called 'my friend' (Is 41:8; cf Gen 18:17–19).

2. Lot

Lot never caught the vision that drew Abraham out of Ur. He seemed to tag along, no doubt admiring his uncle, and holding on to his coat tails (Gen 12:4; 13:1). But you can't get very far on someone else's vision and faith. Self-examination is needed (2 Cor 13:5). Lot is described as 'a righteous man' (2 Pet 2:7), but because he didn't have the heavenly vision he was compelled to part company with his uncle (Gen 13:5–9). Abraham couldn't pursue the heavenly calling with someone who only had an earthly vision, even if he was righteous.

Lot, it seems, wasn't too sold on the tent-dwelling life of Uncle Abraham. He didn't feel comfortable as 'a stranger and an exile' in the land. Of the faith pioneers we read, 'If they had been thinking of the country they had left, they would have had opportunity to return (Heb 11:15)—but they didn't. They were hooked. Tent-dwelling or city-dwelling is not a matter of location but of heart attitude. Lot was a man who had 'opportunity to return', and took it. Why? His heart was not in the other lifestyle. Faced with the choice he turned back, and soon he was again a city-dweller—in a city even more wicked than Ur. Consider the fatal steps he took:

'Lot looked up and saw . . . ' (Gen 13:10). How we look is vital.

'Lot chose for himself' (v.11). Material advantage was the motive.

'Lot...pitched his tents near Sodom' (v.12). Swim near the whirlpool and then:

'Lot...was living in Sodom' (14:12).

'Lot was sitting in the gateway of the city' (19:1). He had achieved a position of authority (Prov 31:23).

The world will always applaud the Lots. A man gets praise when he does well for himself (Ps 49:18). But in the end he lost everything—his wife, his home, his possessions, the chastity of his daughters and his self-respect (Gen 19). And it all sprang from a wrong choice—a choice that every Christian has to face throughout his life. There will always be 'opportunity to return'—for those who want to take it. Pioneers of the heavenly way are volunteers, not conscripts.

The prize of the heavenward call

1. The need of a goal

The more things we have to do the more we need envisioning and motivating. In the Philippian epistle Paul draws aside the curtain and shows us his inner life. We see what made him tick spiritually (3:12–14). We too need a goal that is more than a stimulus for immediate progress and personal fulfilment. It must be big enough to offset the back tow of the world, the flesh and the devil, and all that prevents us pressing on for the prize.

2. Forgetting what is behind

Paul knew that the memory of his past could hinder him. Many of us are hindered by our track record. 'Forgetting what is behind' (Phil 3:13). What do we need to forget?

Sin that we have confessed which God has forgiven,

but for which we haven't forgiven ourselves. Injured pride is usually the root. When we *humble* ourselves, *receive* God's forgiveness, and then *forget*, we are through.

The memory of mistakes and failures. Satan tells us that they disqualify us. He is a liar. See what kind of people God chooses (1 Cor 1:27–29). Praise God, we all qualify! We are old clay pots, weak and unworthy, so that it's all by God's grace, and God gets the glory (2 Cor 4:7, 15).

Living in the memory of past blessings. That can be a source of pride. We are wrongly limiting God, only expecting him to do in the future what we have seen him do in the past (see Ephesians 3:20).

3. Reaching out to take hold

Taking hold of what? 'That for which Christ Jesus took hold of me' (Phil 3:12). On the road to Damascus Paul was 'arrested' by the long arm of God's grace. He was never again free—to do his own thing. He was only free to do the will of the One who had arrested him. Our understanding of that purpose for which Christ took hold of us doesn't all come at once, it is a progressive revelation. To know God's will and do it was, for Paul, not a pastime but a passion. It was all bound up with knowing Christ, and he pursued it relentlessly. Everything else was 'rubbish' (Phil 3:8). It was the prize for which God had called him heavenwards (v.14).

But this was not just for Paul. He goes on say, '*All of us who are mature* should take such a view of things' (v.15, italics mine). Such an attitude to life is an indispensable mark of the mature believer. In striking contrast, note what he goes on to say about those whose 'mind is on earthly things' (vv.18–19).

4. The prize that awaits

Enlisting for the race doesn't secure the prize. There are many competitors, but few prize-winners. 'I press on...to win the prize.' In verse 8 he speaks of his desire to 'gain Christ'. In this race, 'Christ is the path and Christ the prize'. Gaining Christ could mean a deeper and more intimate relationship with him. When he found himself at last on 'the home straight' he had the assurance that he had fully laid hold, and that the prize of the heavenward call was his.

> The time has come for my departure. I have fought the good fight, I have finished the race, I have kept the faith. Now there is in store for me the crown of righteousness, which the Lord, the righteous Judge, will award to me on that day —and not only to me, but also to all who have longed for his appearing (2 Tim 4:6–8).

That last sentence could include you. The prize is not just for the Pauls and other great characters, it's for all—all who have had the heavenly vision, who have set their affection on things above, 'who have longed for his appearing'. This is what it means to be mature.

Memorize

One thing I do: Forgetting what is behind and straining towards what is ahead, I press on towards the goal to win the prize for which God has called me heavenwards in Christ Jesus (Phil 3:13–14).

Home task

1. An enterprising firm, learning that a sizeable proportion of the community were 'Bible-believing Christians', and eager to cash in on this market, decided to investigate in what way these people differed from the rest of the community, in lifestyle habits, likes and dislikes, etc. Their report? 'They are no different!'

(a) In what ways should citizens of heaven be different?

(b) As you note each point ask yourself, 'Am I different here?'

2. In pressing towards the goal for the prize, we spoke of the 'back tow' from the world around us.

(a) Make a list of the things you find the greatest hindrance and talk to God about them, claiming such promises as John 16:33; 1 John 4:4; 5:4.

(b) How would you help a Christian who feels he (or she) has never had 'the heavenly vision' (Jer 29:11–13; 33:3; Mt 7:7–8)?

For further study

1. Christians are called to be spiritually influential in the world. Someone has said, 'The world has been much more successful in influencing the church than the church has in influencing the world.' The story of Lot has something to teach us here.

(a) What do you think caused Lot to make the decision described in Genesis 13:10–11?

(b) Why do you think God allowed him to be carried away captive while living in Sodom, and then rescued by Abraham (Gen 14)?

(c) How did Lot's residing in Sodom affect his influence on the people around him (Gen 19:9, 14, 26, 31–36)?

(d) Study Lot's situation in the light of these scriptures:

1 Corinthians 15:33; 2 Corinthians 6:14–18; Ephesians 5:8–13.

2. Why does Hebrews 11 emphasize so strongly that these *men and women of faith* were also *characterized by possessing a heavenly vision* (see the reading)? What is the connection?

INTO
BATTLE

Arthur Wallis

CHRISTIAN LITERATURE CRUSADE
ALRESFORD
and
KINGSWAY PUBLICATIONS
EASTBOURNE

CONTENTS

5

CONTENTS

INTRODUCTION

MODERN warfare is horrifying. I know because I have seen it—in real life. Many young people today don't want to know. Talk of tanks and guns, blitzed cities and blasted homes, turns them off. I don't blame them. But we cannot live in a 'dream world' from which all thought of war has been excluded. We are dealing with an ugly but inescapable fact of human experience. 'Wars and rumours of wars' there have always been, and the Bible warns us that they will be with us to the end. The soldier is one member of society who is not likely to face redundancy.

Equally inescapable is the fact of spiritual warfare. A man turns his face towards Christ and hits a mountain of opposition. He presses through, but is often tempted to throw it all in. Prayer is often such hard going. Old temptations return with a new lease of life. It is such a battle to witness. What does it all mean? It is simply discovering what the Bible everywhere teaches, that the call of Christ is a call to arms. The Christian life means warfare. This is not to use a metaphor or a figure of speech but to state a literal fact. It is simply that the sphere, the weapons, and the foe, are all spiritual rather than material. In using the military analogy throughout this book I am not expressing any sympathy with the brutality of human warfare. I am simply taking my cue from the Bible. Much of Old Testament history is devoted to the wars of Israel, to teach us how to 'fight the good fight of faith'. In the New Testament the whole concept of Christ's kingdom coming to men is presented in terms of a military invasion. Jesus used a parable about two kings making war to emphasise the cost of discipleship. He also stated that He had not come to bring peace on earth but a sword. In the epistles there are several references to the Christian life as spiritual warfare, while the atmosphere of the battlefield seems to pervade the book of Revelation which looks forward to the final triumph.

There have always been those who wanted the blessings of the Christian life without the battles, who 'say to the seers . . . "Speak to us smooth things".' When God brought Israel out of Egypt to lead them into the promised land, He 'did not lead them by way of the land of the Philistines, although that was near; for God said, "Lest the people repent when they see war, and return to Egypt".' In the end they spent the rest of their days wandering in the wilderness. Many are wandering in a spiritual wilderness today for the same reason. There is no room in Christ's army for those who want to play at Christianity, seeking the thrills and the frills, but shirking the cut and thrust of battle.

The mention of military life conjures up in many

minds such ideas as discipline, hardship, suffering, and other nasty words. But these inevitably have their counterpart in spiritual experience. If these soldierly qualities had been lacking in those first disciples, Christianity would never have got off the ground. The lack of them today is one reason why so much of our Christianity is anaemic, when it ought to be robust and strong.

This book is a battle manual of the Christian life. Here the would-be-soldier of Christ is first shown how to enlist, and then led on to the subsequent steps of faith and obedience essential for spiritual warfare. Most of the practical aspects of the Christian life have been covered. It answers such questions as, 'How can I become a committed Christian?' and 'If I become one, what will this involve?' Others who are already committed, and eager to be out where the action is, will find here much that will help to instruct and equip them for battle.

Today young people are being drawn to Christ in ever increasing numbers. I have written especially with them in mind. The conflict is becoming fiercer and the issues more sharply defined as the end of the age draws near. I rejoice that this hour of challenge is producing so many soldiers of Christ as dedicated and fearless as any who have gone before. To them, with whom lies the hope of tomorrow, I dedicate this book. May the Lord teach their hands to war and their fingers to fight.

I am deeply indebted to Denis Clark and David

Lillie who went through the manuscript with great care and whose suggestions have been most valuable. Also to Loren Cunningham of Youth With A Mission who helped to give me the American slant, and Major Mike Stevens who vetted it from the military aspect.

Those who wish to use this book as a basis of study would do well to read it straight through first, and then go over it a second time, carefully examining the Scripture references that are given at the close of each chapter. Unless otherwise indicated Old Testament quotations are taken from the REVISED STANDARD VERSION (RSV) and the New Testament from TODAY'S ENGLISH VERSION (TEV), otherwise known as GOOD NEWS FOR MODERN MAN. Both are available in cheap paperback editions. Where the AUTHORIZED (KING JAMES) VERSION, has been quoted this is also indicated after the reference (AV). Any matter in square brackets is mine.

ARTHUR WALLIS

INTO BATTLE

ON WHOSE SIDE?

WE live in a world at war. If it isn't 'hot war' it's 'cold war'. There is mounting tension between different nations and ideologies, between East and West, between Capital and Labour, between Black and White. Our homes are no refuge, for even there, so often, there is strife between husband and wife, between parents and children. People search in vain for a way out. Said an army instructor to a cadet, 'Your platoon is almost surrounded, you have lost several men, and you are running out of ammunition. As platoon commander what steps would you take?' 'Long ones, Sir,' was the reply. But man cannot take long steps to escape from his dilemma. He is like a hunted animal with nowhere to hide.

It is one thing to recognise the symptoms, quite another to diagnose the complaint and prescribe the cure. The fact is, man is at war with man because man is at war with God. Behind the human battle there is a spiritual battle. It is the age-long fight between light and darkness, between good and evil, between God and Satan. We are caught up in it willy-nilly. Neutrality is quite impossible.[1] It all began before man appeared on the scene, and will continue until

God's last enemy has been destroyed.[2] If you believe that God is God you cannot doubt who will win. To fight for the wrong cause is not only to lose, but because of the stakes, to lose for ever.[3] So the vital question is, On whose side are you?

Let us trace the river back to its source. In the beginning God made man after His likeness, to obey His laws and to find fulfilment in the enjoyment of His friendship. For a very brief span earth experienced a real Utopia as man lived in harmony with his God, and so in harmony with both his environment and himself. God had created him a free agent because He wanted voluntary, not compulsory obedience—obedience that sprang from love and trust.

Then tragedy struck. Man rebelled, thinking he could pull off a better deal with God's arch-enemy. By believing Satan's lie instead of God's truth he put himself in the enemy camp. The tragic results of his decision are not only all around us, they are within us.[4] Ever since, mankind has been suffering from an hereditary disease called sin. In infancy he has to be taught how to walk and talk, but needs no instruction in how to lie, cheat, and lose his temper.[5] Sin comes as natural as breathing. He seems to have a built-in bias against the will of God, and in favour of pleasing himself. 'All we like sheep have gone astray; we have turned every one to his own way.'[6] This is sin in its essence, turning to our own way instead of to God's.

By living our lives without reference to God we

have played into Satan's hands and put ourselves under his authority. Most people are completely ignorant of what the score is here. They find it hard to accept that the respectable, the moral, and even the religious are in the same boat as the avowed sinner. 'There is no difference at all,' the Bible says, 'all men have sinned and are far away from God's saving presence.'[7]

It is here we have to grasp the nettle. To acknowledge that we are part of the problem is the first step in discovering the solution. Many who air their views on 'What's wrong with the world' have never faced up to this home truth. Some years ago there was a discussion on this theme in the correspondence columns of THE TIMES. The following letter from the well-known author brought the matter down to earth with a bump: 'Dear Sir, What's wrong with the world? I am! Yours faithfully, G. K. Chesterton.'

One of the greatest obstacles to man's salvation is the pride of his own heart that will not permit him to face up to the facts. God says in effect, 'You have failed to measure up. You are weighed in the divine balances and found wanting. You have put yourself in the enemy camp.' But man's response is one of argument, of excuse, of self-justification.[8] What has your attitude been?

Jesus emphasised in His teaching that only as a man humbled himself to acknowledge his need could he receive salvation. Addressing the Pharisees, a group that suffered from an overdose of self-righteousness, He said, 'People who are well do not need a doctor, but only those who are sick. I have not come to call the respectable people, but the outcasts.'[9] In other words, 'If you Pharisees want me to heal your souls, stop pretending you are spiritually well and join the sick queue with the rest.'

Are you now ready, if you have never done it before, to bow your head and humbly acknowledge, 'All that God says about me in the Bible is true. I have broken God's law times without number. I have failed to love God with all my heart, and to love my neighbour as myself. In refusing Christ's rule in my life I have made myself His enemy.[10] I fully deserve God's wrath. I cannot alter this situation by any self-effort. I can only plead for mercy.' If you are able sincerely to make such a confession there is good news to come.

[1] Mat. 12. 30   [2] 1 Cor. 15. 24–26   [3] Mat. 13. 40–42
[4] Rom. 5. 12   [5] Psa. 58. 3   [6] Isa. 53. 6   [7] Rom. 3. 22–23   [8] Luke 10. 29   [9] Mark 2. 17   [10] Luke 19. 27

2

THE RESCUE OPERATION

FED by science fiction and reports of 'flying saucers', many have seriously wondered if the earth would one day be invaded by 'beings' from outer space. The Bible is the record of an invasion that was launched from heaven to rescue earth-dwellers from the clutches of a ruthless enemy, and to restore the kingdom of earth to its rightful Ruler.

You may recall the story drama of a famous French climber who was marooned for days on a narrow shelf of rock high up in the Alps. The temperature was sub-zero. Beside him was the dead body of his climbing companion. With a blizzard raging the prospects of a rescue looked bleak. Then, when the climber had reached the limits of human endurance, a helicopter appeared overhead, and the man was winched to safety. Weeping, he told his rescuers, 'I had given up all hope.'

The Bible is the record of a far greater rescue operation. It tells of God's intervention to save man from a predicament of his own making. He, too, was helpless and hopeless, and what was worse, he had made himself the enemy of the only One who could save him from his desperate plight. Consequently he had forfeited any claim to mercy or compassion. God had every reason to obliterate him or at least to leave him to his fate. Alternatively, He could have waited for him to come to terms. Instead He took the initiative and regardless of the personal cost, He launched a rescue operation to bring man back.

The price God had to pay to reclaim His rebel kingdom was the life of His Son. Here's how the Bible puts it: 'For when we were still helpless, Christ died for the wicked . . .' It is a difficult thing for someone to die for a righteous person. It may be that someone might dare to die for a good person. But God has shown us how much He loves us; it was while we were still sinners that Christ died for us! By His death we are now put right with God . . . We were God's enemies, but He made us His friends through the death of His Son.'[1]

If man's sin has alienated him from God, how is it that the death of Christ two thousand years ago is able to effect a reconciliation? We must first understand what God has to say about the consequences of sin. The truth that 'sin pays its wage—death'[2] is all too clearly seen in the history of man. Before Adam sinned he possessed a life that was not subject to death. In theory he could have lived for ever. But God put him to the test. There was one rule that he had to keep, and God warned him that the day he broke it he would die.[3] He did break it with the inevitable result.

Though man did not die physically there and then,

the moment he sinned death entered in a twofold way. First, he died spiritually; that is, he died in that part of his inner being that gave him contact with God. If you have ever stood at the open grave of someone you loved very dearly, you will know that death means separation. Spiritual death means separation from God, and if the situation is not recovered that separation becomes final. This is the meaning of hell, otherwise called 'the lake of fire' or 'the second death'.[4]

Then the same day Adam died spiritually he also began to die physically. The process of human decay set in, and in due course his body returned to the dust from which it was made. So, from the time of Adam there has been a reign of death over the creation, which means that man is cut off from his Creator, and his decaying body bears silent proof of the fact.

Unless we understand this truth concerning sin and death, we cannot appreciate the wonder and wisdom of God's rescue operation. This was the supreme purpose of Jesus coming down to live as a man among men.[5] The great climax was reached when Jesus gave Himself up to die on the cross. He was not an unwilling victim, for a way out was always open to Him had he chosen to take it.[6] Instead He trod with quiet determination the thorny path that led to the lonely hill top. He had said earlier, 'No one takes my life away from me. I give it up of My own free will.'[7]

When Jesus rose from the dead He explained to His bewildered disciples that His death by crucifixion had not been a ghastly mistake. Nor was it an heroic attempt to save a cause that was all but lost. It had been in the plan from the beginning, foretold by all the prophets.[8] Why was it necessary? Because death was the penalty for breaking God's law. If man had been left to face the music the race would have died eternally, banished for ever from the presence of God. Instead Christ had intervened, accepted responsibility for man's sin, and by dying Himself, had become 'the Saviour of the world'.[9]

Here then is the greatest drama in human history. The only Man on earth who never deserved to die willingly did so in order that men, who fully deserve to die, might not have to. The finest deeds of human heroism pale beside this supreme act of self-sacrifice. It is now possible for all who are the enemies of God because of their rebellion, to be reconciled to Him. You may now be rescued from the kingdom of darkness and death, and transferred to the Kingdom of His Son.[10] The way is wide open for you to quit Satan's service and enlist in the army of the Lord. But this will require a definite response on your part. If God is working in you He wants you to co-operate with Him.

---

[1] Rom. 5. 6–10   [2] Rom. 6. 23   [3] Gen. 2. 17   [4] Rev. 20. 14–15   [5] John 3. 13–17   [6] Mat. 26. 53   [7] John 10. 18   [8] Luke 24. 25–27; Acts 2. 23   [9] John 4. 42   [10] Col. 1. 13

3

TIME TO ENLIST

AN important transaction must take place if a civilian is to become a soldier. He must *enlist*, and this will mean not only terminating his civilian employment but accepting a radical change in his whole way of life. The enlisting of the soldier of Christ is usually called 'conversion'. In this chapter I want to explain just what this transaction entails.

It is necessary to realise that there are two sides to the conversion experience. God has His part to play and we have ours. In the marriage ceremony there is usually an officiating minister who 'ties the knot', but the wedding pair are required to respond by affirming that their hearts and wills are in this union. Even so with conversion, it is God's work to free us from our old allegiance and to join us to Christ. But He requires our willing co-operation.

The Bible often speaks of this experience as a spiritual rebirth.[1] But birth is not brought about by the struggles of the baby but by the action of the mother. We do not become children of God by our own efforts, we must be 'born of the Spirit'.[2] There is a danger of so emphasising the personal response that we lose sight of the fact that it is God, by His

Holy Spirit, who convinces us of our need, enlightens us concerning the truth, and leads us to Christ.

On the other side of the fence there is a danger of some sitting back and waiting for God to take things into His own hands completely and convert them at a stroke. I once spoke to a man about his need of Christ. His defence was, 'Some day I will no doubt see the light', as though he had no further responsibility in the matter. No, we are required to seek the Lord with all our hearts.[3] We are commanded to turn away from our sins ('repent' is the old-fashioned word) and believe the Good News.[4] In this chapter I shall be explaining what this involves, but remember, salvation is God's work. If you are now seeking Christ, it is because God is drawing you.[5] You can only repent and believe because He is working in you.[6]

If you genuinely desire to enlist in the army of the Lord and become a soldier of Christ, then God requires of you a twofold response. First you must quit the service of Satan; that means *repent*. Then you must be joined to the Lord; that means *believe*. Repentance and faith are the two legs by which we enter God's kingdom.[7] People so often misunderstand these two words that I must say something about them.

'Repent' was a note sounded out by John the Baptist, by Christ Himself, and by His apostles. 'God commands all men everywhere to repent' (RSV), or 'turn away from their evil ways' (TEV). We cannot

22

come into a personal relationship with Christ until we obey. Repentance is more than simply 'sorrow for sin'. If I were caught for speeding and given a heavy fine, I should certainly be very sorry, but that would not prove my repentance. I might just be sorry that I got caught! Repentance would mean sorrow for a good and wise law that I had broken, not just a resolve to keep a sharper look out for the speed cop!

Judas confessed with deep remorse, 'I have sinned by betraying an innocent man to death.'[9] Had there been true repentance in Judas's heart he would have experienced God's forgiveness, and that would have saved him from a suicide's death. You may remember that he flung those silver coins, the sordid price of his betrayal, on the temple floor. If, instead, he had flung himself at the feet of his offended God he could have found mercy.

To repent means to change one's mind. When a man repents he ceases to justify himself. Instead of excusing his sin he exposes it. Instead of siding with himself against God he sides with God against himself.[10] It is not that he is able himself to break the chains of sin—that is God's work. But God will only do this when a man's attitude towards his sin has changed.

Repentance always leads to *confession*. 'He who conceals his transgressions will not prosper, but he who *confesses* and forsakes them will obtain mercy.'[11] We must first confess to God, for all sin is primarily against Him.[12] If particular sins trouble us we should

23

name them. But where we have sinned against others we must confess to them too, and where necessary make restitution—that is, do all in our power to make good the damage done. For example, money or goods stolen must be restored with interest.[13]

True repentance will always produce a changed life. The verse just quoted requires us to *forsake* as well as confess our transgressions. In other words the change of mind (repentance) will result in a change of course. We have an example of this in a very simple parable of Jesus. A father told his two sons to go and work in his vineyard. One refused point-blank, but on his way home he had a change of heart. He turned round and headed for the vineyard.[14] That is repentance.

For a true conversion experience repentance must always be accompanied by faith, the other leg by which we enter the kingdom. It is faith in Christ that saves. Man finds a strong temptation to trust his own good deeds for acceptance with God instead of Christ alone. This boosts his ego. But God rejects and condemns outright all such pride of heart. Salvation, He tells us, is a gift, not a wage. This rules out all boasting. 'For it is by God's grace that you have been saved, through faith. It is not your own doing, but God's gift. There is nothing here to boast of, since it is not the result of your own efforts.'[15]

This faith that saves is much more than assent to mental facts about Jesus. I believe *about* Mao Tse Tung, but I don't believe *in* him. 'The demons also believe (about God)—and tremble with fear.'[16] but their faith doesn't save them. To believe *in* someone means to trust yourself to that person. If you are suffering from heart trouble and you really believe in a certain heart specialist you will be willing to put your case in his hands. Believing in Christ as Saviour means committing yourself to Him for salvation. Believing in Him as Lord means submitting to His control.

It is often at this point that someone who is earnestly seeking salvation is tempted to postpone the moment of decision. They presume that the matter is left to them, and that they can turn to Christ when they like. God has only one time for men to answer His call, and that is NOW. When we hear God speak and are conscious of His Spirit pleading with us, that is the time to respond. 'This is the hour to receive God's favour, today is the day to be saved.'[17] God makes no promises about tomorrow.

Has God been speaking to you through these pages? Do you sense that gentle pressure of the Holy Spirit within, urging you to turn to Christ now? If so, then you need to express this to God in a simple prayer. The Bible says, 'Everyone who calls on the name of the Lord will be saved.'[18] Find a quiet place. Kneel down, if this will help you to humble yourself before God. Then from your heart make confession to God and call on Christ to save you. It is not the phraseology that you use that counts, but the fact that your prayer, however stammering, really comes from the heart, and is a real expression of faith, however weak. Do it now.

Did you call on Him? Did you sense that He heard your cry—and has done a work in your heart? In that case do not delay to confess Christ. The Bible tells us that salvation includes confessing with the mouth as well as believing with the heart. 'If you declare with your lips, "Jesus is Lord," and believe in your heart that God raised Him from the dead, you will be saved.'[19] Tell that one who is closest to you that Jesus is now your Saviour and Lord. Do not be ashamed of Him. It will certainly do something for your new-found faith, and bring a real release of joy. And who knows what it may do for the one to whom you witness?

[1] John 3. 3–7   [2] John 3. 8   [3] Jer. 29. 13   [4] Mark 1. 15; cf. Acts 17. 30   [5] John 6. 44   [6] Phil. 2. 13   [7] Acts 20. 21 RSV   [8] Acts 17. 30   [9] Mat. 27. 4   [10] Luke 18. 9–14   [11] Prov. 28. 13   [12] Psa. 51. 4   [13] Lev. 6. 5; Luke 19. 8   [14] Mat. 21. 28–29   [15] Eph. 2. 8–9   [16] Jam. 2. 19   [17] 2 Cor. 6. 2   [18] Rom. 10. 13   [19] Rom. 10. 9–10

4

PUT ON THE UNIFORM

ONE day early in the Second World War I walked
into a recruiting office as a civilian and walked out as
a soldier. I had enlisted—yet to all outward appearances I was still a civilian. The world outside knew
nothing of what had taken place in that recruiting
office. A few months later I was called to a training
regiment and donned the King's uniform. Now I was
a soldier for all to see.

Water baptism may be likened to the enlisted
soldier putting on his uniform. The Bible expresses it
this way: 'For as many of you as were baptised into
Christ have *put on* Christ.'[1] To the man who has
dedicated himself to becoming a soldier, the putting
on of the uniform is a joyful and exhilarating moment.
It does something for his morale, his bearing, his
esprit de corps. All this and more, water baptism
should be to the newly-enlisted soldier of Christ.[2] I
once stood on a Californian beach and watched
about 150 'Jesus people' being baptised in the sea.
The 'love-joy' in their faces as they came out of the
water and then embraced the leader who had baptised them was a sight I shall long remember.

Of course it is enlisting, not putting on the uniform, that makes a man a soldier. Just so it is faith in Christ, not baptism, that makes a man a Christian. Nevertheless, baptism is a significant step of obedience that brings its own blessing. It should never be viewed as a denominational issue. It does not signify adherence to any particular branch of the church. The New Testament teaches that a believer is baptised *into Christ*,[3] not into a particular church or denomination. This is a matter between you and the Lord.

How important is water baptism? It was the focal point in the ministry of John the Baptist, the Forerunner of Christ.[4] Jesus Himself was baptised in water,[5] and baptism had an important place in His ministry.[6] It was universally practised by the early church.[7]

Some of the most important teaching in the New Testament on the Christian life—how we may put to death the old nature and live in the new—is based on this rite of baptism.[8] God intends that as we submit to it there will be a release of faith enabling us to enter into all that baptism signifies. Very often, especially in heathen communities, when a person first professes faith in Christ, opposition and persecution do not break out until the convert takes the step of baptism. Certainly the devil takes baptism seriously.

'Baptise' is a Greek word that has been anglicised rather than translated into English. For this reason its basic meaning, to dip or immerse, has been obscured. New Testament baptism consisted of dipping the candidate in water. When our Lord was baptised He 'came up out of the water'.[9] Similarly, when Philip baptised the eunuch, they both 'went down into the water' and 'came up out of the water'.[10] This agrees with Paul's explanation of baptism as signifying a spiritual burial in the waters of death, followed by a spiritual resurrection.[8]

The command of Jesus to His followers to preach the gospel to the whole world has been called 'the marching orders of the Christian Church'. This great commission included a twofold command concerning baptism. He laid the onus first on the preacher, and then on his convert. The preacher is to make disciples from all nations, baptising them in the name of the Father, and of the Son, and of the Holy Spirit.[11] Those to whom he preaches are commanded to believe and be baptised for salvation.[12] At Pentecost when those who had heard Peter's message asked, 'What shall we do?' Peter replied, 'Repent and be baptised.'[7] Notice that baptism followed repentance and faith.

Baptism has a threefold significance. First it speaks of *purification*. In the hot dusty lands of the East the bathing of the body was an important part of daily hygiene. Sin in Scripture is often described as moral defilement, and its removal as a cleansing. This was the main feature of John's baptism, for it was accompanied by confession of sin.[13] The disciple Ananias exhorted the newly converted Saul of Tarsus, 'Rise and be baptised, *and wash away your sins*, calling on His name'.[14] So we see that in baptism we have an outward washing, corresponding to the inner cleansing the Lord is performing in the heart and life of the believer.

Second, baptism implies *confession*. It is an open declaration for all to see that the one baptised has truly enlisted in the service of Jesus Christ. This is why, as I said earlier, it may be likened to putting on the uniform. Baptism was never intended to be a 'hush-hush' affair. It was normally performed, as in the case of our Lord, right out in the open in rivers or city pools. Today, when a Christian is baptised, whether indoors or out, he is declaring unashamedly, 'I have decided to follow Jesus—no turning back, no turning back.' No wonder it is a joyous occasion.

Finally, baptism signifies *union*. It means that the believer is united with Christ in His death and resurrection. This great truth is unfolded by Paul in Romans 6. 1–11. We have to think of the baptismal pool as the grave and the believer's body as the corpse. As Christ voluntarily yielded Himself up to death, so by a voluntary act of faith we are united with the Christ who was put to death.[15] As loving hands then carried away that dead body and hid it from sight in the rock-hewn tomb, so in the baptismal waters we are symbolically 'buried with Him';[3] that speaks of complete deliverance from the power of our old life.[16] As on the third day Christ rose from the dead, so we rise out of the water, expressing the spiritual reality of our union with Him in resurrection, to 'walk in newness of life'.[17]

It is not necessary for the full significance of all this to be understood for a baptism to be valid in the sight of God. If the Roman believers to whom Paul addressed the epistle had fully understood the significance of their baptism, Paul would never have needed to give them the teaching of Chapter 6. In baptism we are primarily following Christ's example and obeying Christ's command. Once a person has truly turned to Christ and desires to obey this ordinance no one has the right to refuse his plea for baptism. If you are concerned about this matter go carefully through the chapter again looking up the scripture references. Ask the Lord to make His will clear to you, and then, 'Do whatever He tells you.'[18]

---

[1] Gal. 3. 27 RSV   [2] Acts 8. 39   [3] Rom. 6. 3   [4] Mark 1. 4–5   [5] Mark 1. 9   [6] John 4. 1   [7] Acts 2. 38, 41, etc.   [8] Rom. 6. 1–11   [9] Mark 1. 10   [10] Acts 8. 38–39   [11] Mat. 28. 19   [12] Mark 16. 16   [13] Mat. 3. 6   [14] Acts 22. 16 RSV   [15] Gal. 2. 20   [16] Rom. 6. 6   [17] Rom. 6. 4 RSV   [18] John 2. 5

5

EQUIPPED

THERE is another baptism the Christian soldier must experience, that is, if he is to be equipped to serve Christ effectively. Though in the New Testament it is closely associated with baptism in water, it is nevertheless quite distinct—the baptism in the Holy Spirit.[1] It is not an optional extra, but part and parcel of the full salvation procured for us.

It is important to understand that the Holy Spirit is not just a power or influence proceeding from God, but that He is just as much a Person as the Father or the Son. Notice how Scripture speaks of 'Him' and 'He' in relation to the Spirit, rather than 'it'.[2] When we first sensed our spiritual need it was the Holy Spirit who was at work in our hearts. Apart from His action we cannot be born into God's family [3] or enlist as a soldier of Christ. A man devoid of the Spirit is not a Christian at all.[4] It may help us to distinguish the work of the Holy Spirit from the work of Christ by saying: the Holy Spirit comes to do *in* and *through* us, all that Christ did *for* us by His saving work. It is by the Holy Spirit that God is at work in our lives.

Though it may happen at conversion, the baptism

in the Spirit is usually a subsequent and more powerful encounter with the Holy Spirit. It is when 'the power from above comes down *upon* you',[5] to quote Christ's own words. Notice that word 'upon'. It occurs constantly when the New Testament describes this experience. Even our Lord experienced the Spirit coming upon Him at the outset of His public ministry.[6] From that point the power of God was with Him in a way that startled and stumbled the worshippers in the synagogue of Nazareth, where He had been brought up.[7] His very last words to His followers before returning to heaven were to the effect that they would very soon experience the Holy Spirit coming upon them and empowering them to be His witnesses.[8] This was what happened at Pentecost.[9]

Years ago as I was reading in the Acts the history of the early church, I began to wonder what it was these first Christians possessed that I so sadly lacked. Certainly they were unsophisticated, almost naïve, by our modern standards. But what authority! what boldness! what joyous freedom! Our modern Christianity appeared drab by comparison. Later on I came to the conclusion that these people really knew the Holy Spirit, whereas so many of us only know about Him.

The Holy Spirit wants to possess us wholly. This is the meaning of being 'filled with the Holy Spirit'.[10] He wants to energise all our activity and to invade every realm of our spiritual being. Under His direction prayer becomes effectual and the Bible an open treasure store. There is a new release of our personalities in praise and worship. We begin to enjoy a lively sense of the presence and nearness of Christ. We are made aware of power at our disposal to witness and to serve Christ effectively. The Holy Spirit is the dynamic of Christianity.

The Acts of the Apostles records five instances of the Holy Spirit coming upon people.[11] In each case it was a distinct experience, and those on whom the Spirit came knew that something wonderful had happened. Generally they spoke with tongues, that is, languages that were new to them, which they did not even understand. Always there appears to have been some distinct manifestation of the Spirit's presence. From then on they seemed to be at home in the realm of the Spirit. Christianity to them was undoubtedly supernatural. Signs and wonders accompanied their preaching.[12] They healed the sick and cast out demons. In their churches they spoke in unknown tongues with interpretation. They prophesied and received revelations by the Spirit.[13]

Such were the weapons in the hands of these first Christian soldiers, and how effective they were to the pulling down of enemy strongholds! Of course not all were issued with the same weapons, but every soldier was equipped. 'Each one is given some proof of the Spirit's presence for the good of all.'[14] These weapons are still needed and still issued. Come to God, then, with open heart that He may equip *you* with all that you need to be an effective soldier of Christ.[15]

How is one to receive the baptism of the Spirit? The early church did not look upon it as a graduation diploma. Nor was it reserved for those who had attained a certain standard of knowledge, piety, or maturity. In every case following Pentecost it was upon new converts that the Spirit came. Therefore any believer may qualify. First there must be *an uncondemned heart*.[16] As for any other blessing we may seek from God, we must deal with all unconfessed sin. We must come before Him with a clear conscience. If a cloud has come between God and us since we first believed, then we must remove it by confession of that sin to God.

Second there must be a *thirsty heart*. 'Whosoever is thirsty should come to me and drink,'[17] said Jesus in this very connection. It is not that we covet someone else's experience, or wish to keep abreast with others in spiritual things. We must really *thirst for God* as a man marooned on a desert island would thirst for water. If you are not yet thirsty, ask God to show you why. The Holy Spirit is waiting to create that thirst as well as to satisfy it.

Then, there must be *an obedient heart* because 'The Holy Spirit . . . is God's gift to those who obey Him.'[18] Power is dangerous when placed in irresponsible hands. God's power is reserved for those who have submitted to His rule. The power is not given to enable us to carry out schemes of our own which we think may serve the interests of God's kingdom, but to do His will. The coming of the Spirit should mean that Jesus is Lord, for the Spirit comes to glorify Christ through the life that He possesses.

Finally, there must be *a believing heart*. The promise of the Spirit is received by faith.[19] The hands of faith that reached out to receive the Saviour's pardon must now reach out to receive the Spirit's power. Where people genuinely seek but do not receive, the cause is often unbelief. When God shows us unbelief in our hearts we need to confess it for the sin it is, seek full release from it, and ask God to give us the faith of a little child.

One thing more. God has put within His church the ministry of laying on of hands for the reception of the Spirit.[20] Of course, only the Lord Jesus can impart the Holy Spirit. He alone is the baptiser. But we see that He often uses the laying on of hands. Those who minister in this way, with the Lord's authority and direction, become spiritual 'power conductors' as they exercise faith on behalf of those who are seeking. You may be in touch with those who would be ready to pray for you in this way. But if not God will meet with you on your own. Do not rest until you have received the power of the Holy Spirit coming upon you. Without this you are ill-equipped for the battle.

[1] Mat. 3. 11   [2] John 14. 16–17   [3] John 3. 5–8   [4] Rom. 8. 9   [5] Luke 24. 49   [6] Luke 3. 21–22   [7] Mat. 13. 53–57

[8] Acts 1. 4, 5, 8   [9] Acts 2. 1–4   [10] Acts 4. 31   [11] Acts 2. 1–4; 8. 14–17; 9. 17; 10. 44–47; 19. 1–6   [12] Heb. 2. 3–4   [13] 1 Cor. 14. 26   [14] 1 Cor. 12. 7   [15] Heb. 13. 21 RSV   [16] 1 John 3. 21–22   [17] John 7. 37   [18] Acts 5. 32   [19] Gal. 3. 2, 14   [20] Acts 8. 17–18

6

ENEMY COUNTER-ATTACK

IT was during the Italian campaign in the Second
World War. The Allies had advanced on a broad
front dispossessing the enemy of the commanding
position he had held. Immediately the order was
given to consolidate, that is, to strengthen their hold
on the newly occupied territory. As sure as night
follows day, the enemy would be sure to stage a
counter-attack. Troops are never more vulnerable
than when they have just occupied but have not yet
established their grip on new territory. Victory may
be turned into defeat unless advance is followed by
consolidation.

All this is so true in spiritual conflict. We are up
against a wily foe, about whom I shall have more to
say later. He knows when and where we are most
vulnerable. The life of Christ has something to teach
us here. There was a physical attempt on His life
shortly after His birth. Herod was the agent but
Satan was the instigator. Then there was a spiritual
attack by Satan after His baptism and anointing
with the Holy Spirit at the Jordan. Finally, in the
garden of Gethsemane, facing the death of the cross,
Satan had His last desperate fling. It is often so in

Christian experience. After we have been born into the family of God, after the Holy Spirit has come upon us, and then when we come to cross that 'last lone river', we are especially liable to the attacks of the Devil.

First a word or two about temptation in general. God permits it but does not promote it.[1] It is the Devil who is called 'the tempter'.[2] But there is still within us a tendency towards evil even though we now have new desires as God's children. The part played in temptation by this sinful tendency which Scripture calls 'the flesh', is well described by James: 'A person is tempted when he is drawn away and trapped by his own evil desire. Then his evil desire conceives and gives birth to sin.'[3]

Temptation is not sin. It only becomes sin when we yield to it. Jesus, the Scripture tells us, 'was tempted in every way that we are, but did not sin'.[4] Temptation has in fact a very important part to play in the development of our Christian character. A great athlete will subject his muscles to ever greater tests of endurance in order to reach his peak. A tree swept by the mighty wind will send its roots deeper into the soil. Just so God intends that the testings in the race of life shall serve to purify and develop our spiritual character to the full, and that the winds of temptation shall send the roots of our faith deeper into His love.

Though God does not cause temptation, He does control it. He 'tempers the wind to the shorn lamb'.

'Every temptation that comes your way is the kind that normally comes to people. For God keeps His promise, and He will not allow you to be tempted beyond your power to resist; but at the time you are tempted He will give you the strength to endure it, and so provide you with a way out.' [5] Job chapters 1 and 2 provide us with a very interesting back-stage view of temptation. It is seen as part of the age-long conflict between God and Satan, with man as the battle-ground. God put definite limitations on what Satan was allowed to do to Job, and did not permit him to over-step those bounds. It is so with us.

We are not simply the unfortunate victims of the malice of our arch-enemy, but the children of a Father who is all-loving, all-wise, and all-powerful. He is in complete control of the situation. He over-rules temptation for our good. He even promises a special reward to those who endure. [6] Little wonder James exhorts us to consider ourselves both fortunate and happy when we have to endure such trials. [7] Jesus also taught that persecution, which can be a very real temptation of the Devil, should cause us to 'dance for joy', so great would be our reward in heaven. [8]

There is one special counter-attack we need to watch. Being saved by Christ and being filled with the Spirit are experiences that bring very real joy. But feelings are variable, and that gives Satan his opportunity. We wake up with a splitting head, or the day seems to go all wrong. Our joy vanishes away. And then we are tempted to feel that perhaps this new experience, that seemed so real the night before, was just a passing emotion, and we are filled with doubt.

It is here we have to learn a very important lesson. Though God gave us emotions, and spiritual feelings of joy or peace are valuable accompaniments of our salvation, they are not the heart and soul of the matter. The Christian life is based, not on changeable feelings but on changeless facts. If my faith is ruled by my feelings it will fluctuate like the weather. If it holds fast to the promises of God,[9] not only will I keep on an even keel but my feelings will soon begin to behave, and the sunshine of God's love and joy will soon break through my overcast sky.

Someone has suggested that this kind of temptation is like three men, Fact, Faith, and Feeling, walking along the top of a wall. So long as Faith in the middle keeps his eye on Fact in front, Feeling tags along quite happily behind. But when he turns around to look at Feeling he loses his balance, falls off, dragging Feeling with him!

Now about doubting. Despite what some people seem to think, there is nothing pious about spiritual uncertainty, nor anything presumptuous about an assured faith. We are not required to live in uncertainty. When a person is asked, 'Are you a Christian?' and he can only reply, 'I hope so,' it is not a sign of humility, but may often be an indication that he is not resting on the true foundation. God wants us to be sure. 'I write you this so that you may know that you have eternal life,'[10] wrote John to his little children in the faith.

So often Satan counter-attacks the new Christian with a fusillade of doubts. Our feelings and our reasonings are no defence. Faith must be our shield.[11] What does God's Word say? 'I will never turn away anyone who comes to Me.'[12] 'If you declare with your lips, "Jesus is Lord", and believe in your heart that God raised Him from the dead, you will be saved.'[13] 'To all who did receive Him, to those who have yielded Him their allegiance, He gave the right to become children of God.'[14] Did I come to Him? Did I receive Him and yield to Him? Did I confess Him? Did I then have the assurance of His response? Right then, let me rest on His word, whatever my feelings. God will never break His promises.

One thing more. This 'full assurance of faith'[15] is part of our heritage, but it depends on our giving continued allegiance to the Lord. If we rebel and take the bit between our teeth we must not be surprised to find that we lose the assurance of our relationship with God. The backslider will be troubled with doubts. The remedy is simple. To confess our sin, turn from going our own way, and put our hand afresh in His. Then we can lift up our heads to the world and declare with a ring of assurance, 'I know whom I have trusted, and I am sure that He is able to keep safe until that Day what He has entrusted to me.'[16] This is what the world is wanting. 'Give me the benefit of your convictions, if you have any,' wrote the German philosopher Goethe, 'Keep your doubts to yourself—I have enough of my own.'

[1] Jam. 1. 13   [2] Mat. 4. 3 RSV   [3] Jam. 1. 14–15
[4] Heb. 4. 15   [5] 1 Cor. 10. 13   [6] Jam. 1. 12   [7] Jam. 1. 2, 12   [8] Luke 6. 23   [9] Heb. 10. 23   [10] 1 John 5. 13
[11] Eph. 6. 16   [12] John 6. 37   [13] Rom. 10. 9   [14] John 1. 12 NEB   [15] Heb. 10. 22 RSV   [16] 2 Tim. 1. 12

7

DAILY RATIONS

THERE is more than a pinch of truth in the old saying, 'An army marches on its stomach'. Every commander knows that poor food means discontent, low morale, lack of strength and stamina. These in turn affect fighting efficiency.

Daily rations are no less important for the well-being of the Christian soldier. God has provided for us a wholesome and appetising diet in His Word, the Bible.[1] I trust that as you have read these few chapters your 'inner man' has been fed and strengthened. Though we are often nourished by spiritual food that others have gathered and placed before us—as is the the case with books we read or addresses we hear— it is even more important that we learn to fend for ourselves. This is essential if we are to become strong, stable, and effective soldiers.

The Bible claims to be God's word to men—the only holy book that makes such a bold claim. The proof is found within its pages, not in the arguments of those who would try to defend it. Spurgeon, a pulpit giant of the last century, said, 'I would no more think of defending the Bible than I would of defending a caged lion. The thing to do is to let it

44

out!' Over the centuries it has been banned and burned, reviled and ridiculed, attacked by the critics and the sceptics. Still it stands unscathed, the most read, the most loved, indeed the most wonderful book in the world. Behind the great diversity of human authorship is the divine Author.[2] This alone could account for its amazing unity and harmony. Though it was men who spoke and wrote, they were men who were inspired by the Spirit of God.[3] Here then is the mind of God in print. The more acquainted we become with this book the more convinced we are that it is God's truth.[4]

One thing that the new Christian will notice: a new relationship with God brings a new relationship with His Word. How could you love the God of the Book, and have no affinity with the Book of your God? 'I'm fed up with this dry old novel,' said the daughter. 'Very well,' said the mother, 'Choose another, there are plenty more.' Imagine the mother's surprise when some months later she found her daughter avidly devouring the book she had thrown down in disgust. The secret? She had been introduced to the author and had fallen in love with him! That's why your attitude to the Bible changed so radically when you found Christ—a personal relationship with the Author.

Because of its unique nature we must handle this Book differently from other books. We do not read it as an intellectual exercise, nor even for its beautiful prose or its historic interest. Since the Spirit breathes through it, God speaks to us in its pages, and by this means our souls are fed. By it we are instructed, corrected, and encouraged.

How much nourishment we receive will largely depend upon our attitude as we approach the Bible. A good appetite is essential. Peter tells us that we are to desire it as newborn babes their mother's milk.[5] Beware of the periodical, the paperback, the TV programme that takes away your appetite for God's word. 'This Book will keep you from sin or sin will keep you from this Book.'[6] We must approach the Book with faith, expecting God to speak, and that we shall be nourished, strengthened, and blessed. We read of Israel, 'They heard the message but it did them no good, because when they heard it they did not receive it with faith.'[7]

Now for a few practical hints. *A regular time* for feeding our souls is just as important as regular meals for feeding our bodies. We need an hour when our minds are fresh, and when we shall be least liable to interruption. The early morning is the obvious choice. The discipline of getting up that much earlier is valuable, and our time with God prepares us spiritually for the day ahead. Why tune the fiddle when the band has shut down for the night?

If you do not already possess one, invest in *a well-bound Bible* with clear print. It is worth buying the best. What version? Even if your mind is already steeped in the King James English of the Authorised Version, why not consider the advantages of thinking

46

God's thoughts in twentieth-century English? It helps when it comes to communicating those thoughts to others. But some versions are so 'free' that they tend to be interpretations rather than translations. The Revised Standard Version and the new American Standard Bible strike a happy balance. But stick to one version for regular use, keeping others for reference.

It was a bishop who gave me, one of a crowd of youngsters, the best tip I ever received on reading the Bible for greatest profit. Here is his recipe:

1. Read it through
2. Think it over
3. Write it down
4. Pray it in
5. Live it out
6. Pass it on.

Read it through. But where to begin? Start with one of the four gospels. John is a favourite with new Christians, but it contains some deep teaching, so that others may find that Mark, the Gospel of action, is a better starting point. The books of the Bible were written as books, so read them through as books. Select each day a portion of suitable length, but don't bite off more than you can chew.

Think it over. This is where the chewing comes in. It is not enough to read, memorise, or even study the Scriptures. We must learn to *meditate* on them. Ask yourself, 'What is God wanting to teach me through this passage? How do these words apply to me?'

Joshua was one of God's great soldiers in Old Testament times. Joshua 1. 8 teaches us that meditation was one of the secrets of his success. Don't try to meditate in a hurry. It can't be done. Persevere, for it will take time to learn how to extract the nourishment from your spiritual food.

Write it down. Keep a notebook with your Bible and record the thoughts that come to you. 'Much reading maketh a full man. Much writing maketh an exact man. Much speaking maketh a ready man', wrote Francis Bacon. Writing down your thoughts will help to clarify and crystallise them, as well as imprinting them on your memory.

Pray it in. This is very important if we are to be 'doers of the word, and not hearers only'. Often we shall find that meditation is punctuated by prayer, or changes into prayer almost unconsciously. And it won't all be for ourselves, there will be intercession for others too.

Live it out. The Spirit of God may apply the most unlikely passages to your life. Who would have thought the book of Revelation contained much of practical application to us today? Yet we read in the first paragraph, 'Happy are those who . . . obey what is written in this book!' [8] This, of course, is true of the whole Bible. The blessing of reading is fulfilled in obeying.

Pass it on. This is how we share Christ with others, and so increase the blessing and the joy. A blessing shared is a blessing doubled, just as a burden shared is a burden halved. Don't be selfish, share your rations with others!

Jehoiachin, king of Judah, had been exiled in Babylon. One day his royal captor freed him, just as you and I have been freed. Then we read, 'And every day of his life he dined regularly at the king's table.'[9] This is our high privilege. Let us not neglect it.

---

[1] Jer. 15. 16   [2] 2 Tim. 3. 16   [3] 2 Pet. 1. 20–21   [4] John 17. 17   [5] 1 Pet. 2. 2.   [6] cf. Psa. 119. 11   [7] Heb. 4. 2   [8] Rev. 1. 3   [9] 2 Kings 25. 29

8

LINES OF COMMUNICATION (1)

DURING the fighting in North Africa in the Second World War, the battle swayed to and fro across the desert, with neither army able to clinch the victory. The reason? The problem of maintaining a fighting force that had swept a hundred miles or more beyond its supply base. Lines of communication are lines of supply, and when these are severed or stretched beyond breaking point the finest army will grind to a halt.

Prayer is our life-line in the spiritual battle. By this means we communicate with heaven and bring down spiritual supplies vital for the conflict. Let our lines of communication become over-stretched by too much doing and too little praying, or cut by direct enemy action, and we are soon in serious trouble. So let's talk about this very important matter of prayer.

In the opening chapters we saw that man at first was living in harmony with God, but when sin came there was estrangement and separation. Through Christ's work on the cross we saw how communication with God was restored. In fact, we now have a closer relationship with God than Adam ever knew.

Of all the blessings of our salvation, none is greater than fellowship with God in prayer. It is as vital to us as breathing, and should be as natural.

The point was made in the previous chapter that our new relationship with God is the secret of a new love for His Word. Similarly a right relationship with God is the basis of prayer. When as a kid I had done wrong and knew that my father knew, I could not look him in the face or enjoy his companionship as before. I did not cease to be his child, but I did cease to enjoy his fellowship until I had said, 'Sorry, Dad.' It is so with God. Walking in the light, or having nothing between us and God, is the basis of fellowship;[1] and this in turn is the soil in which an effective prayer life will flourish. The Bible states quite bluntly that God will not listen to us if we harbour sin in our lives.[2]

Often prayer is made to seem so complicated, but basically it is nothing more than the child talking freely and naturally to his Father. No special building, ritual, posture or phraseology are needed. Don't get tied up trying to imitate the 'Thee' and 'Thou', 'willest' and 'wouldest', used by some Christians. It may be a comfort to know that in the Hebrew and Greek of the Bible there isn't any special 'reverent' form of address for the Almighty, different from that used to address one's fellow, and that goes for many modern languages. True, there must be reverence, but God looks for this in the heart and spirit of the one who prays rather than in his phraseology.

First of all we should see prayer, not so much as a duty or a discipline (though it is both of these), but as a delight. The God who made us for His pleasure and glory, who reconciled us to Himself through the death of His Son, craves our fellowship. Jesus, our heavenly Bridegroom, says to us, in the words of Solomon's love song: 'Let Me see your face, let Me hear your voice; for your voice is pleasant, your face is lovely'.[3] Does a girl drag her feet when she goes to meet her lover? Does she find conversation with him a bore? Not unless there is something seriously wrong with their relationship.

If at first you find it difficult to become aware of God's presence, speak out the words of the Psalmist, 'The Lord is near to *all* who call upon Him, to *all* who call upon Him in truth.'[4] Remind yourself of the promise, 'Come near to God and He will come near to you.'[5] Then, in the assurance that He is listening, open your heart to Him. Begin to praise and give thanks to Him, for this is how we are told to 'enter His gates'.[6] If you find this difficult let the psalmist help you. Turn, say, to Psalm 34 and address David's words to the Lord until you find the Holy Spirit giving you words of your own.

Jesus spoke much about *asking* prayer, which the Bible calls 'petition', 'supplication' or 'intercession'. On the night of His betrayal He said to His disciples, 'Until now you have not asked for anything in My name; ask and you will receive, so that your happiness may be complete.'[7] So He has given us the right to use His name in prayer, or as a lawyer would say, 'the power of attorney'. What a privilege! He wants us to experience not only the joy of doing this, but that joy completed as the answer is received.

No matter is too small and none too big to take to God in prayer. When you come across prayer promises in the course of your daily Bible reading, note them carefully, and start to use them in your praying. God loves to be reminded of His promises, and they serve as nothing else to strengthen our faith for the answer. No time or place is unsuitable for prayer. Travelling to work, waiting for an interview, wrestling with an exam paper, handling a tricky situation. In the crisis of difficulty or danger, of temptation or trial, prayer should be instinctive. When his Persian monarch suddenly asked Nehemiah a crucial question, he found time to flash a prayer to heaven before replying.[8] That shows he was well practised in the art.

It is not essential to shut your eyes when you pray. If you pray, as I constantly do, driving the car, it is rather important that you don't! Incidentally, there is nothing in Scripture about shutting one's eyes. If it helps you to concentrate your thoughts, fine. Jesus lifted up His eyes when He prayed, as though looking up to His Father in heaven, and being a Jew He probably lifted up His hands too. Anything is helpful that stimulates your faith to realise that you are actually addressing a God who is right *there*.

Jesus once said, 'Give to others, and God will give

to you.'[9] This is a principle with God and applies to prayer, as well as to what we do with our pounds and pence. Just as we can be selfish over our material possessions, so we can in our praying. The remedy is intercession. It is right at times to pray, 'Lord bless me,' but it is wrong if we are never reaching out to others in prayer. This is the meaning of intercession. Reach out beyond your family to that needy family down the road. Reach out beyond your church, its ministers and people, to other churches in town. As you give in prayer, God will give back to you, and you will discover that God uses a bigger shovel than you do!

'Doesn't the Bible say that if we want our prayers answered we must pray according to God's will?' That's right.[10] 'But how can I know if I am praying according to God's will?' That is a very important question, and it touches another side altogether of this matter of *lines of communication*. Communications are not all from the soldier to his Headquarters. What about from Headquarters to the soldier? We've said a lot about our talking to God. What about His speaking to us? That is the subject of the following chapter.

[1] I John 1. 6–9   [2] Isa. 59. 2   [3] Song of Sol. 2. 14 NEB
[4] Psa. 145. 18   [5] Jam. 4. 8   [6] Psa. 100. 4   [7] John 16. 24   [8] Neh. 2. 4–5   [9] Luke 6. 38   [10] I John 5. 14

9

LINES OF COMMUNICATION (2)

IMPORTANT as it is that the forward troops should be able to communicate with Headquarters, to report on the situation or call for supplies, it is equally important that intelligence reports and battle orders should be getting through from Headquarters to the men at the front. There are many believers who know how to call on the Lord for their needs, but are unskilled in the art of hearing God's voice and discerning His will. So they never become seasoned soldiers, and their usefulness is limited.

Referring to Himself as the Shepherd, Jesus said, 'My sheep listen to My voice . . . and they follow Me.'[1] Don't think that this ability to hear His voice is a faculty that only some outstanding believers have, or that requires years of experience. Jesus is saying that it is characteristic of His sheep to listen to His voice and so be led. If you are one of His sheep then the desire and ability to hear His voice is within you.

God has made us dependent on Him for everything. As the soldier should not move without orders, neither should we. Jeremiah reminds us, 'It is not in man who walks to direct His steps,'[2] and Solomon warns us, 'Do not rely on your own insight'[3] or human judgment. In addition to the directing of our steps that we usually call guidance, we stand in continual need of counsel, rebuke, warning, teaching, and encouragement. At the close of the last chapter we posed the question young Christians so often ask, 'How can I pray according to God's will?' It is often the case that we need to hear God speaking to us before we know how to speak to Him.

How do we hear God's voice? Firstly through His word. I am speaking of something more definite and specific than the general comfort and strengthening we should receive when we read the Scriptures or listen to them being explained. Often after preaching I shake hands with the people at the door. Many may thank me sincerely for the message, but when someone grips me tightly by the hand and says with glowing face, 'Something you said really touched my heart tonight,' I know God has truly spoken.

It may be the text for the day on the tear-off calendar. It may be a 'chance' remark dropped in conversation or said in a letter. The Holy Spirit causes it to register deep within, and we recognise it as the voice of the Shepherd.

The Bible also teaches us that when we love God and our lives are yielded to Him, He orders and overrules our affairs for good.[4] So it is not surprising to find that He sometimes speaks through our circumstances. He may say 'No' by shutting one door, 'Yes' by opening another. When things go wrong you can be sure that God is speaking.[5] It may be in a sickness, an accident, a disappointment, a defeat, or through some unanswered prayer of long standing. It is no help to brush the thing aside and press on as though nothing had happened. If we would only seek the Lord about it with purpose of heart we would get the message.

When it is merely a question of getting the green light or the red light on some proposed course of action, God will often guide you by putting His peace in your heart, or by taking that peace away. There are many situations in which 'the peace that Christ gives is to be the judge (of what is right or wrong) in your hearts'.[6]

When there is a particular issue in which you need the Lord's direction, pray about it, and then wait in silence to hear God speak. When we read 'the word of the Lord came to' this one or that in Bible times it was rarely they heard an audible voice. Usually it was the 'still small voice' deep within. How does this work? I believe it is the Holy Spirit, resident in the human spirit, speaking to the human mind the thoughts of God. This means that under the control of the Holy Spirit we begin to think God's thoughts after Him. 'But is there not a danger here that we are merely thinking our own thoughts or even hearing the whisper of Satan?' Of course, there is this danger. We are in a spiritual battle, and battles tend to be dangerous, and inevitably there are some casualties.

57

But spiritually this is only when God's safeguards are ignored.

The question we have to ask is not, 'Is it dangerous?' but 'Is it Scriptural?' If God spoke in this way to men in Bible times, nothing has happened to make it any more dangerous now than it was then. It is by this means that spiritual gifts like prophecy operate. Of course, all prophecy has to be weighed and judged.[7] In the same way you will need to weigh what you believe is the voice of God. And do not be offended that others will want to weigh too what you believe you have received before accepting it. We shall make mistakes, but if our hearts are humble and teachable God will use our mistakes to teach us much.

Now for a few principles that will help us to tune in and hear heaven's signals, loud and clear. Although our minds come into play, it is with our hearts that we need to be concerned. Listening in to God is a heart rather than a head matter. What follows is not a technique in four easy stages, but four principles that will condition our hearts to hear His voice.

First of all, *humility*. Pride lays us open to enemy interference. It will also make us liable to self-deception,[8] thinking our own thoughts and desires are God's. When a person is arrogant or fanatical, not open to reason or willing to submit to others, you may be sure that the pride of his heart has deceived him. 'Humble yourselves'[9] is an oft-repeated command of Scripture. It is something *we* are required to do.

Then *submission*. It is here the will has such an important part to play. We may seek the will of God sincerely without realising how our minds are still influenced by our selfish desires, preferences and ambitions. God cannot get through to us unless we are willing for His will, even if this runs counter to our human desires. Jesus was talking about His doctrine when He said, 'Whoever is willing to do what God wants will know . . .'[10] It is equally true in relation to knowing the will of God in general.

Then there must be *spiritual sensitivity*. As we practise 'tuning in' our spiritual receivers will become increasingly sensitive to heaven's transmissions. There are so many Christians who have never exercised themselves in this matter, and so have remained 'dull of hearing'.[11] But even those who seek God in this way need to beware of those influences that come from the world that may so easily dull our spiritual sensitivity.

Finally there is *patience*, easy to talk about but hard to learn. It is right to seek God for direction. It is right to wait silently on God to hear His voice. But beware of trying to force God to share His secrets before His time has come. There are situations in which God will speak at once, but others when He keeps us waiting. It may be that developing patience within us while we wait is as important as receiving the message when it comes.[12] Of one thing you may be sure, God *will* speak, and speak clearly, if you will seek Him with all your heart.

[1] John 10.27   [2] Jer. 10.23   [3] Prov. 3.5   [4] Rom. 8.28; Eph. 1.11   [5] Josh. 7.7–11   [6] Col. 3.15   [7] 1 Thes. 5.20–21   [8] Obad. 3   [9] 1 Pet. 5.6   [10] John 7.17   [11] Heb. 5.11 RSV   [12] Heb. 10.36

10

POSTED TO A UNIT

It is impossible for a soldier to be an individualist in the way that a civilian may be. He is compelled to work in close co-operation with others. Every fighting unit is a *team*. If we have had the impression thus far that the Christian life is a very individualistic matter, the New Testament teaching on the church will provide a needful corrective. The Lord's army certainly does not consist of a bunch of individuals all doing their own thing. He has planned that it shall consist of many units, or local churches.

In thinking God's thoughts about the church we may have to rid our minds of some popular misconceptions. To many the church is simply the sum total of the various denominations, each with its own particular organisation. But the New Testament has nothing to say about denominations. All that we find there is 'the church'!—and very little organisation. Others speak of the building where people meet for worship as 'the church'. But again, the New Testament never refers to a building in this way. In that first century there weren't any special buildings set apart for worship.

We must listen to the Head of the church Himself

to find the right answer. Christ only made two statements about the church, but they contain the germ
of all that we need to know. When Peter had confessed, 'You are the Messiah, the Son of the living
God,' Jesus replied, 'You are a rock, Peter, and
on this rock foundation I will build My church.'[1]
This that Christ called 'My church' and which He
Himself promised to build, is what Bishop Ryle
called, 'the one true church'. Only those who are
able to confess from the heart who Jesus is, as Peter
did, are on this one foundation, living stones in this
spiritual temple. All true believers then, regardless of
colour, race, or tradition, comprise the church. It is
the worldwide community of God's own people.

Later Jesus was instructing His disciples on how to
deal with a sinning brother. If he will not listen to
you, nor to the one or two others you take along with
you, you are to 'tell the whole thing to the church'.[2]
Obviously Jesus couldn't have meant, Tell it to 'the
worldwide community of God's own people'! Here
then is a different concept of the church. He could
only have meant the local congregation. A few verses
later He described it in its simplest form as 'two or
three come together in My name'.[3] Again note, the
church is not viewed as an organisation, nor as a
building, but as a company of people. Where
believers meet together, even if it be in field or
forest, cave or catacomb, *there* is the church.

These are the two concepts of the church that
Jesus gave us, the worldwide community and the

local congregation. And these are the only concepts that we will find in the New Testament. It is very important, as we pick our way through the confused situation we call 'Christendom', to keep God's blueprint always before us. It is not enough for a man to enlist as a soldier. Sooner or later he must be posted to a unit. It is not enough that you commit yourself to Christ and so belong to the universal church; you need also to belong to a local congregation. This is implied throughout the New Testament. There is also the exhortation, 'Let us not give up the habit of meeting together, as some are doing.'[4] Christians who live in isolation or who wander from church to church are robbing God, robbing His people, and robbing themselves.

The local church should be the place for further spiritual training. As we fellowship with others the corners will be rubbed off and our spiritual lives developed. Paul talks much of the church as Christ's body. As we discover our place in 'the body' we shall begin to function as a hand or a foot, an eye or an ear. We shall also begin to appreciate our need of the other members. Those who can't get along with their fellow Christians, and become 'lone wolfers' are usually unstable and immature.

In the tabernacle of Moses we see a foreshadowing of the church. There were two sections: the Holy Place where the priests ministered, and the inner shrine or Holy of Holies, where God dwelt. In the Holy Place were the table with its special bread, the altar of incense, and the golden lampstand.[5] These teach us what should be the functions of the local church.

The table speaks firstly of *food*. The local church should be a place where the Bible is honoured as God's word, and its truths faithfully taught Besides our own Bible digging, we need the help of those with greater experience whom God has equipped to shepherd and feed the flock.[6] The first church at Jerusalem devoted themselves to four things and the first of these was 'the apostles' teaching'.[7]

The table also speaks of *fellowship*. When we invite someone for a meal it is for fellowship, nqt just for food. The local church should be the place where we share our life in Christ with others. Of course, this is impossible where there is no life. Unlit coals in a grate don't make a fire. But once ignited, the coals need to be kept together to ensure a good blaze. This is a picture of fellowship—the second thing to which those first Christians devoted themselves.[7] Differences of background, temperament or tradition are no problem when we begin to taste the new wine of fellowship in the Spirit.

Then there was the altar of incense, with its fragrant smoke curling upwards. This in Scripture is a picture of *prayer and worship*.[8] The first call of the Christian is not to be a worker, or a witness, but a worshipper. This is our highest function. There should be scope in the local church for each member to participate in praise and worship as well as in prayer.[9] As believers we are all priests unto God, and there should be liberty to exercise our priestly functions.[10] This includes using any spiritual gift that God has given us for the blessing of the rest. The early church certainly made good use of the altar, for we read that they devoted themselves to prayers.[7]

Finally, there was the seven-branched lampstand giving *light*. This speaks of *testimony*. The local church was never intended to be an inward looking group taken up with its own blessings, but a lighthouse in the darkness of this world. Christ told us that we were to be salt and light in the world.[11] He expects us to be involved, just as He was, in the spiritual and social needs of the men and women around us. Certainly there was nothing inward-looking about the Jerusalem church. So bright was their light that we read, 'And every day the Lord added to their group those who were being saved.'[12]

A soldier is posted to a unit. He is not free to chose one that takes his fancy. You will need to seek the will of God as to where you should make your spiritual home. You will be limited of course to what is available in your locality, and only rarely will you find anything that approximates to the New Testament ideal. At all events give the local church that you attend your loyal and whole-hearted support. Whether or not it is a denominational church, keep yourself free from a denominational spirit. You belong firstly to the body of Christ, that is the worldwide community of God's children, and then to *that* local congregation of believers. Scripture does not require you to belong to anything more. This will help you to maintain the unity of the Spirit with God's people everywhere.[13]

If before your conversion you were linked with a church where the Bible is not truly preached, and where there is no living fellowship, don't assume that you are to cut yourself off forthwith. God may still want you there, at least for a time, humbly to bear your testimony to Christ. The Christians in Jerusalem continued to worship in temple and synagogue, until they were thrown out![14] But *that* wasn't their church. The fellowship we have been talking about they found in the homes where the believers met together. And if your former place of worship is unable to meet your need of food, fellowship and an outlet for service, though you still maintain contact with it, you will need to find live fellowship elsewhere, even if you have to travel a distance.

When we look at the worldwide picture of the church we see that a wonderful thing is happening as a result of the visitation of the Spirit. Barriers are crumbling as God's people discover the truth of what they have so often sung 'We are not divided, all one body we.' The situation has been likened to a flock of ducks, all from the same family, yet separated in different pens. Their only contact is to quack at each other through the fence! Then the flood comes and the ducks become water-borne. Soon they are swimming over the tops of the submerged fences, overjoyed to discover that they are one after all.

Jesus made this prediction concerning His sheep, 'They will become one flock with one shepherd.'[15] Also in that great prayer just before the cross He asked the Father that all His people may be one, just as He was one with the Father.[16] God is remembering that prayer. It will yet be fully answered. Let us not hinder this by sectarianism, exclusivism, or by any other sectional interest. Instead, let this goal of true spiritual unity be as dear to our hearts as it is to His.

[1] Mat. 16. 16–18   [2] Mat. 18. 16–17   [3] Mat. 18. 20
[4] Heb. 10. 25   [5] Exod. 37. 10–28   [6] Acts 20. 28
[7] Acts 2. 42 RSV   [8] Rev. 8. 4   [9] 1 Cor. 14. 26   [10] 1 Pet. 2. 5   [11] Mat. 5. 13–14   [12] Acts 2. 47   [13] Eph. 4. 3
[14] Acts 2. 46; 3. 1   [15] John 10. 16   [16] John 17. 11, 21–23

11

AN IMPORTANT COMMAND

MUCH of a soldier's life is taken up with receiving commands and obeying them. As soon as God had saved His people out of Egypt He taught them that obedience was the price of His continued protection and blessing.[1] I am now going to speak about an important command that is closely connected with the teaching just given on the local church. It is the command to eat bread and drink wine in remembrance of Christ.

Baptism in water and the Communion are the two great ordinances of the church. An ordinance is a statute or decree, and these two were given by the Head of the church Himself. This ordinance is variously called the Communion, the Sacrament, the Eucharist, the Lord's Supper, or the Breaking of Bread. It was foreshadowed in the Old Testament by the Jewish Passover.

The homes of the Israelites in Egypt had been delivered from the destroying angel by each household killing a lamb and sprinkling its blood on the doorposts of each home. God had said, 'When I see the blood I will pass over you.' The lamb was then roasted and eaten. From then on the Passover was celebrated annually at God's command, 'as an ordinance for ever'.[2] It was on Passover night centuries later that Jesus, in the company of the Twelve, instituted this memorial Supper to remind them of their Master who was so very soon to become the true Passover lamb, shedding His blood for their salvation.

All that the New Testament tells us about this ordinance is confined to its institution as recorded in the first three Gospels,[3] two passages in the Acts,[4] and two in 1 Corinthians.[5] It is interesting to compare the two ordinances. Both point to the heart of the Christian faith, Christ's death on the cross and our union with Him. Baptism, however, is a rite of initiation, and so does not need to be repeated. The Communion on the other hand, like the Passover, was to be repeated again and again—'as often as you eat this bread and drink the cup.'[6]

When the Lord took the bread He said, 'This is My body.' When He took the cup He said, 'This is My blood.' We are not to understand by this that anything magical or mystical took place in the elements, any more than any change took place in His body when He said, 'I am the door' or 'I am the vine.' He was using symbolism, and referring to unseen spiritual realities. This is another feature of an ordinance, it is a kind of enacted parable that uses the outward material thing to signify what is inward and spiritual.

We must not assume that our Lord's words referred only to His death. He did not say, 'This do in remembrance of My death,' but 'in remembrance of Me.' He knew that when the time came for them to do it He would no longer be dead, but very much alive. The Supper speaks of the results of His death as well as the death itself. For example, the bread not only symbolises His physical body, but His spiritual body, of which we are all members.[7] The cup not only speaks of His blood shed for us, but of the resultant life which is now within that spiritual body, 'For the life of the flesh is in the blood.'[8]

Breaking bread is an act of *commemoration*. The emphasis on remembrance is very strong. In asking His disciples to do this Jesus is saying, 'I want this meal to remind you of Me, and of all that I did for you.' We tend to forget so quickly. When, as all too often happens, I have to leave home for a while, I like to take with me a photo of my wife. But when I return home I don't worry much about the photo. Why should I, when I have the real thing? The Bible tells us that we are only required to obey this command 'until the Lord comes'[6] referring to Christ's personal return. When we see Him face to face we shall no longer need this reminder.

Breaking bread is also an act of *confession*. Here again it is very similar to baptism. Paul reminds us, 'as often as you eat this bread and drink the cup, you proclaim the Lord's death.'[6] It is not uncommon for an unbeliever witnessing the Communion service to find Christ, and the believer to receive a fresh vision of the cross.

Finally, breaking of bread is an act of *communion*. Paul tells us that the bread and the cup are 'the communion' of the body and blood of Christ.[9] In the passover it was not enough for the Israelite to slay the lamb and sprinkle its blood on the doorway, the lamb had then to be eaten, roasted with fire. In instituting this memorial Supper Jesus did not say, 'Look at the bread and cup on the table, in remembrance of Me.' He told us to *eat* and to *drink*.

Earlier in His ministry Our Lord had said that those who ate His flesh and drank His blood had eternal life.[10] 'But,' someone will say, 'I thought it was receiving Christ by faith that gave us eternal life, not taking Communion.' True. But receiving Christ is but the first act of feeding on Christ. By this I mean, assimilating into one's spiritual being His life and virtue, just as eating food means receiving its strengthening and nourishment. This is but the beginning of a life of communion. And the Communion service is intended to stimulate us 'to feed on Him in our hearts by faith',[11] not just as we partake of the elements, but continually. That's why the service is so much more than a remembrance of His death.

It is worth noting that this simple yet beautiful ordinance was instituted by Jesus in a private home, on a weeknight, and in connection with a social meal. It is a pity that its simplicity has so often been obscured by ritual and tradition. How often should we break bread? Here again, man has made rules where the Holy Spirit has made none. After Pentecost it would seem that the Christians broke bread every day; later on probably less frequently. All that Jesus said was, 'As often as you eat . . . and drink'[6] leaving the frequency an open question. Circumstances, and the mutual desire to do this will vary from church to church. Scripture, however, says nothing about a special time or place or official leader being required before the ordinance may be kept.

Though there is much joy and blessing in obeying this command of Christ, a word of warning is needed. It is possible to partake of this Supper 'in an improper manner'.[12] This is liable to bring the Lord's judgment upon the person concerned. Because of serious division among the Corinthians and misbehaviour at the Lord's table, some in the church had been afflicted with weakness and sickness, and some had died. Carelessness here may expose Christ's soldier to enemy attack. Before partaking of the elements 'Everyone should examine himself'[13] to see that his conscience is without offence toward God and man. If things are not right it is much better to refrain from partaking until they are put right.

Jesus said, 'If you love Me you will obey My commandments.'[14] Let us see to it that we are found regularly at His table, with pure hearts overflowing with praise and gratitude. In this way we shall be following in the steps of those first Christians who 'devoted themselves . . . to the breaking of bread'.[15]

[1] Exod. 15. 26   [2] Exod. 12. 14   [3] Mat. 26. 26–29; Mark 14. 22–25; Luke 22. 14–20   [4] Acts 2. 42, 46; 20. 7   [5] 1 Cor. 10. 16–17; 11. 20–34   [6] 1 Cor. 11. 26 RSV   [7] 1 Cor. 10. 17   [8] Lev. 17. 11   [9] 1 Cor. 10. 16–17 AV   [10] John 6. 53–54   [11] Communion Service, Book of Common Prayer   [12] 1 Cor. 11. 27   [13] 1 Cor. 11. 28   [14] John 14 . 15   [15] Acts 2. 42 RSV

12

KNOW YOUR ENEMY

An army will make use of all possible means to obtain information about the enemy and his tactics. The Christian soldier, however, has an infallible handbook that will tell him all that he needs to know. From the Bible we learn that our enemy is threefold— the world, the flesh, and the devil. The world is the *external* enemy, the flesh is the *internal* enemy, and the devil is the *infernal* enemy! By 'the world' is meant the anti-God system that dominates mankind. By 'the flesh' is meant our fallen nature with its sinful tendencies. By 'the devil' is meant one who is not only evil, but the originator of evil. Of course, these three are very closely related in their working, as we learn from Ephesians 2. 2–3. But in this chapter I shall be concentrating on our arch-enemy, the devil.

One result of becoming a child of God is that the invisible and spiritual world, that hardly existed for us before, becomes real. The unbeliever, on the other hand, is dominated in his thinking by the material world. But the unseen world does not simply consist of God and His angels, it includes a rebel kingdom, with someone called Satan as its ruler. This is not fancy but fact.

Is it not rather old-fashioned to believe in the existence of a personal devil? Very!—as old-fashioned as the Bible itself. It commences, 'In the beginning God'—without stopping to explain Him or prove His existence. In the same way the Book introduces Satan, a personality standing in opposition to God, without explaining his origin, though clues are scattered throughout the record.

I believe in the existence of a personal devil *because my reason tells me so*. You cannot have spiritual power without spiritual personality. That force of good in the world which transforms and ennobles, implies the existence of a spiritual Being who is good. Similarly, that force of evil in the world which corrupts and destroys, implies the existence of a spiritual being who is evil.

I believe in the existence of a personal devil *because my experience tells me so*. Who has not known a sudden and inexplicable urge to do wrong that passed off as it was resisted? Also in dealing with those who have opened their lives to occult powers, I have been made aware of a powerful evil presence that could not be explained in human terms.

I believe in the existence of a personal devil *because Jesus did*. He had good reason. At the outset of His public ministry He was tempted by the devil for forty days, ending with a face to face encounter.[1] It is here that the usual arguments against a personal devil break down. Jesus was alone in the wilderness, away from other human beings, so He

75

could hardly have been tempted by the world. Nor had He a sinful nature, so He could not have been tempted from within. How then was He tempted, unless by some personality outside Himself?

I believe in the existence of a personal devil *because to deny this makes nonsense of almost all the references to him in the Bible.* If there is no devil then what is this spiritual conflict that runs through Scripture all about? Who are we fighting? Not our fellow human beings. The Bible says they have been blinded by Satan.[2] Perhaps that's why so many of them don't believe he exists! 'We are *not* fighting against human beings,' declares Paul, 'but against the wicked spiritual forces in the heavenly world'[3] under the leadership of the devil. When it comes to the invisible world it is safer to trust divine revelation than human reason.

As to Satan's origin, it appears that he was created by God with the rest of the angelic host. He was 'full of wisdom and perfect in beauty'. He was evidently blameless in His ways until he rebelled. Eminent among the angels of God, he wanted to be pre-eminent. Pride in his beauty, avarice, and a desire to usurp the position of God Himself, are the causes given for his downfall. He was ejected from heaven.[4] Jesus said He saw him fall like lightning.[6] A considerable number of the angelic host was involved in his rebellion and also cast out. These fallen angels are the hierarchy of evil against which we fight.[3] Beneath them again are the demon powers that strive to take possession of human beings. Satan is spoken of as the prince or ruler of demons.[5]

Satan, then, is a created and hence a finite being. He is *not* all-powerful, all-knowing, nor personally omnipresent, although his influence is felt everywhere since his evil agents encircle the globe. He is under God's authority and can only act with God's permission.[7] We have already seen in the case of Job how God may overrule Satan's work for our good. No doubt this is one reason why he is still around.

The names and titles of our enemy reveal his character. *Satan* means adversary. He sets himself in opposition to all that is of God. *Devil* means Accuser, accusing God's people before God day and night.[8] The story of Job is a perfect example of this. Then *Abaddon* and *Apollyon* mean destroyer.[9] He is dedicated to the destruction of God's work. Three descriptive names tell us more. Because of his cunning he is called the *serpent*.[8] In his ability to intimidate he is like a *roaring lion*[10] hunting for prey. Finally we see him as *the dragon*,[8] a ferocious winged monster, with supernatural powers. He is called the wicked one, the tempter, the thief, the liar, and the murderer. Surely the personification of all evil.

Three titles reveal his present position in relation to this world. Jesus called him *the ruler of this world*.[11] It was no empty boast when he offered Jesus all the kingdoms of the world if He would fall down and worship him. He is called *the prince or ruler of the power of the air*,[12] so that his sphere of operations is the heavens that envelop this earth. Lastly, he is *the god of this world*.[13] It has ever been his evil intention to seduce men to worship him instead of God. No wonder John says, 'the whole world is in the power of the evil one.'[14]

This battle between God and Satan is the conflict of history. The cross of Christ is 'the climax of history'.[15] It was there that Satan was decisively beaten. On the eve of that stupendous victory Jesus said, 'Now the ruler of this world will be overthrown.' And so he was. His authority was destroyed, and final victory guaranteed.[16] The cross is the only basis on which the soldier of Christ is able to resist Satan and stand victorious on the field of battle. Does it seem that our enemy, despite the victory of Christ, is still having immense success? The fact remains that the high court of heaven has passed sentence. His ultimate doom is assured. Meanwhile God gives him plenty of rope. But the day is coming when the sentence will be executed, and the devil and his angels will be cast into the lake of fire.[17] But for the moment he is a force to be reckoned with. In the next chapter I want to speak about his tactics.

[1] Mat. 4. 1–11   [2] 2 Cor. 4. 4   [3] Eph. 6. 11–12   [4] Isa. 14. 12–15; Ezek. 28. 11–17   [5] Mat. 12. 24   [6] Luke 10. 18   [7] Job 1 . 12; 2. 6   [8] Rev. 12. 9–10   [9] Rev. 9. 11   [10] 1 Pet. 5. 8   [11] John 12. 31; 14. 30; 16. 11   [12] Eph. 2 . 2 RSV   [13] 2 Cor. 4. 4   [14] 1 John 5. 19 RSV   [15] Heb. 9. 26 NEB   [16] Heb. 2. 14   [17] Rev. 20. 10

13

ENEMY TACTICS

THOUGH himself invisible, Satan has left his foot-
prints on the sands of history for all discerning eyes
to see. The subject is vast, so that we shall only deal
here with the two great examples of his tactics in
Scripture. These will help us to identify the tempter's
trail. The rest the Holy Spirit will teach us through
Scripture and experience.

Satan's first appearance in human history is recorded in Genesis 3. 1–7. He came in the guise of a
serpent to tempt our first parents, and we are told
that he was 'more subtle' than any other of God's
creatures. There are three instructive words in the
New Testament that refer to this characteristic of
Satan. It speaks of his '*plans*'[1] (designs RSV). He is a
clever strategist with thousands of years of experience.
He lays his plans carefully and pursues them with
relentless determination. Then it speaks of his
'*tricks*'[2] (wiles RSV). This warns us of his cunning,
stealth, and power to deceive. It speaks too of his
'*trap*'[3] (snare RSV), the method by which the un-
wary are lured and taken.

When Satan tempted the first pair in the garden,
he chose a flank attack rather than a frontal assault.

He attacked the man through the woman. Adam was not deceived by the serpent, but Eve was.[4] The serpent then used the woman to tempt the man. The enemy will often attack us indirectly through those who are closest to us, especially if the relationship is not wholly yielded to God.

Notice the subtlety of Satan's approach to the woman. 'Did God say, "You shall not eat of every tree of the garden?"' The answer was, 'No' for only the one tree had been forbidden. But the question was calculated to create doubt and confusion, the 'softening up' process before the main strike. Though Eve parried the thrust, it was followed by another that penetrated her defences. 'You will not die. For God knows that when you eat of it your eyes will be opened, and you will be like God, knowing good and evil.'

This was intended to blacken God's character, suggesting that God had lied to them in telling them they would die, and that His motive in doing so was to deny them what would be for their advancement. The woman was also being lured with the bait of self-interest. The fire of unholy ambition—to be like God—was kindling within her. This was how Satan himself had fallen, and now he is seeding that same rebellion in the woman's heart. Having undermined God's authority he is encouraging her to assert her own.

Eve began to contemplate the forbidden fruit. She saw it was 'good for food'. Temptation often comes through our bodily appetites. She saw it was 'a delight to the eyes'. Through eyegate—the word that is read or the picture that is seen—Satan is still capturing the minds of men. Finally, she was convinced that it was a tree 'to be desired to make one wise'. This was a temptation to pride. This wisdom was not the sort that comes down from heaven, but what is 'earthly, unspiritual, devilish'.[5] John might have been summarising this temptation in the garden when he said, 'For all that is in the world, the lust of the flesh and the lust of the eyes and the pride of life, is not of the Father but is of the world.'[6] So Eve took the forbidden fruit and shared it with her husband. Round One to Satan.

Four thousand years later Christ, 'the last Adam',[7] was also tempted to eat. This was not in Eden but in the wilderness. Nor had He a body well nourished by the produce of a garden, but one gripped by intense hunger after forty days of fasting. Where Adam fell Christ triumphed. Read the account in Matthew 4. 1–11.[8] 'If you are God's Son, order these stones to turn into bread.' No doubt our Lord was conscious of those supernatural powers, as yet unused, stirring within Him. Had they not been given to prove that He was truly the Son of God? Could He not now use them to vindicate Himself before the eyes of the unseen world, and at the same time to satisfy His intense but quite legitimate hunger?

But Jesus knew it was the Father's business to vindicate His Servant. The Spirit of God had led

Him into the desert where there was no food. He gladly accepted the situation, hunger and all, as part of heaven's plan. Those supernatural powers had been given Him, not to escape from the will of God, but to do the will of God. He would not use them at the suggestion of the devil, but only at the Father's direction.

'Man cannot live on bread alone, but on every word that God speaks.' How right were His priorities. The spiritual took precedence over the material, pleasing the Father over pleasing Himself. As He later expressed it, 'My food . . . is to obey the will of Him who sent Me.'[9] Satan had invited Him to vindicate Himself. Instead He had vindicated the will of God His Father.

Again the devil attacked. Taking Jesus to the Holy City he set Him on the highest point of the Temple and said, 'If you are God's Son throw yourself down to the ground,' backing up the point with a Scripture that promised angelic protection. Satan is good at quoting and misapplying scripture to suit his own ends. Now Jesus was being tempted to vindicate Himself before the eyes of men.

The Jews were mistakenly looking for one who would set them free from the Roman yoke. If He now made a supernatural descent into the midst of the temple worshippers, would they not acclaim Him as the Son of God? Would they not believe that the ancient prophecy of Malachi was being fulfilled: 'The Lord whom you seek will suddenly come to

His temple?'[10] What a dramatic commencement to His ministry!

Jesus perceived at once the evil that lay at the root of Satan's suggestion. To act in a way that would require God to intervene for His Son's protection would be to tempt providence, and again to act in independence of God. It is sinful to try to force God's hand. 'You must not put the Lord your God to the test,' quoted Jesus. To have flung Himself down would not have been an act of faith, but of presumption. It is wrong to wrest the initiative from God.

Finally, from a very high mountain the devil showed Jesus all the kingdoms of the world and their greatness. 'All this I will give you . . . if you kneel down and worship me.' Satan asserted that he had authority to make the offer,[11] and Jesus never questioned this. In fact He later referred to him as 'the ruler of this world'.[12]

Jesus knew that one day those kingdoms would be His, for the Father had promised Him this.[13] But now the rebel ruler was offering Him this on the cheap. No rejection, no suffering, no crucifixion. It was the crown without the cross, but on Satan's terms—'if you kneel down and worship me'—in other words, 'If you acknowledge me as God.' This is Satan's one passion, to be acclaimed as God. Jesus finally repulsed Satan by quoting, 'Worship the Lord your God and serve only Him.'

As with the first pair, Satan tempted Jesus to act

contrary to God's will for personal advantage. Jesus met each temptation as a man, wielded the sword of the Spirit which is God's word, and vanquished the enemy.

Remember Satan is a spirit and so his working is supernatural. Notice how he transported Christ to the pinnacle of the temple and to the high mountain, and then showed Him the world in the flash of a second. Because something is supernatural is no proof that it is of God. Satan tries to counterfeit everything that God does. That's why we are told to 'test the spirits'.[14] 'Even Satan can change himself to look like an angel of light!'[15]

The supernatural realm that Satan operates we call 'the occult'. It includes all forms of spiritism, magic (black or white), fortune telling, astrology, horoscopes, ouija etc. Steer completely clear of all these. Real powers are operating, but they are evil and plainly forbidden.[16] Other things like hypnotism, clairvoyance, colour therapy etc. may not necessarily be occult, but may very easily become so, and one is wise to leave them completely alone. If you have dabbled in any of these before you became a Christian, even in fun, it is important that you confess this to the Lord, and in Jesus' name claim deliverance from any 'brush off' which could affect spirit, mind, or body.

Finally, try not to see Satan any bigger or smaller than you see him in the Scripture. Some Christians seem to have a very big Satan and a very small Jesus.

This ends up in a bondage of fear. Others have so minimised his influence that they are blind to much of his activity, and so play into his hands. Just as every ship is built to float and every plane to fly, so every Christian has been created to overcome Satan and all his works.

[1] 2 Cor. 2. 11   [2] Eph. 6. 11   [3] 1 Tim. 3. 7; 2 Tim. 2. 26
[4] 1 Tim. 2. 14   [5] Jam. 3. 15 RSV   [6] 1 John 2. 16 RSV
[7] 1 Cor. 15. 45   [8] See also Luke 4. 1–13   [9] John 4. 34
[10] Mal. 3. 1   [11] Luke 4. 6   [12] John 12. 31   [13] Heb. 1.
2; Rev. 11. 15   [14] 1 John 4. 1 RSV   [15] 2. Cor. 11. 14
[16] Lev. 19. 26, 31; Deut. 18. 10–14; Acts 16. 16–19; 2 Thess. 2.
9–11

14

DEFENSIVE WARFARE

CONTINUOUS victory depends on learning the secrets
of defensive warfare. God can never use us to attack
the enemy's position until we have first learned to
defend our own. What is our position? It is summed
up in that little expression, 'in Christ'. By this is
meant our union with Christ and all the blessing that
results from that union. Look at the epistle to the
Ephesians. In the first chapter we learn of our blessings in Christ in the heavenly world,[1] and in the last
chapter of our battles.[2] The blessings are to fit us for
the battles.

We have already seen something of our union with
Christ in His death, burial, and resurrection, as
signified by water baptism. Now we must see in
Ephesians our union with Christ in His ascension.[3]
The power at work in us is the very same as that
which raised Christ from the dead, and seated Him
at the Father's right hand. Every power in the universe is now beneath His feet,[4] and so beneath our
feet too since we are in Him. This is the position of
victory that Christ has won for us.

God has '*made* us sit with Him'.[5] We didn't climb

up there by our own efforts, He put us there. Read Ephesians 1. 16–2. 7 and ask God to show you how you can have your feet on terra firma and yet spiritually be seated with Christ in that heavenly realm. It is not enough to grasp it with the mind, you must believe it in your heart. The effect in your Christian life will be far-reaching. Instead of fighting *for* a position of victory you will be fighting *from* a position of victory. What a difference when we are looking down on the enemy, as Christ is, instead of looking up at him.

The warfare of Ephesians 6. 10–17 which we shall consider in this chapter is primarily a holding operation. The armour is all defensive; it is to enable you to 'stand up against . . . resist . . . hold your ground'.[6] In this battle it is the devil that has to do the attacking. For complete victory you have only to defend what Christ has won.

Before we don the armour Paul tells us, 'Build up your strength in union with the Lord.'[7] Try lifting a suit of armour and you will know what Paul is talking about! In himself the Christian is as weak spiritually as any other man. He must confess his weakness continually and by faith draw his strength from the Lord.

What then is the armour, viewed as a whole? Elsewhere we are told, 'Put on the Lord Jesus Christ.'[8] In a word, the armour is Christ. This accords with Old Testament teaching where the Lord is ever His people's defence. 'The Lord is my rock, and my fortress, and my deliverer . . . in whom I take refuge, my shield . . . my stronghold.'[9] Considered in detail, the armour is the varied protection we have in Christ. By faith we must take it piece by piece. Twice Paul instructs us to use 'the *whole* armour of God'.[10] The devil is no fool. He will attack where we are unprotected.

In studying the armour, I shall quote from the RSV. The first three are basic pieces to be put on *in preparation* for the battle. Notice the past tense: 'Stand therefore, *having girded . . . having put on . . . having shod*.' Then the tense changes: '*taking* the shield . . . *take* the helmet . . . and the sword.' These may be seized and used in the moment of battle. Another writer has put it very aptly: 'A soldier is sitting in his tent and he is waiting for the battle call. He has on his belt, his breastplate and his boots; and suddenly the bugle blows. He picks up his shield, he puts on his helmet, he grasps his sword—and he is ready for battle!'[11]

The girdle is rather different from the belt of the modern soldier. The oriental wore a long robe. Girding the loins signifies gathering it at the waist with a girdle. It was loosened for rest and tightened for action. If a soldier was not girded he would certainly be impeded, and most probably tripped, in the battle. In naval language it means 'clearing the decks for action'.

To express this in practical terms, we must deal with every encumbrance that would hinder us in the fight. In another passage a similar thought is expressed when the Christian life is likened to a marathon: 'Let us rid ourselves, then, of everything that gets in the way, and the sin which holds on to us so tightly, and let us run with determination the race.'[12] 'Everything that gets in the way' may include things which are not in themselves sinful. 'All things are lawful for me,' says Paul, 'but not all things are helpful.'[13] It may not be against the rules for an Olympic miler to wear a heavy overcoat, but it certainly wouldn't be helpful! There may be habits, ambitions, pastimes, attitudes, and so on, that may be alright for the Christian 'civilian' (a contradiction in terms) but not for the Christian soldier.

We are to gird our loins with *truth*. Jesus said 'the truth will make you free;' and again, 'the Son makes you free.'[14] *He* then is the truth. *He* is the girdle. Don't wait for the dust and din of battle before you deal with those hindering things. Come in faith to the Son and let Him free you now.

Next is *the breastplate of righteousness*. The breast suggests our affections, emotions, and desires. Remember how the enemy darts penetrated first Eve's heart, stirring up unholy desires, and then Adam's. One of Solomon's wisest sayings was, 'Keep [i.e. guard] your heart with all vigilance; for from it flow the springs of life.'[15] Solomon would have been wiser still had he practised what he preached! He 'clung . . . in love' to many foreign women who turned away his heart from God and led him into idolatry.[16] He became a casualty through neglecting the breastplate.

The breastplate is righteousness, and Christ is our righteousness.[17] The moment we believed, the righteousness of Christ was paid into our heavenly account which was 'in the red' to the tune of thousands. Of course this radically altered our standing in heaven. But now we have to learn to use the cheque book of faith and live on these heavenly resources. This is practical righteousness. This means trusting Christ for grace to think right and act right, especially in our relationships with our fellow men.

The third piece of basic equipment is our *gospel sandals*. 'Having shod your feet with the equipment of the gospel of peace.' There is of course a place for aggressive witness, but the sandals, like the rest of the equipment, are to enable us to stand, not to march. The older versions have, 'the *preparation* of the gospel of peace', again something which is put on *before* the battle. What soldier would want to be caught by the enemy with his boots off?

The gospel sandals which enable the soldier to hold his ground refer, no doubt, to 'the defence and confirmation of the gospel'.[18] This will become increasingly important in the warfare of the end-time. Stephen was well shod when he made his great defence before the Council. Christ had warned His followers they would have to stand before rulers to bear witness. Writing to persecuted Christians Peter says, 'Be ready at all times to answer anyone who asks you to explain the hope you have in you.'[19] In other words, 'Be ready with your boots on.'

The Acts of the Apostles teaches us that to preach the gospel is to preach Christ. He is the gospel. A young friend asked my advice on how to handle some Jehovah Witnesses who were coming round for a talk. I said, 'Don't argue about doctrine, but preach Christ. Testify to what He has done for you.' Standing in these wonderful sandals we will never be moved from the faith of the gospel.

Now for the last three pieces, that we can seize and use in the moment of emergency. 'Above all taking *the shield of faith*.' 'Above all' because the shield is the large variety affording protection to the whole body, ideal for defensive warfare. When soldiers stand with these, shoulder to shoulder, they present an impenetrable wall. David often said that the Lord was his shield, but Paul says that faith is our shield. He becomes our shield as we exercise faith, but it must be faith in *Him*.

'With which you can quench all the flaming darts of the evil one.' If only our first parents had stood firm in their faith in God's love and wisdom, those flaming darts that ignited their unholy desires would have been put out at once. When later Christ was attacked with these they were immediately quenched, enabling Him to wield the sword with devastating effect. 'Do not throw away your confidence.'[20] Often the devil will use adverse circumstances to tempt us to abandon our shield. It was so with Peter when he denied His Lord. Jesus said, 'I have prayed for you that your *faith* may not fail.'

It is practically impossible to hold up one of these body shields and look down. To hold up the shield means to 'keep our eyes fixed on Jesus'.[21] Remember Peter walking on the water? When his eyes were on Jesus his faith was invincible. But when he looked at his circumstances the shield was lowered and swift came the darts of doubt and fear.

Increasingly is the mind of the believer becoming a battle-ground. Hence the importance of '*the helmet of salvation*'. We can say with David, 'The Lord is . . . my salvation.' He is the helmet. Salvation may be expressed in three tenses:

Past Tense: I have been saved from the *penalty* of sin.

Present Tense: I am being saved from the *power* of sin.

Future Tense: I will be saved from the *presence* of sin. The devil's attacks on the mind also come along these three lines. Even though our sins have been confessed and forgiven, he will try to attack us on our past record, and bring us into condemnation. Put on the helmet. 'There is no condemnation now for those who live in union with Christ Jesus . . . Who will accuse God's chosen people? God Himself declares them not guilty!'[22]

With others it is more the present relationships of life, the pressures and the problems that adversely affect their thought life. They are tempted to give way to bitter, jealous, proud or impure thoughts. There is complete deliverance and protection from all of these in the salvation of Christ.[23] As to the future, so many are haunted by fears of the unknown tomorrow, their health, their jobs, their finances, their families. The thought of nuclear war fills them with dread. They are afraid of death. What a need for the helmet of salvation. I *shall be* saved. Jesus is coming back to reign. My future is in His hands and He does all things well. Elsewhere Paul refers to the helmet as 'our hope of salvation'.[24] Only the Christian has justification for being an optimist. But more of this in the closing chapter.

Finally, we are to take '*the sword of the Spirit* which is the word of God'. Here again the sword is defensive, to enable us to stand. Some say that 'the sword' is the Bible, yet there are many Christians who hold the Bible in their hands and even store it in their minds, who have never used this sword. 'Word' here means *utterance*. 'The sword of the spirit which is the utterance that comes from God.' To wield the sword we must *speak* to Satan, and say in faith as Jesus did, 'It is written.' This will compel him to leave.

As with each other part of the soldier's equipment, the sword refers to Christ. He is 'the word of God'. There is great power in declaring His name, His character, His victory. You will find the scriptures in the appendix on 'Our Authority over Satan' will help. They are worth memorising. But remember it is the Spirit's sword. There is nothing magical in the

93

words. But when the Spirit inspires them they will be effective.

In this armour God has made provision for our complete protection. Clad in it the enemy will not be able to touch us. He may make repeated attacks but he will never move us from our position of victory in Christ. And then, great will be our joy, 'having fought to the end, to remain victors on the field.'[25]

---

[1] Eph. 1. 3   [2] Eph. 6. 12   [3] Eph. 2. 4–6   [4] Eph. 1. 19–21
[5] Eph. 2. 6 RSV   [6] Eph. 6. 11, 13   [7] verse 10   [8] Rom.
13. 14 RSV   [9] Psa. 18. 2   [10] verses 11, 13   [11] *God's Freedom Fighters* by David C. K. Watson (p. 76)   [12] Heb. 12. 1
[13] 1 Cor. 6. 12 RSV   [14] John 8. 32, 36   [15] Prov. 4. 23
[16] 1 Kings 11. 1–4   [17] 1 Cor. 1. 30 RSV   [18] Phil. 1. 7
RSV   [19] 1 Pet. 3. 15   [20] Heb. 10. 35 RSV   [21] Heb.
12. 2   [22] Rom. 8. 1, 33   [23] Eph. 4. 22–24   [24] 1 Thess.
5. 8   [25] verse 13 Weymouth's Translation

15

ENTANGLEMENTS

A SOLDIER's life calls for great dedication. He cannot get deeply involved in outside interests and at the same time be an effective soldier. Paul puts it this way: 'A soldier in active service wants to please his commanding officer, and so does not get mixed up (entangled RSV) in the affairs of civilian life.'[1] The world in which we are called to serve Christ is full of entanglements. Many promising soldiers of Christ have become ineffective or have even deserted through the lure of the world. Paul recounted with great sadness, 'Demas fell in love with this present world and has deserted me.'[2]

In the parable of the Sower, Jesus warned us of some of these dangers. The thorns that choked the good seed He interpreted as being 'the worries about this life, the love for riches, and all other kinds of desires'.[3] In James's view, for one united to Christ to court the friendship of the world is to commit spiritual adultery.[4] According to John, to have in your heart the love of the world is to be devoid of the love of the Father.[5]

Let us look at these worries, riches, and desires of which Jesus spoke. Take note that worrying is a form of worldliness, for Jesus classed it with the love of money and worldly pleasure. The root of worrying is unbelief. Is not a soldier's food, clothing and every other necessity the responsibility of his commander? 'So do not start worrying: "Where will my food come from? or my drink? or my clothes?" (These are the things the heathen are always after.) Your Father in heaven knows that you need all these things.'

Then there is 'the love for riches' which Paul said was 'a source of all kinds of evil'.[7] Money is not evil in itself since we need it to live. It is when it gets into our hearts that the trouble begins. Men do not love money for itself, but for the power, influence and prestige that it brings, and the material things it will procure. Greed for money lies behind much political activity and most industrial unrest. It is a powerful weapon in the hands of Satan.

The man of the world looks upon earthly treasure as his security. But Jesus showed how insecure this was. Earthly treasure could be ruined—'moths and rust destroy'. It could be removed—'robbers break in and steal'. You could be taken from it—'You fool! This very night you will have to give up your life; then who will get all these things . . .?'[8] No wonder the Bible speaks of riches as 'an uncertain thing'.[9]

How are we to safeguard ourselves against this snare of the devil? First we are to resist the spirit of the age that is always greedy for more, and to cultivate a spirit of contentment. 'Keep your lives free from the love of money, and be satisfied with what you have.'[10] Then, we are to recognize that the money that God permits us to handle is a sacred trust. We are not to be mean, selfish, or extravagant. We are to give generously—to the work of God and the servants of God and the needy—as the Lord prospers and directs us. The Israelite gave a 'tithe' (tenth) of his income to God as a basic minimum. The New Testament Christian certainly should not give less. 'God loves the one who gives gladly.'[11]

Finally, instead of placing our 'hope' on riches, we are to place it 'on God, who generously gives us everything for us to enjoy'.[9] This is true security for He has promised to take care of all the needs of His children. What a privilege to trust such a rich and generous Heavenly Father.

The third entanglement Jesus mentioned was 'all other kinds of desires'. A great variety of things may come under this category. Like riches, many of them will not be sinful in themselves, but become an entanglement because of the place that is given to them in the heart and life. The thorns 'choked' the good seed. If a desire is arresting my spiritual growth then let me free myself from it, even if this means taking drastic action.

In Luke's account of this parable, these 'desires' are referred to as the 'pleasures of life'.[12] Though we live in a pleasure-mad world, we should not assume that 'pleasure' is necessarily a dirty word. Very many who make no profession of faith look upon Christianity as going to church on the one hand, and giving up all pleasures on the other. How boring!

In certain Christian circles worldliness has almost been reduced to a set of 'Thou shalt nots'. This living by a legal code is a snare into which the Pharisees fell. It led them to emphasise the wrong thing and to make a wrong judgment of others. They even accused our Lord of being a worldling. 'Look at this man!' they cried, 'He is a glutton and wine-drinker, and a friend of tax collectors and outcasts.'[13] It led to inconsistency, taking pride in the scrupulous observance of what was incidental, while neglecting the things that really mattered. Christ called them 'Blind guides!' adding, with a touch of ironic humour, 'You strain a fly out of your drink, but swallow a camel!'[14]

No, following Christ will never 'cramp our style'. Not only does God give all things generously for our enjoyment, but promises to withhold 'no good thing' if we walk uprightly.[15] It is the devil's lie, often sustained by the wrong attitude of believers, that Christianity is a 'kill-joy' affair, and 'goodbye' to a full and satisfying life. The very reverse is the truth. We have been called to a life of liberty, not restriction. The Lord denies us nothing, except that which would injure us, or maybe others.

Though the soldier of Christ is not to be entangled by the world, nor is he to be isolated from it. Separation to Christ and His cause does not mean seclusion. Christ told us to be 'salt', that is, to be His preservative in a decaying society. You cannot preserve fish by putting the fish in one barrel and the salt in another! Nor can we segregate ourselves, and at the same time permeate and preserve society. Jesus was rightly called 'the friend of sinners', and yet in His spirit and standard He was always a Man apart. He never compromised His convictions. We are called to be like Him.

There are no set rules in Scripture on these matters, only guiding principles. It is important that we apply these carefully, and so avoid being entangled. They will enable us to decide for ourselves many other doubtful matters. But God's word is very clear—we are not to judge others who decide differently.[16] Speaking of 'doubtful things' Paul says, 'Nothing is unclean of itself'.[17] What may be wrong for one may be right for another. What may be wrong for me in this set of circumstances may be right in that. These are the questions I need to ask:

Can I do this with a clear conscience and a heart at peace? 'Happy is the man who does not feel himself condemned when he does what he approves of!'[18]

Can I enter into it wholeheartedly? 'Whatever your hand finds to do, do it with your might.'[19]

Can I do this to the glory of God? 'Whatever you do, whether you eat or drink, do it all for God's glory.'[20]

Can I do this in Christ's name (i.e. as His representative)? 'Everything you do or say, then, should be done in the name of the Lord Jesus.'[21]

Can I kneel down and thank God for this thing? 'Everything you do or say, then, should be done . . . as you give thanks . . . to God the Father.'[21]

Will it be helpful to my spiritual life? '"All things are lawful" but not all things are helpful. "All things are lawful" but not all things build up.'[22]

Will it enslave me? 'I could say, "I am allowed to do anything"; but I am not going to let anything make a slave of me.'[23]

Will it endanger my health? 'Don't you know that your body is the temple of the Holy Spirit, who lives in you . . . Use your bodies for God's glory.'[24]

Will it minister to my fallen nature or lead me into temptation? 'Stop giving attention to your sinful nature, to satisfy its desires.'[25]

Is it in keeping with a proper stewardship of time and money? 'Look carefully then how you walk, not as unwise men but as wise, making the most of the time.'[26] 'The man to whom much is given, of him much is required.'[27]

Will it stumble my brother who may be weaker than I? 'Be careful, however, and do not let your freedom of action make those who are weak in the faith fall into sin.'[28]

Is it likely to be misunderstood? 'So do not let what is good to you be spoken of as evil . . . Let us then pursue what makes for peace and for mutual up-building.'[29]

Of course no one will ask all these questions every time, but as you imbibe the principles your conviction of what is right or wrong for you will most often be instinctive.

Susannah Wesley in a letter to her son Charles, later to become the gifted hymn writer, summarises much of what has been said:

Whatever dulls the sensitiveness of my spirit towards God, or takes the fine edge off my thought of Him—must be ruled out, for *He is my Lord.*

Whatever injures or weakens my body, or affects the mastery of it—must be ruled out, for *it is the temple of the Lord.*

Whatever adversely affects the clearness of my witness to Jesus Christ before others—must be ruled out, for it was *His parting wish that I should be a witness of Him.*

Whatever may cause my brother to stumble in his Christian life—must be ruled out, for *that would grieve Jesus.*

As Christ's soldiers let us be dedicated to Him and avoid being entangled.

---

[1] 2 Tim. 2. 4   [2] 2 Tim. 4. 10   [3] Mark 4. 19   [4] Jam. 4. 4 AV   [5] 1 John 2. 15   [6] Mat. 6. 31–32   [7] 1 Tim. 6. 10   [8] Mat. 6. 19; Luke 12. 20   [9] 1 Tim. 6. 17   [10] Heb. 13. 5; 1 Tim. 6. 6–9   [11] 2 Cor. 9. 7   [12] Luke 8. 14   [13] Luke 11. 19   [14] Mat. 23. 23–24   [15] Psa. 84. 11   [16] Rom. 4. 1–4, 10–13   [17] Rom. 4. 14   [18] Rom. 14. 22; Acts 24. 16; Col. 3. 15   [19] Eccl. 9. 10; Col. 3. 23   [20] 1 Cor. 10. 31   [21] Col. 3. 17   [22] 1 Cor. 10. 23 RSV   [23] 1 Cor. 6. 12   [24] 2 Cor. 6. 19–20   [25] Rom. 13. 14; Gal. 5. 13   [26] Eph. 5. 15–16 RSV   [27] Luke 12. 48   [28] 1 Cor. 8. 9; Rom. 15. 1–2   [29] Rom. 14. 16, 19 RSV

16

DISCIPLINE

IF discipline is weak, even the best equipped army is liable to crack when faced with hardship or adversity. Of course discipline is an unpopular word in a society where authority is being attacked and undermined. Here the attitude of the Christian soldier must stand out in sharpest contrast to the spirit of the age. We are called to be disciples, that is, disciplined men. This is a vital element in Christian soldiering.

It is a tremendous truth that we 'do not live under law but under God's grace'.[1] This is setting many free from a life of struggling and bringing them into victory. Trying to live the Christian life by rules and regulations only leads to defeat and frustration. 'Christ has set us free!' exclaims Paul, 'Stand, then, as free men, and do not allow yourselves to become slaves again.'[2] But we must not forget that he goes on to say, 'Do not let this freedom become an excuse for letting your physical desires rule you'.[3] When liberty leads to licence you end up with a worse kind of slavery. It's great to step on the accelerator, but if you don't know how to apply the brake you're heading for trouble! Liberty must be balanced by discipline.

A child needs to be disciplined by parents and teachers. But this is only to help him to discipline himself and so be fitted for responsibility. How can he control others if he has never learned to control himself? So it is self-discipline, or 'self-control'[4] to use the Bible word, which I want to emphasise in this chapter. This means firstly facing up to the temptations of the body.

Our bodies are only evil in so far as they are dominated by our fallen nature. Through grace we are freed from this dominion.[5] Then the body becomes an instrument to serve the plan of God. It is like a telephone by which the world communicates with us, and we with the world. This is why we are told to present our bodies to God[6] that Christ may be expressed through us.

The Creator has placed within us bodily desires, for food, for sleep, and for sex. Through 'the fall' these appetites, given for our enjoyment as well as the necessary preservation of life, have got out of hand. Very often they master us when we should master them. A hearty appetite degenerates into gluttony, a healthy desire for sleep into laziness, and normal sex desire, which God designed for marriage, into lust and licentiousness. Self-discipline means gaining the mastery over our appetites just as a colt has to be broken in. Paul puts it this way: 'I could say, "I am allowed to do anything"; but I am not going to let anything make a slave of me.'[7]

The seeking of sensual pleasure only proves the

truth of Jesus' words, 'Whoever drinks this water will get thirsty again'. But dissatisfaction and frustration are not the most serious consequences of throwing self-restraint to the winds. The door of the human personality is thus opened to evil spirits. Drug-taking has the same effect. 'A man without self-control is like a city broken into and left without walls.'[8]

Where a nation makes sensual pleasure its goal, as did ancient Rome, it is sowing the seeds of its own destruction. It is here the Christian soldier must fight for Christian standards. He is to be salt in a decaying society. But what if the salt has lost its taste? What if the Christian himself is enslaved to his own appetites? How can he fight the corruption around him? Vigilance will always be needed, for even great men have lapsed badly here. Noah is described as a blameless man who walked with God, and yet his son found him in his tent drunk and naked.[9]

Self-discipline, however, is not simply a question of overcoming the sins of the flesh. It enables the Christian to win the prize in the spiritual contest. 'Every athlete in training submits to strict discipline;' explains Paul, 'he does so in order to be crowned with a wreath that will not last; but we do it for one that will last for ever.'[10] If the athlete does not exercise self-discipline that 'extra' he needs in the race will not be there, and someone else will breast the tape first. Similarly, the soldier will be unable to endure suffering, to hold out in the day of adversity, and will win no decoration for his part in the battle.

So the matter is one of great importance if we have an eye for the coming day of reckoning and reward.

The disciplining of the mind is no less important than that of the body. Our minds are under constant bombardment by enemy propaganda. How easily the thought life becomes infected by pride, uncleanness, ambition, or jealousy. We are afflicted with wandering thoughts or we waste time in foolish daydreaming. The New Testament makes it quite clear that we are responsible to discipline our minds.

Peter writes to believers facing end-time persecutions and pressures—a message which will become increasingly relevant as the age draws to its close. He has some important things to say about the mind.[11] 'Have your minds ready for action,' or as the older versions have it, 'Gird up the loins of your mind'—a fitting word for the scatter-brained! Later he says, 'The end of all things is near. You must be self-controlled and alert [keep sane and sober RSV], to be able to pray.' Both words suggest a disciplined state of mind, not intoxicated by the spirit of the age. Paul is even more explicit. He says, 'We take every thought captive and make it obey Christ.'[12]

Closely associated with the mind are the emotions and affections. These too must be disciplined. In his Patmos vision John sees the glorified Son of Man 'with a golden girdle round his breast',[13] that is, His affections and emotions are controlled by His divine character. Though at times Jesus displayed deep emotion He was never carried away by His feelings. If we find ourselves overcome by excitement, fear, anger or resentment we need to take our emotions in hand. Paul reminded Timothy, 'God did not give us a spirit of timidity but of power and love and self-control.'[14]

Perhaps it is the tongue that calls for the greatest self-control of all. What irreparable damage has been done to the cause of Christ by criticism, gossip, slander, back-biting, misrepresentation, exaggeration, and many other activities of that small unruly member. James, who has most to say about this, insists that a man's religion is worthless if he hasn't learned to control his tongue, but that the man who never slips up here is perfect, and is able to control his whole body.[15] 'No man has ever been able to tame the tongue,'[16] declares James, and yet the tongue *must* be tamed. What is impossible to man is possible to God.

How is all this self-discipline to be accomplished? First we must recognise that it is not only needed but commanded of us as soldiers of Christ, therefore it must be possible. To assert otherwise would be to make God a tyrant. Second we must admit that we cannot do it ourselves. It is not dependent on our strength of will, so we are all in the same boat here.

Thirdly, there must be within us a God-given determination to take ourselves in hand with the strength that He gives. Discipleship means saying 'No!' to self by embracing the cross.[17] So many of us pamper when we ought to pummel. Paul says, 'I harden my body with blows and bring it under complete control.'[18] And again, 'Endure hardness, as a good soldier of Jesus Christ.'[19] Augustine spoke of having toward God a heart of flame, toward man a heart of love, and toward himself *a heart of steel*.

Finally, we must reckon on the fact of the cross, and of the indwelling Spirit. Look again at the opening of Romans 6. Remember what happened to us when Jesus died. Move on to chapter 8 and read Paul's triumphant declaration: 'The law of the Spirit, which brings us life in union with Christ Jesus, has set me free from the law of sin and death.'[20] Remember, 'self-control' (literally, 'inward strength') is not the fruit of our striving but 'the fruit of the Spirit'.[21]

Fasting, a practice encouraged in the Bible, may greatly help us in this whole matter of self-discipline. This is fully dealt with in my book, GOD'S CHOSEN FAST (see back cover).

---

[1] Rom. 6. 14   [2] Gal. 5. 1   [3] ver. 13   [4] Gal. 5. 23 (temperance AV) [5] Rom. 8. 1–4   [6] Rom. 12. 1 RSV [7] 1 Cor. 6. 12   [8] Prov. 25. 28   [9] Gen. 6. 9; 9. 21   [10] 1 Cor. 9. 25   [11] 1 Pet. 1. 13; 4. 7; cf. 5. 8   [12] 2 Cor. 10. 5 [13] Rev. 1. 13 RSV   [14] 2 Tim. 1. 7 RSV   [15] Jam. 1. 26; 3. 2   [16] Jam. 3. 8   [17] Luke 9. 23 RSV   [18] 1 Cor. 9. 27 [19] 2 Tim. 2. 3 AV   [20] Rom. 8. 2   [21] Gal. 5. 22–23 RSV

17

MORALE

Psychological warfare is nothing new. The redskin practised it when he brandished his tomahawk and charged the foe with a blood-curdling yell! In every battle morale has always been of crucial importance. The finest and best equipped army becomes an easy prey once it is demoralised. Occasionally God Himself employed psychological warfare when He thundered against Israel's enemies before ever battle was joined. The devil too uses the psychological approach when he comes 'as a roaring lion', and we have already seen how we must be protected by 'the helmet of salvation'. I want now to show how to maintain a morale of the highest order, even in the midst of the fiercest battle.

The devil is a pastmaster at attacking the Christian soldier with doubt and fear, discouragement and depression. In addition to the protection afforded by our armour, we need to know how we may hit back and even seize the initiative. There are two weapons we must learn to use—joy and praise. They are the greatest morale-boosters I know, and the enemy finds them thoroughly demoralising.

Joy, like self-control, is part of 'the fruit of the

Spirit', and joy is one way in which the Spirit's power is expressed. If you are a joyful Christian you are a strong Christian, 'for the joy of the Lord is your strength'.[1] It was the radiant joy-filled lives of those early believers that took the Roman Empire by storm. Satan had no answer, and multitudes were drawn like a magnet to Christ.

It was not that these early Christians found their new life a bed of roses. Far from it. Deprivation, suffering, persecution, and even death were the order of the day. But this only caused their joy to stand out in sharper relief, and to prove that it was no superficial emotion. Christ's disciples had seen this same joy in the life of their Master. He had spoken of His joy being in them and had prayed to the Father that they would experience it fully.[2]

There is a paradox here. Jesus was 'a man of sorrows' and yet He knew this deep abiding joy. At the cross His cup of sorrow was full, yet even there 'because of the joy that was waiting for Him, He thought nothing of the disgrace of dying on the cross'.[3] It was the same with Paul. Called to endure the most intense suffering and hardship, he calmly declares, 'although saddened, we are always glad.'[4] And again, 'I am happy about my sufferings for you.'[5]

Let us visit the apostle in the prison at Rome. Shackled day and night to the soldier that guards him, he dictates a letter to the believers at Philippi. Not a word of complaint or self-pity, but a letter brim-full of joy. 'Rejoice in the Lord always,' quotes

Paul. The scribe lifts his quill from the parchment and looks up at the kindly face lined by years of suffering. 'Did you say "*always*", Paul?' 'Yes, always —and I'll say it again, Rejoice.'[6]

The Lord had told His disciples to 'dance for joy'[7] when they were persecuted for His sake. Such a command is quite ridiculous to those who only know a happiness that depends on happenings. Jesus never promised us blue skies and calm seas; in fact He warned of storms and tempests,[8] but promised that we would have His joy. It is strange but true that the persecuted Christians of Eastern Europe know much more about this 'great and glorious joy, which words cannot express'[9] than their brothers in the free West.

Paul names joy as one of the three characteristic features of the kingdom of God,[10] so we are not dealing here with a secondary matter. He often links it with peace, and shows us that it is the product of faith.[11] One thing is clear: we can never dissociate it from the ministry of the Holy Spirit.[12] Because He comes to make Christ real, fulness of the Spirit and fulness of joy go hand in hand.[13]

This joy of the Holy Spirit inevitably finds its outlet in expression of praise to God. Praise, according to the Psalmist, is joy's safety valve,[14] while James asks, 'Is anyone happy? He should sing praises.'[15] Thanksgiving and praise honour God,[16] and there is no higher service that we can render. It often releases the power of God to work in extraordinary ways. As soon as Jonah in the belly of the great fish raised 'the voice of thanksgiving', ascribing deliverance to the Lord, he *was* immediately delivered.[17] Paul and Silas in the inner dungeon, their backs bleeding and their feet fixed in the stocks, spent the midnight hour 'praying and singing hymns to God'.[18] The Lord responded with an earthquake which freed them from their fetters—and the jailer from his sins!

Perhaps the outstanding example of the power of praise as a weapon against the enemy is when Israel was invaded in the reign of Jehoshaphat. He called the nation to prayer and fasting, and God gave the assurance of victory. Next day they went into battle with a choir as their vanguard 'who were to sing to the Lord and praise Him in holy array'.[19] The moment the choir began to praise, God routed the enemy. Satan trembles when soldiers of Christ have 'the high praises of God . . . in their throats and two-edged swords in their hands'.[20]

Scripture often speaks of the *sacrifice* of praise or thanksgiving. This is a timely reminder that this weapon costs something to wield. People often say, 'But I just don't feel like praising.' I don't suppose Jonah felt like it. He probably felt a bit hot and clammy! I don't suppose Paul and Silas felt like it, with bleeding backs in a dark, dank, smelly dungeon. We are not invited to praise when we feel like it; we are commanded to praise continually,[21] to give thanks *for* everything and *in* everything.[22] This is what God wants, and this is the *sacrifice* that glorifies Him.

III

Like joy, praise is so very much the overflow of the
Spirit-filled life. So many testify to a wonderful
release in praise when the Lord Jesus baptised them
in the Holy Spirit. The Ephesian believers had been
filled, but Paul exhorts them, 'Go on being filled with
the Spirit' (literal translation) and show it by singing
'hymns and psalms to the Lord, with praise in your
hearts'.[23] Note that last phrase. It is so important
that it is a heart matter and not simply a form of
words. A 'praise patter' is obnoxious both to the
ear of God and man. But when praise wells up from a
heart that is inspired by the Holy Spirit it will both
honour God and harass the devil. So train yourself
to use the weapons of joy and praise.

[1] Neh. 8. 10   [2] John 15. 11; 17. 13   [3] Heb. 12. 2   [4] 2
Cor. 6. 10   [5] Col. 1. 24   [6] Based on Phil. 4. 4 RSV
[7] Luke 6. 23   [8] John 16. 2, 33   [9] 1 Pet. 1. 8   [10] Rom.
14. 17   [11] Rom. 15. 13   [12] Gal. 5. 22; 1 Thess. 1. 6 etc.
[13] Acts 13. 52   [14] Psa. 47. 1   [15] Jam. 5. 13   [16] Psa. 50.
23   [17] Jonah 2. 9–10   [18] Acts 16. 25   [19] 2 Chron. 20.
21–22   [20] Psa. 149. 6   [21] Heb. 13. 15   [22] Eph. 5. 20;
1 Thess. 5. 18   [23] Eph. 5. 18–19

18

THE FINAL BATTLE

IN the opening chapter I spoke of the nature of this conflict that inevitably involves us all. It is the fight between light and darkness, between good and evil, between God and Satan. But how is the battle going? Anyone trying to assess this impartially might be excused for concluding that the devil was winning hands down! But the man who studies Bible prophecy is neither surprised nor dismayed. He knows that God never promised that the gospel would gradually christianise the world. He knows that God's present purpose is to call out of the world a people for Christ called the church.[1] He knows that while God is accomplishing this, often with powerful movements of His Spirit, the world situation will continue to worsen, with increasing tribulation, lawlessness and evil.[2]

How then will it all end? Imagine a game of chess, Right versus Wrong, in which Wrong seems to be sweeping the board. But Right is calmly waiting for that strategic moment when He will move One Piece, and say to Wrong, 'Checkmate!' Yes, it is God, not Satan, who will have the last move, and that will be the promised return of Jesus Christ to Planet

Earth. Not this time in humility and obscurity, but
with myriads of angels as His escort, in the most
dazzling display of power and splendour this world
has ever seen.

Both Old and New Testaments abound with pre-
dictions of this great event. In fact there are many
more prophecies concerning Christ's second coming
than His first. It will be the vindication of God's
whole plan of redemption, for it will involve the
overthrow of Satan and all his hosts. The book of
Revelation provides a fitting climax to the Bible, for
this final battle and the events leading up to it are
its central theme.

Though Christians are basically agreed on the fact
of Christ's return, there are considerable differences
in the interpretation of prophecy. Much of it is
obscure or capable of more than one interpretation,
especially the book of Revelation with its vivid
symbolism. God could have made it all perfectly
plain, so there is a wise reason why He has not done
so. We are dealing with 'God's secret wisdom, hidden
from men',[3] so no computer, whether mechanical or
human, is capable of feeding us with the right
answers. We are shut up to the teaching of the Holy
Spirit that we may be preserved from human specu-
lation. In this chapter I shall be dealing with basic
facts rather than controversial details.

At the end of His earthly life Jesus spoke to His
disciples of His departure to His Father's abode to
prepare a home for them there. Then He added, 'And

after I go and prepare a place for you, I will come back and take you to myself, so that you will be where I am.'[4] This promise was not fulfilled by His coming back to them in resurrection, nor by His coming in the person of the Holy Spirit, nor in the sense in which He came to them at death. What Jesus meant was made plain to them on the Mount of Olives.

In the act of blessing them Jesus was parted from them. They watched Him soar heavenwards till a cloud obscured Him from their sight. Still gazing upwards with the forlorn hope that perhaps He might reappear, they were startled by voices beside them. 'This Jesus,' said the two angels, 'who was taken up from you into heaven, will come back in the same way that you saw Him go to heaven.'[5]

'This Jesus'—not God the Father; not even Jesus in the person of the Holy Spirit—but Jesus Himself 'will come back'. That means His return will be *personal*. Then He would come back 'in the same way'. He had left them in a real body, for Thomas had been invited to put his hand into his Master's wounded side. So His return would be *physical*. Then in Revelation we read, 'Look! He is coming with the clouds! Everyone will see Him.'[6] That means His return will also be *visible*. There is a prophecy that suggests He will even return to earth at the very same spot, the Mount of Olives.[7]

God revealed to Paul that this great event in its first phase would involve the rapture (carrying away) of the saints. 'There will be the shout of command, the archangel's voice, the sound of God's trumpet, and the Lord Himself will come down from heaven! Those who have died believing in Christ will be raised to life first; then we who are living at that time will all be gathered up along with them in the clouds to meet the Lord in the air. And so we will always be with the Lord.'[8]

Concluding a great chapter on the resurrection of the body, Paul states: 'Listen to this secret: we shall not all die, but in an instant we shall all be changed, as quickly as the blinking of an eye, when the last trumpet sounds. For when it sounds, the dead will be raised immortal beings, and we shall all be changed.'[9] This change, of course, refers to our resurrection bodies rather than a moral or spiritual transformation. It is in this sense that we shall then be made like Christ.[10] The change will be instantaneous and permanent, and will fit us for a new mode of existence where we shall dwell in the presence of the Lord for ever.

What will this second coming of Christ mean for the world? For those who have rejected Him it will mean judgment. In His parables Jesus often taught that His coming at the end of the age would mean the punishment and destruction of the ungodly.[11] Paul referred to the coming of the Lord as being with flaming fire to punish the godless and unrepentant with 'eternal destruction.'[12] This solemn prospect should sober us up and send us out to reach others while grace still holds the door open.

What will Christ's coming mean to the careless or disloyal soldier of Christ? Jesus warned His disciples repeatedly that His coming would be sudden and unexpected, like a thief in the night.[13] For this reason they were to be watchful and prayerful, and not be caught unawares like the rest of mankind.[14] The command to watch is now more necessary than ever for the temptation to fall asleep is that much greater just before the dawn. Some believers will evidently be found unprepared for this sudden meeting with the Lord, else why the oft-repeated warnings?

Both the gospels and the epistles teach that when Christ returns He will judge the character and conduct of His servants, and deal with them accordingly.[15] The soldier who has been disloyal, guilty of misconduct, or who is found unprepared can only expect rebuke from his Commander, loss of privilege, and to have his wrong-doing exposed and dealt with.[16] This is why John urges us to abide in Christ 'so that we may be full of courage when He appears and need not hide in shame from Him on the Day He comes'.[17] No wonder John speaks of this great event as a purifying hope.[18]

What will that day mean to the loyal soldier of Christ, with no back-log of unconfessed sin, who has kept alert and prayerful, waiting for His Commander to appear? He will be able to look His Master in the face, see His smile of approval, and hear Him say, 'Well done, good and faithful servant.'[19] All the travail and tears, the sorrow and suffering that he was called upon to bear will then seem as nothing for the supreme joy of that moment. Best of all will be to enjoy the presence of his Master for ever, a joint-heir of His throne and His glory.[20]

Finally, what will that day mean for the great Commander Himself? Already He has waited almost two thousand years for His enemies to be made His footstool.[21] This then will be the hour of fulfilment, when the victory won on the cross will be vindicated before the whole universe.[22] This will be His coronation day, for not only shall every eye see Him, but 'all beings in heaven, and on earth, and in the world below will fall on their knees, and all will openly proclaim that Jesus Christ is the Lord'.[23] Perhaps His greatest joy will be to see in His glorified saints 'the fruit of the travail of His soul and be satisfied'.[24]

The story is told of a mother and daughter who steadfastly refused to yield to the Roman Emperor the allegiance due to Christ. Romans throng the Colosseum as they are led out to die. For one moment there is a hush as the two stand alone in the centre of the arena. Suddenly from high up in the gallery a voice rings out, vibrant and strong, across the great amphitheatre: 'Maranatha!'[25] ('Our Lord come' in Aramaic, the watchword of the early church). The lords and ladies turn to see whence comes this barbaric cry. Matron and maid lift their heads and a smile from another world lights up their faces. Then with a roar the lions are upon them, and two most valiant soldiers have fought their last fight.

This hope that sustained saints and martyrs in their darkest hour will do so to the end of time. Men may take away from the Christian his position, his property, and even his very life, but they cannot rob him of his hope—that Christ will surely come, that his fidelity will be rewarded and his faith vindicated, that the end will be certain victory. As Peter would say, this is no 'cunningly devised fable', but sure and sober truth. Let it fill your vision, fortify your faith, purify your heart, and steel you for the fight. And then, having fought to the end, you too will stand with Christ at last, victor on the field of battle.

[1] Acts 15. 14; 1 Pet. 2. 9   [2] Mat. 24. 4–12; 2 Tim. 3. 1–5, 12–13; 4. 3–4 etc.   [3] 1 Cor. 2. 7   [4] John 14. 3   [5] Acts 1. 11   [6] Rev. 1. 7   [7] Zech. 14. 4   [8] 1 Thess. 4. 16–17 [9] 1 Cor. 15. 51–52   [10] Phil. 3. 20–21; 1 John 3. 2   [11] Mat. 13. 40–42, 49–50; 25. 41–46   [12] 2 Thess. 1. 6–9   [13] Luke 12. 39–40; cf. 1 Thess. 5. 2   [14] Luke 21. 34–36   [15] Mat. 25. 19; Luke 19. 15; Rom. 14. 10–12; 2 Cor. 5. 10 [16] Luke 19. 22; 1 Cor. 3. 12–15; 1 Cor. 4. 5; Col. 3. 25 [17] 1 John 2. 28   [18] 1 John 3. 3   [19] Mat. 25. 21   [20] Rom. 8. 17 RSV   [21] Heb. 10. 12–13   [22] Isa. 53. 12   [23] Phil. 2. 10, 11   [24] Isa. 53. 11   [25] 1 Cor. 16. 22

OUR AUTHORITY OVER SATAN

IF you memorise the following Scriptures they will become weapons in your armoury. These are taken from *Good News for Modern Man.* (*Today's English Version*), but you memorise them in the version which you generally use.

Eph. 6. 11, 17 Put on all the armour that God gives you, so that you will stand up against the devil's evil tricks.
And accept . . . the word of God as the sword that the Spirit gives you.

Luke 10. 18–19 I saw Satan fall like lightning from heaven. Listen! I have given you authority . . . over all the power of the Enemy, and nothing will hurt you.

Jam. 4. 7 Submit yourselves to God. Resist the devil, and he will run away from you.

Col. 2. 15 And on that cross Christ freed Himself from the power of the spiritual rulers and authorities; He made a public spectacle of them by leading them as captives in His victory procession.

1 John 3. 8   The Son of God appeared for this very reason, to destroy the devil's works.

Heb. 2. 14–15   That through His death He might destroy the devil, who has the power over death, and so set free those who were slaves all their lives because of their fear of death.

1 John 4. 4   The Spirit who is in you is more powerful than the spirit in those who belong to the world.

Rev. 12. 11   Our brothers won the victory over him (Satan) by the blood of the Lamb, and by the truth which they proclaimed.

Mat. 12. 29   No one can break into a strong man's house and take away his belongings unless he ties up the strong man first; then he can plunder his house.

Mat. 18. 18–19   What you prohibit on earth will be prohibited in heaven; what you permit on earth will be permitted in heaven. . . . whenever two of you on earth agree about anything you pray for, it will be done for you by My Father in heaven.

1 Cor. 15. 57 But thanks be to God who gives us the victory through our Lord Jesus Christ!